ONE FOOT IN BOUNDS

Defining and Defying Boarding School Limits

By *David Phillips*

David K. Phillips

Copyright © 2012 by David K. Phillips

One Foot In Bounds
Defining and Defying Boarding School Limits
by David K. Phillips

Printed in the United States of America

ISBN 9781622304936

All rights reserved solely by the author. The author guarantees all contents are original and do not infringe upon the legal rights of any other person or work. No part of this book may be reproduced in any form without the permission of the author. The views expressed in this book are not necessarily those of the publisher.

Unless otherwise indicated, Bible quotations are taken from the Authorized Version. Copyright © 1952 by A. J. Holman Company, Philadelphia, PA.

The Library of Congress has catalogued the edition as follows:

The well-known hymn, Amazing Grace, is in the public domain. The writer guarantees that all material in this volume is original in nature.

www.xulonpress.com

"As any merchant officer well knows,
the hardest times on a voyage are the beginning and the end,
the departure and the ultimate landfall.

Once well at sea, life settles into a routine
that is only occasionally disrupted by storms or accident.

But the approach to land, in thick weather,
at night, or even in the clear light of day, is always hard."

THE NEW-FOUNDE-LAND:
A Personal Voyage of Discovery
By Farley Mowat

For Elizabeth and Jennifer

Whose loving presence in our home extended our boundaries

beyond anything we could ever have thought or asked for,

and whose loving witness continues to inspire.

TABLE OF CONTENTS

Map of Kenya and East Africa... xi

Introduction... xiii

PART 1 – THE HATCHERY

Chapter 1 The Bubble Gum Gang...17
Chapter 2 The Mau Mau...23
Chapter 3 The Hatchery..32
Chapter 4 MacKinnon Road Prison Camp..40
Chapter 5 The Hardest Part of Forgiveness......................................48
Chapter 6 Green Tree..51
Chapter 7 My Best Christmas Gift, Ever!..55
Chapter 8 Trips, Games and Letters...59
Chapter 9 Manyani Prison Camp: the Ultimate Freedom................63
Chapter 10 Visitors with Unique Gifts...71
Chapter 11 Ma Reed, Livingstones and the Cow Trough..................76

PART 2 – KEDONG DORM

Chapter 12 Karibuni Cottage 85
Chapter 13 Pa Hollenbeck and Band Practice 96
Chapter 14 The Tool Cupboard, Debagging and the Fire................100
Chapter 15 Coals of Fire 107
Chapter 16 The View from Mount Longonot 111
Chapter 17 The Comolli Family Disasters.......................................115
Chapter 18 In the Twinkling of an Eye 121

PART 3 – WESTERVELT DORM

Chapter 19 Nicknames and Changing Boundaries 127
Chapter 20 Slingshots and a Humming Primus 137
Chapter 21 Warts, Dumas and Hugo..142
Chapter 22 A Secret Swimming Pool and the Space Age................147
Chapter 23 Broken Airplanes, Pioneer Camp and a Stolen Salary 151
Chapter 24 The Radio Transmitter, Clubs and Rugby 156
Chapter 25 Enforcing the Point System, and the Lasse Family.......164

Chapter 26 Senior Safari 172
Chapter 27 Over Niagara Falls 181

After Words 187

After RVA 189

Forth-coming Books 191

Map of Kenya and East Africa

INTRODUCTION

О ur family wanted a unique gift for Elizabeth, our daughter, as she turned 12 on February 29, 1988. Over the years I had told our daughters events from my growing up years; my childhood and school experience took place almost entirely in Kenya, in the six locations mentioned in this book of memories.

My parents had served the Lord with Africa Inland Mission, AIM, an agency founded in 1895. From its humble beginnings it had grown to include missionaries from many countries, and its purpose, as an evangelical and interdenominational mission, was to evangelize African linguistic groups that had not previously heard the Gospel.

My parents both went to Africa with the AIM in 1938, my father leaving England for northwestern Kenya, with the intention of work among the Turkana people. My mother left Winnipeg, Canada to work in south-eastern Kenya, learning the Kamba language. Mother and dad met in Kenya and were married there and I was born in Canada while my parents were on furlough, on home assignment. All my school days were spent at Rift Valley Academy, a missionary kids' boarding school.

* * *

Rift Valley Academy started as a one room school in 1906 for the children of Charles Hurlburt, a school designed to serve up to 10 students. Two years later a generous donation from the Butterworth family made it possible to build a large building, which would serve as a home and school for 40 students. During his remarkable hunting expedition in Africa, ex-President Teddy Roosevelt drew back a small piece of cloth covering the cornerstone of the school's building. On that stone these words are inscribed: "Laid by Hon. T. Roosevelt, Aug. 4, 1909". His expedition took him far and wide; his hunting trek opened American eyes to the marvels of the continent.

Few missionary children could say that they attended a school dedicated by a President of the United States; that slightly-grey stone block is still there for all visitors to gaze at and photograph. The breadth of Roosevelt's travels was reflected in the student body; my classmates, and those of my siblings, came from Kenya, Uganda, Tanganyika, Congo, Sudan, Central Africa Republic and Nyasaland in 1963, when I was in Grade Eleven.

Roosevelt left something besides his name as he proceeded to his famous hunting expedition. He was noted for memorizing details and for his ability to converse on any subject with the smartest people in the highest halls of academia in the USA. After all, Teddy Roosevelt had participated in the Rough Riders, a small regiment sent to Cuba. Perhaps Roosevelt bequeathed his full-bodied masculinity, his devouring of books and his love of history, his strenuous schedule and his leadership to generations of students; young men attending RVA seemed to be infused with a desire to explore, to test the boundaries. This was in our minds from time to time as we lived through the crisis of the Bay of Pigs and President Kennedy's showdown with the USSR over nuclear weapons.

Not only was Roosevelt a cowboy, a hunter and a man passionate to weed out corruption. In 1912, he gave a 90 minute political speech having just been shot, knowing the bullet was in his chest. Of course, that 50 page speech tucked in his shirt pocket helped save him from death in the assassination attempt, but his reference to himself as a "bull moose", in the opening lines of his speech, illustrated his passion to get on with the job, whatever the cost. He was our "man's man", an adventurer who laid the cornerstone. The resulting profile was that of an American hero living surviving danger. We mourned when President Kennedy couldn't survive his assassin's bullet. Young lives in Africa were inextricably linked to the political ebbs and flows of American influence.

Many aspects of Teddy Roosevelt's personality were formed in my fellow students: an ability to hunt wild game, eclectic reading and a memory for details. Perhaps those were simply genes carried as Americans: an enthusiasm for life, a certainty that life demanded an overwhelming commitment and an quest for new experiences.

* * *

Early on I realized how few of this great hero's qualities lay within me. I had a vivid sense of adventure, an admiration of parks and their flora and fauna. My father never spoke about Roosevelt. Rather, his frame of reference included dusty copies of historic magazines, usually the coronation of a British monarch. His black steel trunk also held his school marks, reminding him of the boarding school he had attended in Kent. England was his home and native land.

My mother was more practical, less sentimental. She didn't store her memories from Canada in a trunk; instead she helped the four of us, Dorothy, Pearl, Don and me, as we packed our steel trunks for boarding school every three months. Those trunks held our clothes, and of course our Bibles, along with a few precious items to place beside our beds in boarding school.

The boarding school we attended brought together different strains of human personality. On the one hand, the evangelical and highly dedicated missionary movement of the early 20th Century included a compulsion to pass on conservative Christianity into the lives of missionary children. Teachers from America brought their own culture, usually influenced by Republican ideals. Conduct had to be regulated, and for this purpose the Point Card System was developed. Good doctrine, an American curriculum and academic excellence were the conceptual boundaries that formed our intellectual horizon. Our Principal, Herb Downing, had even set up the curriculum with the hope that RVA would train a future generation of missionaries. "What a hope!" I murmured.

* * *

Just outside of the boundaries of the mission station, which defined RVA's property, stood a thick, green forest. Africa's wild life had inspired Teddy Roosevelt to undertake his amazing African hunting trip. Later, he led an expedition to the Amazon. He loved the outdoors, hunting big and small game. Traveling with a steel trunk of leather-bound volumes, he read a book each day. Numerous museums in the USA, not just the Smithsonian, house his hunting trophies from 1909-1910. He embodied the desire to experience the outdoors, leaving an American imprint in Africa.

Introduction

So we had two foundation stones. One foundation stone was Jesus Christ. Upon this foundation the edifice of character building and academic excellence was erected. Placing the correct building blocks in place was the task our teachers undertook.

At times their task collided with our desire to explore the outdoors since the other foundation stone was, literally, the one laid by Teddy Roosevelt. The physical location of the school at Kijabe, on the side of the Great Rift Valley, brought excitement and exuberance to each day. The divergence involved in these two viewpoints created tension in my growing up years and is an integral part of my story.

* * *

Although RVA had only been functioning since 1907, the foundations of Christian commitment were already seen in its alumni. The school photo of 1921 showed 26 students. Many returned to Africa with the AIM; their sons and daughters sat in the school dining room at meal time, at chapel and in the classrooms each day. Almost half of the first students at RVA returned to Kenya, many as pioneer missionaries. Their names were a legacy in the mission: the Stauffacher family: Richard, Claudon, John and Florence; the Barnett family: Arthur, Paul and Eric; the Propst family, Charles and James; Homer and Paul Bailey and Linnel Davis. That represented just one school picture, the one from 1921. Many families followed in their footsteps, with their sons and daughters returning to Africa.

While the immediate goal was to prepare students for college back in the USA, one of the underlying themes of RVA was preparing students, not only for a Christian life, but also for full-time Christian service. These two themes, academic and spiritual, formed the living DNA of our school.

* * *

Of all his excellent qualities, I wish that one particular characteristic of the famous Teddy Roosevelt could have been acquired simply by having the room where he slept as my dorm. I was born during the frozen days of winter in Winnipeg; I never possessed a memory capable of storing endless details. Roosevelt's amazing memory, his ability to recall names and events, was never mine.

If I had inherited RVA's hero's remarkable ability there would not have been so many small lapses of memory in my narration of events at Rift Valley Academy.

David Phillips May 2012

CHAPTER 1

THE BUBBLE GUM GANG

Our Grade Eight adventure began as an innocent little hike. Saturday mornings occasionally afforded us time for extra long hikes. If we caught Pa Hollenbeck in a good mood or if we had not caused trouble for a while he might extend an extra privilege to us.

Boundaries around the Kijabe missionary station were set by teachers and clearly explained to students; it was important not to disobey. The need for safety evolved over time in response to various crises or dangers. In the minds of the students, however, boundaries keeping us away from forests and the Kedong Plain presented a challenge to be overcome. The sense of adventure beckoned. For the small group of us on that Saturday morning, the urge to explore "way outside the bounds" shone as a beacon, gently tempting under bright sunny skies.

The Hollenbeck family lived at one end of our dorm and all Saturday events needed permission from this stout, generally happy man. We called him "Pa", because he was our dorm parent. Dorm mothers and women teachers were referred to as "Ma"; the men were referred to as "Pa". Jim Hollenbeck's temperament usually enabled him to laugh with heart-felt amusement and he endeared himself to us greatly as he answered, "Yes, just don't get yourselves into trouble and be back by meal time!" Our interpretation of his reply was taken as permission to go "out of bounds". He had given permission to go right to the limit of the school property, but not past that boundary.

"Out of bounds" were words that conveyed a clear meaning, more than just a mental map of the steep hills all around us. "Points off" was a penalty for going beyond the hairpin corner at Dames Stream, on the way to the highway; that was "out of bounds". Other infractions included going up into the forest beyond the railway track, or into the bush below the mission station, or going the other way, or past First Ravine on the road to the township of Kijabe, where the Asian merchants sold their wares in their *dukas,* or stores. RVA's boundary lines were easy to understand.

This morning, though, Pa Hollenbeck seemed in a good mood and that was all the permission we needed. He didn't need to know that we had acquired extra energy from eating several extra slices of the always-soggy toast served at breakfast.

We walked towards the dusty, winding road that would take us out towards the main highway, linking the capital city, Nairobi, with many Kenyan cities further west and north. Within fifteen minutes we had walked down the hill to the African schools, past their playing field, around the sharp corner at Dames Stream and past the last house on the mission station. We had not specified what we meant when we asked Pa Hollenbeck to "take a morning walk along the road out to the highway". On the road, where we were throwing stones at birds, we were now "out of bounds".

The first limits were set between 1906 and 1946 when wild animals were present in the forests. The Mau Mau was an organized uprising by members of several African tribes, which began after World War II, and erupted as a rebellion in 1952; Africans and white settlers were killed in a conflict that began when white settlers moved onto unoccupied tribal lands. Political solutions were gradually taking place for Kenya's independence from Great Britain, but these were not being managed quickly enough. That morning, we were not concerned about those issues, nor were we even aware of them when we took our hike on that Saturday morning.

* * *

In order to keep us "in bounds" and well-behaved, a point card system had developed, known as the Point System. At the beginning of each new term a student began with a clean Point Card, which meant "10.0 points". Some students might even arrive at the end of the term with a clean card, with no points having been withdrawn. For me, that was almost impossible. Arriving late for a meal meant "-0.1" being written in a square on the Point Card. "Out of bounds", a worse trespass, called for "-0.3" points. Talking back to a teacher carried a costly penalty. If one dropped past the cut-off score of "7.6" before the end of the term, three months later, then permission was denied for the term's grand finale, known as Rendezvous, or Mutton Guz. Special food included roasted corn and hamburgers; the entertainment was a movie, a big deal since we rarely saw movies.

We happily made our way out to the Great Rift Valley, far below us, which stretched to the horizon. The Kedong Plains, the floor of the Valley, spread northwards, towards Ethiopia, and Tanganyika lay to the south. On the far horizon, to the west, a faint blue line marked the escarpment, dividing the earth with a gigantic gash a mile deep.

We possessed speed in our new *tackies*, running shoes. Our youthful energy could not possibly give out. Six years of living on the slopes of the Rift Valley had furnished us with the survival skills needed for a simple Saturday hike down to the plains and back up to the township of Kijabe. What could possibly go wrong?

The first four miles were easy. We were six adolescents, carefree and happy, as we talked and laughed, throwing stones at small bushes and eucalyptus trees lining the dirt road. The dirt road out to the Nairobi - Eldoret highway hummed with life; birds, wild flowers, cactus, baboons, monkeys, waterfalls and wild bees. Long slender green vines hung down from upper branches to the ground. Monkey calls, high up the escarpment, vibrated through the forest; we tried to imitate their voices, and then laughed together.

When we arrived at the highway the morning sun had already risen over the brow of the escarpment. Thank God for an early start to the day! It was still relatively cool, but a faint line of sweat ran out from under my cap. A noisy *piki-piki* roared by with black smoke fuming out of its tail pipe. Only two people should be riding a motorcycle, but a man, his wife and a child were balanced on the old, noisy thing. The woman held her child in one arm and a *kikapu*, a basket, full of vegetables in the other hand.

In no time we turned right, and felt the highway sail away beneath our feet, running down to the plains. I rejoiced as gravity pulled me quickly down the escarpment. The turnoff to Kijabe Mission was now behind us; the thrill of reaching the floor of the Rift Valley lay ahead. The next two miles were easy. We loped, almost running, along the edge of the highway; trucks, struggling up-hill, groaned on the first steep gradients of the escarpment, shifting down and then needing an even lower gear.

* * *

Close to the bottom of the long escarpment section a small, white Catholic chapel came into view, set back from the road. It was set in the midst of a small grassy park, full of flowers. Its Italian architectural style proclaimed the nationality of the men who had supervised the construction of this particular stretch of the road.

Peanut, my friend, found the door of the chapel open. "Hey, you guys. *Dig* this! A Catholic saint!"

"Yeah," said *Fish,* another one of my friends, "and money offerings that some poor guys made, too!" *Fish* was tall and loved music, singing and playing instruments of all kinds, while *Peanut* did well in every subject, much better than I ever did. My 13 year-old ethics were nowhere near as noble as those of the original builders who constructed that little chapel. I lagged behind my companions as they left. I heard the voice of the African gardener, a tall, proud Kikuyu tribesman, whose responsibility it was to guard the chapel and keep up the little colorful gardens around the parking lot.

My five companions had left the chapel and talked briefly with the gardener. Now, alone in the small chapel, I pocketed half the coins that lay on the white altar cloth beside the crucifix, and then ran towards the door. My conscience was heavier than my pockets, which were suddenly enriched with three shillings. The gardener looked at me, no expression showing on his face. I took it as an accusation and didn't like him, for some reason. I skipped down the stairs to catch up with the hikers who were already across the road. "Hey, *Flappit,* what kept you so long?" called *Crimson.* I hesitated. "Oh, just looking around in there", I said lamely, but I hated to have to add a lie to my previous misdeed.

The highway rolled off the escarpment like the end of one of the slides on the play area at school and suddenly the road and the flat plains were one and the same. We walked single file along the edge of the highway as tall grasses rolled over themselves in frantic little dances ever time a car whooshed past. Now that we had reached the plains, a disappointing feeling came over me. Mount Longonot seemed farther off than ever. We spotted zebra lazily grazing far in the distance. Wildebeast dotted the land as well, while a black hawk circled higher and higher in the sky, never tired of soaring in wide, lazy circles. We had walked almost an hour on the Kedong Plains, the basement of the Great Rift Valley. For the first time, I walked on the ancient land at the bottom of the Rift Valley.

* * *

In the distance, protruding from the steep side of the Rift Valley wall, a rock shelf about six miles long and a little more than a mile wide was home to about three thousand people. From where we walked on the highway, the sun bounced off the *mbati* corrugated iron roofs of the school buildings. Our school was one of nine schools on the Kijabe Mission Station. The others were African schools for boys and girls, two for elementary students; two for Intermediate students; two for High School students; a Bible School and a Technical School for teaching skills such as carpentry and building. Most of the 2,000 students on the mission station were Africans; we students at RVA numbered less than 130.

We identified each building in relation to the position of the building with the largest shinning roof. That building was Kiambogo, where we had our meals and classes. In much earlier times Cape Buffalo, known in the Swahili language as *kiambogo,* roamed this area. The largest building at Kijabe was named after a dangerous animal.

The government owned the virgin forest around Kijabe and approximately 70 acres were used by RVA for dorms, school buildings, playing fields, a small infirmary and homes for teachers. Missionaries' kids, also known as MK'S, came to this school from Kenya and several other countries in East Africa. The school seemed spread out when we walked up and down the hill, going from one building to the other, but from this distant vantage point it took an effort to figure out which building was which.

We began to slow down a little as the sun sparkled on the distant, bright, tin corrugated roofs; just then Roland Giddings asked, "Why is that truck stopped in such a funny position?" We called him by his last name, *Giddings*, and his mother and father were dorm parents for my sisters. Of course, students referred to them as Ma and Pa Giddings.

"Isn't that a police car?" asked Kenton Fish. We simply called him *Fish*. Both *Giddings* and *Fish* were fortunate because theirs were not real nicknames, not like mine.

"*Flappit*," *Fish* called, his lanky, legs leaping him forward like a gazelle. "Come on!" I hated my nickname. Why couldn't I have a nickname like some of the other guys?

The *lorry*, or truck, was parked with all its wheels on the road, and behind the truck shards of glass lay strewn all over the road. A passenger car had been driving in the same direction as the truck the night before, but the driver had not seen the stalled truck in front of it. The car had crashed into the back of a stalled truck, probably going full speed.

The deaths of the two men happened in a second as the sharp fangs of the bent metal roof decapitated the two men. The metal frame above the windshield, meant to protect people, brought about an instantaneous fatality. Half-eaten carrots lay on the seats. Tiny bits of broken glass covered everything. Danger could appear from the most unexpected, unusual places. The men who died in that car last night never knew how quickly their lives could be snuffed out. The truck had motor trouble; no signal had been put on the road to indicate that danger lay ahead.

* * *

We trudged on for another hour, now beginning to lose energy. The road back to school, where we would start to climb the escarpment, lay another three miles ahead, and I felt hot and sweaty. Our school looked far away. I yelled out, "What happens if a teacher drives by and sees us here, walking out of bounds?" We couldn't do anything about that now. The return trip meant climbing back up that long hill, something much more difficult than walking and running down it. We were starting to get hungry; lunch was being served back at school. Our places at the tables would be empty and we would be missed.

On our left lay the massive mountain, Mount Longonot, which dominated the skyline, reminding us every day that this Great Rift Valley had been born in a cataclysmic rage of fury, eruptions and lava. "Wouldn't it be fun to walk to Mount Longonot?" exclaimed David Campbell. His nickname was *Campbell,* not imaginative and certainly not a hurtful name. He spoke with a singsong voice and was a natural comedian. One never knew whether he was on the verge of getting us into more trouble, or out of trouble. I enjoyed spending time with him and was happy to be on this hike with him. His birthday was on the same day as mine, but he was a year older than me.

If we made it all the way to the mountain, even to the base, not to mention climbing the volcano, we would be heroes for a day at Kedong Dorm. but we had to be back for supper or face the music. We would not hike out to Mount Longonot today.

"I wish there was a *choo* here, but there's no *gudge* anywhere!" I said, wondering about a bathroom break. "Just go in the bushes," said *Fish*.

The sun now shone with a blazing, white light. We were walking on our shadows and our canteens were almost dry. Shimmering heat, extending over the wild grasses, amplified the stillness in the air; the sun had reached to its zenith, meaning we had another three hours before we would start to feel relief. As we walked back toward the school the sharp lines of Mount Longonot receded, but no matter how far we walked in that blazing furnace, we didn't seem to make progress in reaching the first little rise of land, the bottom the escarpment. We still had a long way to go.

The East African Railways and Harbors moved the railway when the track up the escarpment had been upgraded some thirty years before. We arrived at the point where two steel lines crossed the road. To the north, the tracks faded into a shimmering wave; that was the direction to Lake Naivasha. We decide to walk back along the tracks since no teacher in his right mind would be walking along the railway tracks. We competed to see who could walk on the tracks, like circus artists, without falling off. Roger Crimson had the best balance. Roger's father was a pilot for the Missionary Aviation Fellowship, MAF.

I felt jealous; they could walk on the tracks, balancing well, for ages before falling off. I couldn't and I slipped off the track again, not having walked more than 100 paces before losing my balance again. I wanted to be as athletic as each of them. A thought crossed my mind: Why couldn't our family have cars like the ones their dads drove? Why did dad always have to buy a grey Peugeot 203? They all drove Chevrolets.

* * *

"Man! *Dig* that, will you!" *Peanut* called out. Daniel Hahn had keen eyes and he was leaning out over a little cement bridge. During the rainy season a turbulent little river would thunder under that bridge, but today the light brown, sandy soil was dry.

"Are those things marbles?" *Fish* called out excitedly.

"Get off the track and look at this!" *Giddings* said. He was already down on his hands and knees in the little dry creek. We slipped down the steep embankment. *Giddings* rubbed dirt off blue and green balls. In no time at all he was blowing a huge bubble. *Peanut* had the same idea. *Fish* soon had his mouth full, too. I soon had my mouth full of bubble gum, too, but I couldn't blow big bubbles like they did.

"*Severe!* Let's grab some more," yelled *Campbell*. RVA slang was like another language.

"Where did this stuff come from?" shouted *Giddings*.

"Here, grab my shirt!" said *Peanut*. *Crimson* used *Peanut's* shirt to form a small bag, tying the sleeves together.

"Did someone throw boxes full of gum out of the window as the train passed by?" asked *Fish*. "Were they stolen and then tossed away so that someone wouldn't get caught?" The idea of finding stolen loot had a mysterious ring to it. My heavy pockets held gum and metal sounding shillings. I began to feel a guilty conscience.

Peanut was the practical one, excellent when the subject in class was Mathematics. "Tell you what: take off your shirt and take scads of this stuff back to the dorm! Tie the sleeves, use the shirts like a bag, like this, then pass a stick through the top and the bottom and we'll carry it like the Africans carry an animal on their shoulders."

My cheeks were sore. I could hardly chew any more. In my greed I had taken too many balls of bubble gum. The unmanageable mass in my mouth made me repent, so I spit out the mass and formed another wad, a smaller one this time.

We walked up the tracks, the little rest having been good for us, and we trudged under the boiling afternoon sun without T-shirts. A train passed and we stood to the side waving to all the passengers who waved back to us. The passenger train disappeared over the long, flat plains in the direction of the distant pink shores of Lake Naivasha. The distant pink was the accumulated plumage of millions of flamingos, content to rest on one leg at the lake's shores. I wanted to take wing, to fly back to school. In our greed to become heroes, we had walked farther than we could really manage, but we had miles to go.

As the afternoon wore on, my bundle became heavier so I gradually let some gum fall out. We walked on, no longer trying to balance on the narrow steel tracks. The smooth little path along the edge of the train track served us well, and we arrived at Kijabe train station, our place of arrival and departure at the beginning and end of each term. We walked slowly along the long platform; I waved to the stationmaster who was leaning back, his grubby metal chair balanced against the white wall. The front two legs of his chair moved back and forth in the air. I longed for a rest.

Finally, as the afternoon slipped away, we arrived at the long railway cut in the hill above RVA. We were nearly back at our dorm and supplied our fellow dorm students with free gum. The five-minute warning bell rang, giving us just enough time to get to supper on time. As I stood in the lineup outside the dining room waiting for the second bell, I felt painful blisters on my feet. Under a clean shirt, my shoulders already felt the sun burn. The supper bell rang the second time and 100 young people barged in for supper, charging into the Kiambogo dining hall like a wild herd of hungry buffalos.

* * *

"Where were you guys for lunch?" asked Ray Davis at the head of our table. We were assigned our tables for the 13-week term. We were eight boys seated around the table and Ray was the most responsible Grade Eight guy.

"We were out on a hike and got delayed because of this accident we saw." *Crimson* was going to get us out of trouble again by telling another story. One never knew what to believe about Crimson's stories. They seemed too incredible, but then again, his father was an MAF pilot. "Do you want to hear about this most unbelievable adventure?"

"Sure," said Ray, "but you guys are going to get points off for missing lunch."

Life always had a way of finding you out, even if we had chosen a *severe* name for ourselves: "The Bubble Gum Gang". That was a take off on the Sugar Creek Gang books we enjoyed so much three or four years before.

My jaw was so sore I had to force myself to chew my supper, even though I was so hungry. How could you know when something was enough, or when you had gone too far? So often I got myself into a jam. I didn't mean to, but then I was in trouble again.

For example, take the three shillings in my pocket. Why had I not resisted that temptation? And the bubble gum: how could you enjoy something without getting in head over heels? Worse than those two new experiences to think about, it seemed to me that during the last two years things were working up to a head. Things were getting worse and worse for me at Rift Valley Academy.

Why did things always catch up to me? My memory took me back to the first time that I walked along those long, grey, uneven, knot-filled boards of the porch on Kiambogo building. The boarding school was supposed to convey the sense of a home away from home, but not all was well for me; last term I had almost been expelled.

CHAPTER 2

THE MAU MAU

A nagging, never-ending struggle wouldn't leave the pit of my stomach. The pain was most acute when I hear my father say, "It's time for you to go to school." That caused a tussle between what my adults wanted for me and what I planned to avoid. For several months before we went to Canada from Kenya in 1953, I felt that pain. It started when we were still in Eldama Ravine, after I had just turned six. Our parents took us, four young children, on *furlough*, to England and Canada for a six month leave-of-absence from their full time work in Kenya, to speak with friends and supporters. Having arrived in Winnipeg, Manitoba, my parents took me to see a Canadian doctor. "There's nothing to say," said the pediatrician. "He needs a regular diet; keep him away from stressful situations."

Perhaps it wasn't just the word "school". Our whole family seemed to be going to doctors. A year before, I had asked my mother, "Why is daddy going to hospital?" She answered, "He has polio; he was completely paralyzed, but he improved while in the hospital in Eldoret; he was moved to Nairobi and we are sure God will heal him." Many people in different countries prayed for him; six months after being paralyzed he regained his strength. One day, he felt heat flow from his head down to his feet. His return to health was seen as an answer to many prayers.

Dorothy, my sister, who was two years younger than me, apparently had only a mild case. She appeared to have come through her fever with no permanent after-effects, but I was left with one leg slightly shorter than the other. While she was sick I was also in bed; the after effects of polio for me were mild; a slightly shorter leg resulted in my always looking slightly out of balance in photos.

Pearl, my second sister, was barely two years old when she went to the hospital in Eldoret; she came home to our mission station in Kabartonjo with the polio virus. She caught it from a child who had just arrived from England. Later, she came to Eldama Ravine, where we were staying temporarily, wearing a tiny metal brace on her small leg. That was the first time the grumble in my stomach told me things were out of kilter. In Canada Pearl had surgery on her leg and she would use a brace for her whole life.

Donald, my younger brother, six years younger, had been born during the time that we were all recovering from the dreaded disease. He didn't have any effects from the sickness; his happy smiles as a baby fascinated us when everything around us looked glum.

But now we were back in Africa. The DC 3 plane took two days to fly from London to Nairobi, Kenya, stopping overnight in Cairo. That extra effort needed by the noisy engines of the sturdy little two-engine World War II packhorse plane could only have been due to parcels kindly given at the last minute, a demonstration of love and care by our Phillips clan in Dorking, England. While waiting for a new assignment we stayed at the AIM guesthouse in Nairobi.

* * *

The Africa Inland Mission was asking a significant question about Kenneth and Hazel Phillips, my parents. Where would AIM post our family? Previously, we lived in a village, Kabartonjo, in the Nandi Hills, near Lake Baringo, and my parent's work included training Bible School students, starting new Christian congregations, and serving sick people at the medical clinic. However, just before the Mau Mau Emergency, my father had been asked by the Tugen tribal leaders to leave the area. They did not appreciate the stand my parents had taken against female genital mutilation during the annual time of "customs", the long training session for pubescent boys and girls when the ancient customs of the tribe were passed on to the next generation.

Our family had no invitation to return to a mission station, and my father's health was not yet fully recovered to the point that he could participate in pioneer evangelistic work. Wherever the posting was to be, one inescapable decision had been made, as obvious as the magnificent Ngong Hills close to Nairobi, rising sharply out of the plains. I would have to go to boarding school.

"Daddy, I don't want to go to boarding school." I pleaded more than once, my seven year old anxiety making my voice rise higher than normal.

"Now, David, of course you do. All missionary kids want to go to boarding school!" His extra enthusiasm was intended to overcome my growing reluctance.

"I know, but I don't want to go to boarding school." My seven-year old logic had not mastered skills needed to argue with adults.

"You'll get over it. The first few days are the worst. You'll even like it in the end."

"But daddy, I have another tummy ache."

I always had an ache in my tummy, especially when the conversation came around to school. Attending one of the British boarding schools in Nairobi, the Prince of Whales, or the Duke of York, was apparently out of the question. I would have to go to Rift Valley Academy. Daddy carried a British passport, Mommy was Canadian, and an American curriculum had been chosen for me with constant Bible teaching, whose purpose was character building and spiritual formation.

* * *

My seventh birthday arrived and I received a little carpentry tool set. In the tool shed behind the guesthouse I found several new boards, which needed a little work with a strong little hammer. I pounded nails into the boards haphazardly as hard as I could, angry that I couldn't make my father understand me. The wood was very hard and most of the nails got bent so I pulled out the nails, leaving little holes in the boards that had been carefully stored by Mr. Stauffacher for a new expansion on Mayfield guesthouse.

Mayfield was a huge house that could accommodate 20 guests, or more. For four weeks we stayed in the big house. The dining room was a constant buzz of activity with people coming from smaller cities and towns, shopping and visiting, doing their business in Nairobi, the capital city, and then returning to their homes. We had meals with others three times a day and complete strangers would come to our table, saying, "Oh, Ken and Hazel, we've been praying so much for you! We hear you are better, and look at how much David and the children have grown! David, you will soon be going to RVA! You must be excited to go there as soon as the Mission Conference is over!" Comments like that made my tummy ache even more.

I didn't know what else to do so I sat on the steps and looked at the millions of flowers in the bougainvillea bushes close by. Seven-year old logic has its strong points, and I came to the wise conclusion that carpentry was not to be my calling in life. My logic was based solely on early performance.

* * *

The day arrived for the one hour trip to Rift Valley Academy, and the pain in my stomach intensified. When we drove up to the Kiambogo building, the main building of the school, I fingered the sharp, dangerous points on the barbed wire gate. All along the property barbed wire stretched in seemingly endless coils. I was going to be left at a school where there was danger from the Mau Mau; their activities had brought about the political "Emergency". During the previous year many tribal Kenyans and white families died.

Two African soldiers greeted us and daddy returned their greeting, first in Swahili and then in their local dialect. While he was a chaplain in the army, during World War II, daddy had become so attentive to the details of facial features of tribes in Kenya that he learned to guess their native tongue. Consequently, and much to their surprise, he said "Hello" to them in their heart language without being informed of their dialect. He told us he could guess what language they spoke at home by the way their faces had been marked, partly the shape of their heads. "Sometimes it's just a lucky guess," he said.

The long walk along the veranda seemed endless; the Grade One and Two class room was at the far end. Daddy said, "David, this is Miss Barrett and she is going to give you a test." Mommy stopped talking in a low voice to Miss Barrett, and turned to me with the sweetest smile she could muster. Her smile expressed hope and perhaps a bit of fear, too. She hoped that the homeschool teaching at Kabartonjo would bring good results.

Clara Barrett wore a green sweater and had curly hair. "I'm going to give you a little test," she said to me smiling, as if she wanted me to like her. "If you can read, then you'll start in Grade Two. If you can't read, then you'll be in Grade One. You are too young, really, to advance into Grade Two. All the students in Grade Two are a year older than you are. Your birthday falls at the end of December, so I should place you in Grade One, but perhaps you can read well enough to keep up to the Grade Two's."

My stomach churned and I blinked back a tear that wanted to come; I was determined to catch up to the students I had never met. I couldn't win arguments with adults, but I would do my level best in reading.

Miss Barrett wrote ten words on the blackboard, one under the other. The first one was '*r.e.a.d.*' I knew that one and relaxed. "Red," I said. It was like the color of my shirt. I finished all the words quickly and smiled. No tears had come. Read was something past.

"Fine, just one error," she said, as if pronouncing a sentence that could influence the rest of my life. "The first word is "Read" (she said it as in 'reed') "I will give you 90%. You will be in my Grade Two class. We'll see how you do; if you can keep up with the others you will advance with them to Grade Three in August." Then she added, "Of course, you can say 'read'." She agreed with my attempt at the word.

I knew that word could be pronounced two ways. I secretly knew that I was going to like Miss Barrett. She had given me a test and I had passed it.

The next decision was where would I live from January to March. My parents had long-time friends by the name of Wells and Edith Devitt; they lived in a two-story stone house surrounded by a high green hedge. Daddy and Mommy took me to their big house in a small valley. The sweet scent of the cedar hedge and the brightly colored flowers seemed so much more comforting; I had stared at the barbed wire security a few minutes before. Mr. Devitt had previously agreed for me to stay with them for three months since the dorm up at RVA was full. Mrs. Devitt made me feel welcome; she gave me a big smile, and pulled me against her herself, hugging me. "You'll enjoy living with us," she said, smiling.

"Say you are grateful, David!" my mother urged.

"Thank you for letting me stay at your house, Mrs. Devitt," I said. "It's good to meet you, Mr. Devitt." Those words had been practiced several times in the car on the way from Nairobi to Kijabe Mission Station. I had to practice being polite. Practicing for real life was important in our home. We had to stand up if an older person or a woman came into the room. In the Devitt's home I was supposed to show good manners, but that wasn't going to be a problem. I liked them right away.

Wells Devitt was so tall! I looked up at him, my head bent backwards. Then I looked around at their furniture. Everything seemed to be dark brown or almost black but that was because the windows had special protection; the Mau Mau haunted everyone's thoughts.

My parents left me at the Devitt's home. Their daughter Helen was already in high school and she made me feel at home right away; Wells and Edith were very approachable, too. I asked, "Mrs. Devitt, what do soldiers do around the school? Why is there so much barbed wire in front of the school?" I didn't yet know that barbed wire enclosed the entire school, or worse, that the previous year was closed for a term because of the threat to students and teachers.

Edith Devitt looked at her husband. He lifted his eyes ever so slowly and his chin dipped down at the same time. I saw him look at her. Was he pretending not to have heard the question? "Well, David, some bad men live in those forests, bad men who want to hurt people. But, don't worry because you'll be safe here. This is your home now."

I went to my room, the upper bedroom, which looked up at the green forest. I took off one shoe and sat on my bed until it was time for supper. Mrs. Devitt called, "Time for supper, David!" I looked at the stew she had made. I ate a tiny bit and thanked her for the supper. "Thank you for the stew," I said. "I'm going to bed now. I have a sore tummy."

As I left the dining room I looked up. Over the door, several guns hung from the wall. One in particular caught my attention; it had a curved barrel. The talk about bad men in the forests made me upset because it took me back to Kabartonjo, on the Nandi Hills, near Eldoret, where our family had lived until we felt the effects of polio.

* * *

A scene came back from Kabartonjo I was five years old. Earlier in the day I had played with my best friend, Wilson. He and I were inseparable. His father was the African evangelist and taught in the Bible School. The evening I remembered brought me back to a walk with my father. We strolled across the football, soccer, field used by the young men who studied with Wilson's father. A fresh mound of re-brown dirt at the far end of the field marked a new grave; we walked towards the place where Rosalie had been buried, a week before. She had died at the age of 20 from consumption and I was at her bedside when we sang her favorite songs, as she left her bed and went to heaven. Rosalie had been one of my best friends because she took care of me when my mother was attending sick people at the medical clinic. Many people sat around her bed, and I was beside the African pastor, on one side, and my father on the other side, as we held hands around her bed when she breathed her last. We sang her favorite song, "My hope is built on nothing less, than Jesus' blood and righteousness"; we sang in Tugen, the language of the people in the village.

My father held my little hand in his big, strong hand and I said, "Squeeze my hand harder, Daddy." When he squeezed my hand I felt secure. Then I said the same thing again. It was easy, at age 5, to feel secure when he held my hand so tightly.

That night I heard my parents talking about the political situation in Kenya; they thought we were asleep in bed, but I was still thinking about how Rosalie, one of my best African friends, had died. When her relatives had come for the funeral more than 50 members of her family had decided to follow Jesus. I still felt safe, with daddy's strong hand holding mine in the late afternoon, but then I heard my father telling my mother about the dangerous times that were coming. As I lay in bed I heard him say, "The chief is against me for my speaking out about the 'customs'. Outside this area, quite far away, Mau Mau soldiers want white settlers to leave Kenya." It was the first time I heard the strange words and I didn't know what they meant, but I knew it meant big trouble was coming.

I went to sleep with the memories of that day's encounters. First, I remembered the *bunduki*, African *askaris*, or soldiers, guarding the school where I was to study. Then I met Miss Clara Barrett, and now I was going to sleep in the Devitt's home.

The next morning Edith Devitt told me to get up. She asked me what I wanted for breakfast. Her voice was kind and it reminded me of the gentle morning breeze I had enjoyed in Nairobi, the previous morning when we got into the car to come to RVA for the first time.

"Hurry, David," said Helen. She was so much older, someone I could look up to. She patted her horse on the nose as we left their house. As I struggled to keep up to Helen Devitt walking up the fairly steep hill to the school I already had reached three conclusions: First of all, I would like Grade Two and secondly, I would keep up with the boys and girls already studying in school. I would not let Miss Barrett down by failing. She was kind enough to put me ahead, not put me back. Thirdly, Helen, a Grade Nine student, was kind and encouraging; I was going to like her, too.

* * *

After school was out that day, before going back to the Devitt's for supper, some boys were playing marbles on the roundabout in front of the Kiambogo building. Close by was a parking area for cars. In the circle were about a dozen little boys, carefully hoarding marbles, trying to flick them into the tiny hole at the center of a circle.

Suddenly, loud gunshots rang out. I was petrified. Taking protection, I ran up the stairs, the long green stairs towards the boys' dorm. Was that noise thunder? There were no clouds in the sky. I had climbed the green steps to the upper floor of Kiambogo.

"Oh, that! That is just the sound of soldiers target practicing," said a boy my age. "The African *askaris* do target practice at 4:00 every afternoon." I'd seen Raymond Davis in my class during the day. He had brown hair, cut close to his head, a strong set of arms and he knew his way around everything.

"What's your name?" Ray asked.

"David Phillips," I answered quickly.

"Hey everybody, get that! Here's *Flappit*. Did you get that? This guy's name is *Flappit!*"

"No it's not! It's not my name!" I blurted out, running away.

A chorus of calls sounded after me. "Hey, *Flappit*, come back!" yelled a dozen young voices. "Come back and play with us!"

Before walking under the enormous shade tree at the bottom of the long slender path that wound down the hill, I kicked the ground as hard as I could. "My name isn't *Flappit!*" I muttered, but Helen didn't hear me. I walked into the house as slowly as I could.

I lost my home and my name within a day. What was worse: the sound of the guns, at target practice, or an unwanted nick name? Both the sound of the rifles and my new name had come out of nowhere. I found Helen and we walked down the hill to their home; walking through the wooden swing gate at the end of the path I rubbed several delicate leaves together from the tall, green, Cyprus hedge. I inhaled several times and closed the gate carefully, looking back across the knee-high wild grasses. Perhaps wild men were hiding there.

* * *

The Devitt's dark brown horse was standing close to the fence and I wanted to ride it but an inner voice was rebelling at everything. I needed to punish someone and I told myself I would never ride that beautiful horse. I didn't want to dislike everything around me. I was old enough to know right away it was a destructive impulse, one born from sudden dislike of what was happening to me.

Every afternoon that week we heard the sounds of African soldiers at target practice. The King's African Rifles shot successive rounds into the soft earth cliffs at First Ravine, the first sharp curve on the road from the mission station to Kijabe market place. Targets were placed on the opposite side of the deep ravine. Volleys of white chalk spurt into the air as the bullets became embedded in the whitish clay behind the targets. We were never allowed to watch them shooting, but we heard them every afternoon that week and for days afterwards.

* * *

A tall, intimidating wall of barbed wire surrounded our school. If you tried to follow one wire you managed for a while but that single strand of wire became lost in the thousands of other bits making up the effective protection. It kept little children safe from unknown terrors hiding in the forests. The piercing rolls of barbed wire spread out in front of the wall, covering the ground, were almost twice as tall as a man. One of the *big guys* explained to me that the purpose of the barbed wire was to protect us from potential assaults of the Mau Mau. "They vowed to drive the white settlers from Kenya and return the power into the hands of the Africans," he said. "The Kikuyu, Luo, and some Kikamba tribesmen want independence from Great Britain." I didn't know what independence meant.

The barbed wire fence was like a great scar on a man's side after a vicious fight; it wound around the hill, where it sloped downhill, about ten feet high. Endless miles of barbed wire curled to the edge of the small forested area, around the bathrooms and kitchen, to its highest point, at the diesel electric generators, around Westervelt dorm, where the *big guys* slept, and back around to Kiambogo building. Thousands of little grey field mice made their nests in this protected no man's land. Some bigger boys hunted these mice with lots of laughs but the field mice always got away. They were safe there.

Guards kept their positions day and night. The most prominent location was beside the dining room corner, beside the bell on the porch. At the end of the parking lot there were more guards. One never knew when, or where, the Mau Mau might make an attack. These soldiers slept in the basement of Kiambogo building.

Whenever the word Mau Mau came up the tone of the conversation changed. People looked around and talked in a different tone. Several times there were little conversations that I interrupted at the Devitt's home. The Mau Mau meant danger. After all, that was why daddy had just been assigned as the Protestant Chaplain at the MacKinnon Road Detention Prison Camp. I had no idea what those big words meant so Edith Devitt explained, "The mission wants your daddy to go into prisoners' cells every day. Many Mau Mau have been caught and put in prison. Your father goes into prison each day to in tell Mau Mau men about the Bible, about God's love and how He wants to forgive them in Jesus' name. There was a big British Air Force base at MacKinnon Road, a small place near Mombasa. That's where your family lives now. You will go there after this term is over. When you come back next term you will stay in the Hatchery at Kiambogo building."

"Mrs. Devitt, what's a cell?" She struggled, looking for words to explain.

Mr. Devitt answered me, "Well, there are big airplane hangers at MacKinnon Road. The inside each hanger the space is divided into large dormitories; up to 100 men stay in each cell. Your father is going there to talk to these men, to preach the Gospel to them."

I listened, my eyes searching for a clue to say that daddy wasn't actually that close to these men, all day long, locked up in a big room with those dangerous offenders. It sounded so dangerous! Mr. Devitt kept guns in his house to shoot these men, yet my father was sitting down with them. What if they attacked him? I knew the Mau Mau wanted to kill white men, especially British. Daddy was from Dorking, England.

The story went around that the Mau Mau came to burn our station one night they got to the railway track above the station. There, stretching up and down the railway lines, they confronted a wall of fire. They could not get down to the station to burn those foreigners. March 28, 1953 was the night this happened. They never even got to confront the African guards. The only white man on guard that night had been *Chipps*, the British officer.

When we learned of Daniel in our Bible Classes and how God had protected him from great, hungry lions when he was a long way away from home, it wasn't hard to believe in God's ever-present protection and thank him. Hearing about men who wanted to throw spears against missionaries made my stomach boil again.

Soon, the first, long term of 13 weeks was over. I read well enough to keep up. A dozen students studied in Grade Two: Ray Davis, Malcolm Collins, Andrea Propst and several others in that small Grade One and Two classroom. In our class, there were only a few girls. I had a seat at the back of the classroom next to the big warm fireplace. Just before daddy came to get me for vacation, I remembered my tummy ache, but the bell for recess sounded and I forgot to think about that pain as we played dodge ball.

* * *

All the students had bright yellow and red rulers. Half way down the ruler was punctuated with geometric shapes: circles, oblongs, and squares. The rulers came from America. I didn't have a ruler, but I wanted one. One day, walking back to the Devitt's house, I saw a red ruler on the ground. I knew that it didn't belong to me. I leaned over, looked around to make sure no one was looking, and put it with my things in my bag.

A few days later I said to the Edith Devitt, "Look at my new ruler!"

"David, where did you get that?" Her voice had a sharp tone to it.

"Oh, I just got it," I said, trying to act calmly while resisting her question.

"Did you steal it?" A very strict question came from someone standing very straight.

"No I just found it. I promise you I didn't steal it." I had a twang of doubt. Was it stealing something if you picked it off the ground? Why hadn't I reported it as lost?

"You didn't steal it?"

"No. I didn't. By the way, what is that curved gun for?" Was it stealing if you found something on the ground? I knew what Daniel in the Bible would have done. He would have gone to the bad Babylonian king and given him the red ruler. I couldn't do that now, though, after I had said that I didn't steal it.

Edith turned to her husband, Wells. He took me on his knee and said, "Now you must promise me never to tell anyone about my guns, alright?" I nodded; my eyes were as big as saucers at this twin victory, of being able to keep my new red ruler and having maneuvered them into telling me about the mysterious guns. "I use my guns to hunt animals. There are ever so many animals down on the plains. The big gun is for hunting an elephant. The smaller ones are for antelope. The one with a curve is a buffalo gun; if you are ever hunting a buffalo and he corners you behind a tree what will you do?"

I couldn't remember living through a situation like that so I kept silent.

"Well, the buffalo will keep charging. You can kill it with a curved gun though. Shoot it around the tree." Why would anyone want to shoot animals? On the long wall along the porch up at Kiambogo I had seen naked horns, taken from kudu, gazelle and buffalo. They looked so ugly, bare, dead and lifeless, each hanging on a shield. The shield symbolized a victory. I hated seeing buffalo horns on the wall of the porch.

"Now come outdoors and I'll teach you to ride the horse," said Wells. We went outside. "Have you ever ridden a horse?" He appreciated the out-of-doors so much, unlike my father. Here was my chance to become part of another world, to be friendly with horses, pets and the out-of-doors. However, standing so close to the huge animal, the pain in my stomach was almost unbearable. "No, I can't ride it," I answered quickly.

"Come over here, Prince. There, we have the bit and bridle on and now the saddle. Now come here David and get on. I'll help you up."

"I can't ride! I don't know how to ride a horse!" I whined, and felt bad for doing so.

"Don't be afraid. He won't hurt you!" For several minutes they encouraged me, wanting to share their immense joy, their horse, but I was afraid of buffalos and Mau Mau and being caught for taking a ruler that I had found on the ground. I lost the opportunity to overcome some of my fears, listening to kind –hearted people, learning to ride a fine horse.

***

The view of the Rift Valley, with colors changing all day long, had to be one of the worlds' treasures. Perhaps, in order to compensate for such splendor God created something disquieting: the constant winds blowing down the side of the Rift Valley.

The administration set the dress code. The girls' uniform was a white blouse and a grey jumper and skirt, with the RVA symbol in red and white sown above the heart. Girls referred to the uniform as *unipukes*. Guys wore a khaki shirt, British style khaki shorts and an American bomber jacket, tight at the waist and bulky in the chest. The same red and white RVA symbol was worn over our hearts.

Ma Barrett kept a sandbox in the corner of her classroom and if we read well, or finished our work early we could play extra time with the dry, white sand, piling it up into little hills and pretending that we were explorers. Also, she draped a blue apron around me and let me stand in front of an easel with a long paintbrush in my hand. I tried to paint something as nicely as the students around me but couldn't get the brush strokes just right.

It was almost the end of term. Ma Barrett had us perform a little rhythm band piece. She had given the triangle to David Campbell, beside me, the drum to Andrea Propst, and a tambourine to Ray Davis. Carl Barnett rang a small bell. I was to play the cymbals, sounding them about three times in the piece. I enthusiastically clanged them; they were so loud, but they only sounded a few times in a musical piece.

It was my first experience of *Rendezvous* so I didn't know how important the party was to students at the end of the term. It was hot, we were outside and I was feeling mean for being called *Flappit*. We were on the slope at the bottom of the basketball court, perhaps so that classes would not be disturbed by the noise. I couldn't wait for my part so halfway through the band music I crashed the cymbals together as loudly as I could. What a wonderful, big booming sound!

Miss Barrett looked at me, but said nothing. Then, when I did it again, she stopped the band, came and took the cymbals from me and gave them to Malcolm to play. Now he had two instruments and I had none.

The end of term came and with it *Rendezvous*. Corn was boiled or cooked over an outdoor fire, and hot dogs dripped red ketchup and yellow mustard. Shining sparks shot up into the almost black sky. I followed the sparks bobbing upwards until they died out, lost against little stars. I wondered if that was how stars came to be up in the sky.

Mutton Guz, another name for the end of term picnic, really was the best event of the term. Afterwards a black-and-white film flickered on the screen. Candied apples, red and shiny under their overcoats of gooey sugar, brightened up everybody's eyes and left gooey red lines around peoples' mouths. When the band played, I sat back in my chair with my arms stubbornly crossed. In my disappointment, not being able to play, I kicked the cross bar of the gray metal chair under me in time to the music. I knew all of the music off by heart, but Ma Barrett wouldn't even let me bang the cymbals three times.

* * *

No one needed to teach you survival skills because they just came naturally. You feared the Mau Mau and spoke with the Africans who guarded the school, the men who used their afternoons for target practice, aiming at life-sized cardboard figures propped up against the while cliffs at First Ravine. You didn't want to be accused of *cobbing* anyone's stuff because stealing from each other got you in trouble. That meant I couldn't enjoy the bright red ruler I had found on the dirt path for I certainly didn't want to hear anyone say, "Look, *Flappit's* got my ruler! Where did you get that?"

Soon the term was over. I said, "Thank you!" to Wells and Edith Devitt for taking me in for three months. I would be in the *Titchie* Dorm for the third term, after coming back from holidays. Vacation would last four weeks.

When daddy came to get me, my black steel trunk was ready. It had been packed for two long days. A little red ruler was tucked away at the very bottom of the trunk and my clothes were on top.

On the very top of the trunk was my favorite book, *Little Pilgrim's Progress*.

CHAPTER 3

THE HATCHERY

*M*y first holidays passed too quickly at MacKinnon Road; my first train trip to RVA for a new term lay ahead. Holidays passed so quickly. I was standing on the train platform wishing that the brightly painted passenger cars of the EAR&H, East African Railways and Harbors, would never come. My wishes couldn't come true, of course.

The train was to arrive in the tiny, dusty McKinnon Road Railway Station at 4:00 pm. I stood with my parents for a few more minutes. My mother held my brother in her arms. Dorothy and Pearl stood close to my father.

I bit my lower lip and felt the tears coming as the time came for the train to leave. It had been stopped in the station for ten minutes; the time had come to return to school. Mommy was dressed in her best blue dress, which came halfway between her knees and her ankles. The sleeves reached half way down her arm below her elbows.

Daddy was dressed in khaki fatigues. His khaki shirt sported a double row of red bands on each shoulder, letting everyone know that he was a chaplain in the British Army. His long khaki colored-stockings, held up close to his knees with a metal elastic, gave him an official look, as did his thin black belt. My father had prayed with me for protection on the long trip and I felt better after that.

They kissed me and I turned, struggled to get up the three steep steps into the train. The African conductor heaved my steel trunk into the train. I climbed up the three steep steps and followed the conductor along the long, narrow corridor to my compartment. The train lurched forwards once or twice and I leaned out the window as the train left the station. The wheels started a slow beat, gradually going faster as the train pulled away.

Now, the figures of my parents and my three siblings, Dorothy, Pearl and Don were only small dots at the edge of the train track and then they were gone. I examined my compartment. Three men had entered the train in Mombasa; beside them I felt very small as I sat near the window. The brush outside went by faster and faster. An occasional glimpse of an elephant or a giraffe was instantly swallowed up by the next clump of small thorn bushes and dessert trees.

The man beside me wore a large colored cloth on his head, wrapped in such a way as to hide his hair; his beard was neatly woven, somehow tucked into itself, ever so intriguing. He seemed hairy, but nothing about him seemed unruly. The other two men, in the seats across from me, wore long pajama-type clothes, the kind I had seen on the streets in Nairobi and Mombasa. I knew these men had their roots in various provinces in India.

Their conversation, about religion, went on and on, first in English, then in Swahili. I asked the man whose hair was hidden by the orange cloth, "Why do you not cut your hair?" He could cut his fingernails but not his hair, which is what God wanted. The other two men laughed. I felt proud, listening in on conversations involving grown men, even if they were total strangers. I didn't feel afraid; I was curious and questions kept popping up in my mind. They took me to the diner car, telling me to save my supper-in-a-bag for the next day. The men continued to talk when I lay down on the top bunk and their voices, plus the constant rolling of the steel wheels on the tracks, quickly put me to sleep.

The next morning the sun was high in the sky, almost noon, when the train arrived in Nairobi. I waited anxiously on the track beside the train after all the passengers on the train had left. An African porter lifted my steel trunk down. Finally, a white man came to help me; I felt so relieved. "Sorry that I am late, but something happened to delay me," he said. "I told your father that I would meet you and put you on the train to Kijabe."

The tears in my eyes that had somehow appeared during the ten long minutes I was alone in the train station were only a memory. I enjoyed a car ride around the city, my arm out the left side of the Ford truck. The sense of being alone had disappeared; I felt joy at having been picked up by a faithful friend of our family.

I had travelled all night from Kenya's coastal dessert plain and arrived safely in Nairobi. Those three men talked unceasingly. I realized that my parents worked in a world where Asian people held their religious views with tenacity. The train trip and the contact with the three strangers was my first glimpse into the world of such different perspectives. My parents worked in an isolated place, MacKinnon Road, but they weren't inaccessible. Letters formed a link with other missionaries; letters ended up making the world safe. A letter to Nairobi brought a friend to meet me at the train. I couldn't pinpoint the feeling, but suddenly I sensed that the world was bigger than I could ever knew. After lunch the train traveled uphill from Nairobi, stopping briefly at Limuru; then at 3:00 pm it arrived at Kijabe. I was in Grade Two and had been on my own, with strangers, for 23 hours.

* * *

Slowly I learned that the Great Rift Valley, whose jagged edges begin to split the land apart north of the Dead Sea, cut its ruthless way through the crust of the earth, spreading through East Africa, and extending as far south as Malawi and the Zambezi River, all the way into Mozambique. Numerous lakes dot its 3,000-mile, (4,830 km) course, including a long trough in the Red Sea. The Rift Valley splits Kenya apart, like a mighty blow to the back of an unsuspecting foe, exposing geological ribs from which the land was formed long ago. Many volcanoes and lakes left scars upon the land.

Some anthropologists, like the Leakey family from England, were so convinced that this was where humans first appeared, that they dedicated themselves to find ancient, prehistoric bones. Richard Leakey and his family sat on scorching rocks under unforgiving sun, easing tiny bone fragments out of the past. The word was out that deep within the layers of rock, many miles to the north, bones could be found that would push the history of humans back into ages that we knew were impossible. After all, we were taught that the world had been created out of nothing, a little more than 6,000 years before.

Kijabe Railway Station looked over the valley to the opposite side, to the distant escarpment, some fifty miles away, the horizon, which was a faint blue line. Between that distant escarpment on the other side and our narrow light-red brown, dusty road on this side, the sharp triangular peak of Mount Longonot shone with clear pastel colors in the afternoon's sun-kissed sky. The dark void below the peak grasped the nearly circular volcano that had long since ceased to gasp for air. Pre-history stared us in the face every day, stubbornly occupying its ground. Tumultuous, restless little dust-devils, dancing columns of dust, partied around the mountain's base as the up-currents formed each day.

* * *

My trunk was heaved up onto the back of an old blue Chevy and the vehicle made its way along a narrow road cut into the steep sides of the hill. When the truck arrived at Kiambogo building, Malcolm Collins, one of my friends from the previous term, helped me take my trunk up the long, green staircase. His presence comforted me because his dad, Tom, and my father, Ken, were the best of friends.

The steps led to the *hatchery*, the dormitory for boys 7 to 10 years of age. The name of the dormitory combined mystery and progress; perhaps it was a bird's nest, from which baby birds learned to fly, becoming adult birds, or possibly it was a place where little tricks would come to light.

Already a few boys occupied the best beds, the upper berth. There were twelve bunk beds around the room; 24 boys between Grades One and Four slept and played there. This was my new home for the next thirteen weeks. In the center of the room a large square column of stones reached to the high roof; it was the chimney, supporting the roof. Four bulletin boards were attached to each wall of the chimney and to each bulletin board were fastened six white cards. My name was written on the top of one card. The weeks of the term were marked off in columns.

"What's that?" I asked, pointing to my new, white card.

"Your point card," said Malcolm. He explained that if you got up late, after 6:20 am, or if your shoes weren't polished, or if your khaki uniform was dirty, or if you sassed the teacher, or if you were late to meals, then you "got points off". My head was swimming from all the rules. I was trapped and didn't want to be there. Instead, I wanted to be back with Edith and Wells Devitt. I cried myself to sleep the first nights, and then I learned how much fun could be had in the Hatchery.

I chose an upper bunk close to our dorm parent's door, not a good place for me to carry out my plan. I wanted to huddle under the blankets at night. I would read *Black Beauty*; my special gifts for going to school were a torch and a copy of the story of my favorite horse. The blankets would hide the light and I would read a few pages each night. That way I wouldn't mind being away from home so much. Wouldn't it be nice to be free, be able to ride a real horse, like Prince, the Devitt's horse?

Little games were always taking place in one corner or another in the Hatchery and that was fun, but I also learned that there was one corner of the Hatchery where I would get beaten up if I approached anyone of the two bunk beds. They were the older guys and could be mean. That was the corner to stay away from.

* * *

Our dorm parents were the Davis Family. My friend Ray and I were in the same grade; his brother, Allan, was still too little for school. However, he wanted to stay in the hatchery with his big brother, Ray. We were small kids so our homework was not as heavy. If you talked during study hall you got points off.

When it was time for devotions Ma Davis read another Sugar Creek Gang book. We'd all gather around in one corner of the Hatchery, 24 little boys dressed in our pajamas, listening while she read another adventure tale, then she read the Bible and prayed.

"Lord God, Be Thou near all the mommies and daddies. May Thy strong arm be near to protect from all harm and danger," she would pray every night.

I added, under my breath, "Keep daddy safe when he is in the prison with those bad Mau Mau men." The various words used to describe the Mau Mau gave me shivers. Bad, wild, rebellious, dangerous and sly were some of the words I heard repeated repeatedly. I never heard anyone saying anything good about them.

Devotions were soon over. The lights were out. Little boys who had come from Tanganyika, to the south, and Uganda, to the west, and Ethiopia, to the north, settled down to sleep under the care of God's angels and the watchful eyes of the King's African Rifles.

Ma Davis turned the lights off. "O.K. boys. And, I don't want any monkey business. If I hear any monkey business I'll have to take points off." The switch for the lights was located near the door, which opened onto the hall. Her apartment was just down the way. Sometimes Pa Davis, with his silver hair and huge hands and fingers that played the piano better than a radio, came to say "Good night!"

Friday nights were scary. After lights went off, Allan Davis lay with his eyes shut, his hands over his eyes, his pillow covering his hands and the blanket pulled up over the pillow. He knew what happened on Friday nights.

"Ooooohhhh, loooooookkkkk." A dozen spooky voices murmured in the dark. "Heerree comes the White Bush buck."

"Noooo! I don't want to see the White Bush buck tonight," whimpered the little guy from under several layers of protective covering, his voice full of terror.

"The Whiiiiittteeee Buuuushbuck." groaned a voice as the little five-year old head peaked out. Coming towards him was a fiery light, a red circle floating in the dark. An older boy placed a flashlight into his mouth and turned on the switch, lightening up his mouth, producing the effect of an unknown danger. The light danced at the level of the lower bunk with a stunning and terrifying effect.

Suddenly, the little guy could stand it no more. He screamed. His mother came running down the hall. We heard her footsteps when she stepped out of her apartment. Every crooked board in that ancient Kiambogo building possessed its own squeak. Everyone was suddenly in bed, asleep and even snoring.

"Allan, What's the matter?"

"Nothing, it's going to be OK," he said. Several boys had promised to "plaster" him if he squealed on them. Allan may not have known what it meant to be plastered, but it didn't sound inviting.

Some Friday nights the Black Leopard joined White Bushbuck. Two lanterns appeared out of the dark. An older boy joined in the cruel fun. Knowing it was wrong to make a little guy scared, so scared that he might even wet his bed, was worthy of points off. I felt that the game was cruel. Knowing what it was to be a long way away from my home, I couldn't join in that or other cruel little jokes like short sheeting a bed, or putting a frog in someone's bed. Ma Davis, our dorm mother, lived down the hall so she couldn't see what went on after she turned the lights out. She lived so close by, yet had so little idea of what really went on in the *Hatchery*.

* * *

My weekly letter home hardly hinted at the complexities of dorm life. It seemed impossible to correctly describe pranks, and besides, if I did give the whole picture, then what would my parents have thought? Routine stuff was easy, perhaps safer to write about. It was impossible to write what life was like in my dorm. Compartmentalization began to develop: parents didn't want to hear about the realities of dorm life. Something caused me to hesitate, unwilling to tell about the exciting chapter I had just finished in my book last night. I would certainly get points off if Ma Davis or Ma Codor read a letter in which I had just written, "I was reading *Black Beauty* last night under the covers with my flashlight after lights out. . .against the rules. . .and this is what happened in the book."

Furthermore, it didn't seem right to write about the King's African Rifles. "Target practices go on every day at 4:00 p.m., which makes us feel safe. They are practicing to kill the bad men. Yesterday was Saturday and we went to First Ravine and dug a lot of bullets out of the white chalk cliff. I didn't find any, but Carly Barnett already has a dozen bullets." I didn't think mom needed to know about that time when we had gone "out of bounds", returning with spent bullets. It would only make her upset, but for us, it gave a greater incentive to go to First Ravine again.

These were the boundaries set by the school, such as "No flashlight reading after lights out!" Other boundaries were never defined, but were just as real, and these were what we knew parents would approve or disapprove of. I could not write, "I wish you were here because I got in an awful fight yesterday. I got called a bad name, so I shouted an insult, then I got cuffed on the head really hard by one of the *big guys*." I knew my mother would not want to receive a letter like that so I wrote, "I'm learning to play *nyabes*, and I'd like to have some new marbles so I can play better. Carly Barnett is the best player and he won the best *nyab* I had, my cat's eye." I left all the important stuff out of my letters.

At the end of the term two huge events took place. The first was *Rendezvous*, and the second was graduation. It was the first time I had heard of graduation, and its impact gave me much to think about. School had a starting point and an ending point. Some students had spent years at RVA and they were leaving, going to America, never to come back. They seemed so tall, which is why we called them the *big guys*. They were finishing; surely, I thought, I'll never finish school, as these older students just did.

* * *

The wind which sweeps down off the highlands into the valley constantly replaces the hot air that swoops up from the valley's floor into the cooler atmosphere. Kijabe was well named; it means "The Place of the Winds". One night there was even a pent up little scream in the wind's throat, or so it seemed.

As Grade Three began, I saw teachers talking together in a tight little group. They looked up at the hill behind the school. There was a tension in their eyes I had not seen before. Six weeks passed and the tension remained. The fear of men who lived in the bamboo forest at the top of the escarpment was very real.

And then came that Friday night. The guards on duty around the barbed wire fence were tense. It was October 1953. Ma Davis read one of the Sugar Creek Gang books. I was resting on my arm, lying on a top bunk. Little boys were wondering how the Sugar Creek Gang would get out of the latest predicament, another adventure.

I saw a tiny orange flame above the trees, above the top of the hill and sat up. Several others noticed. Ma Davis looked up and saw the tension in our faces and she tried to read faster, securing our attention with the additional energy summoned to her voice.. Our attention was riveted by the flames, which were growing higher, spreading out. We knew that a calamity was taking place; the Mau Mau rebels were burning a village. A village was going up in flames and no one could do anything. She recognized our discomfort and stopped reading. She said a quick prayer and hugged us all.

After the lights had been turned off, Ma Davis came back into the room. She stood by our beds with her arm around some of us as we looked at the hill, standing beside the four windows facing the top of the hill. High on the brow of the escarpment we watched the orange glow. It grew in size but after a long time it died down.

A Mau Mau raid had taken place. An entire village, Lari, had been burned to the ground, just because the elders in that village were loyal to British law and would not deny their belief in Jesus Christ, no matter what the consequences. Because of their refusal to enter into an accord with the men who came from the outer darkness of the forest they all died. The *big guys* whispered, saying all 300 people in the village had been burned to death except for one little boy who escaped into a tree and slipped away to another village where he awoke the villagers there. The slain elders of the village had previously accepted the message of the Christians so they could not take the Mau Mau oaths.

I remembered having heard that word, "the oaths", one day at home when my parents were talking in subdued voices in the kitchen. When daddy saw I had come into the kitchen he stopped talking. I had no idea what the word "oaths" meant, but it sounded ominous, mysterious and dangerous.

* * *

Life in the dorm consisted of endless pranks. One Friday night, almost two years later, during study hall a lot of extra disturbance arose from the end of the table where the *big guys* were studying. I was in Grade Five by this time. There seemed to be extra shuffling of feet and grunts and groans. The teacher on duty, Pa Entwistle, was slightly tense. He was a quiet sort of man, I thought. He kept looking at the *big guys* who were making the noise. I knew something was up, but couldn't figure out what.

Pa Shaffer came down from his house at about 8:00 p.m. to develop pictures taken on his camera. Roy Schaffer had been a student in previous years and had returned to RVA as a staff member, a teacher, so he knew all about pranks. During the Mau Mau he prepared students for the worst. He went to the dark room in the crawl space at the northern end of Kiambogo building, under the far end of the dining room, where we were all studying. Pa Shaffer emerged from the dark room with a frown on his face and talked with Pa Entwistle. The shuffling at the far end of the dining hall, where the *big guys* were studying, stopped. Then there was a total silence in the study hall.

Something was up. Both men went out for a few minutes and then came back. They went straight to one of the last tables and bent down to talk to one of the *big guys*. He stood up and his face was a beet red. Pa Entwistle and Pa Schaffer took the matter to the Principal, Herb Downing. Being sent to see Pa Downing was the school's worst nightmare. They asked him how much time he had spent setting up the Halloween trick.

The student had been caught red-handed on Halloween night with a fantastic Halloween trick, miles beyond the simple game of "Silent Submarines" being played at our table. During the previous weeks he had wired up the lights and wiring system of the Kiambogo building in such a way as to set a timer for 9:00 p.m. As study hall ended he was going to set off an enormous bang. Only he knew how many tricks he had planned with his genius' capabilities to wire the building.

* * *

He had been cheated out of his enormous gag by only a few minutes. The misfortune of having been discovered meant he had to do a hundred hours in "restoration time"; it would make him think how he could help the "community" of which he was a part.

He was made to do that same amount of time on community work projects, painting the walls, cleaning the sports equipment and scraping off the curled-up green paint on the handrail along the edge of the veranda. I thought it was a sign of admiration on the part of the teachers for skills, that they gave him the community project and didn't take off points off from his point card, which would have caused him to miss out on Rendezvous.

* * *

About the same time, one of the boys who didn't know how to stay away from temptation; he was unknown to us, a little professional thief. . .that's what he was. For a while everyone kept loosing things in the dorm, especially food. Everyone had things stolen from the little table by our beds. We knew someone was a pro.

To catch him one boy asked his parents for some chocolate laxative. It disappeared and the thefts stopped, although we never found out who had almost graduated with the degree of Certificate in Uniquely Acquired Properties.

* * *

Another year passed and the tricks became more carefully thought out. Of course, beds were still short-sheeted, and plastic snakes would be put under your pillow. The configurations of dorm rooms changed a bit, with a few boys switching from one room to another. Our dorm parents were now Ma and Pa Senoff, from Canada, but with a distant background in Russia. They were watching over us. Amazing! All those wonderful sermons on Sunday afternoons were supposed to change us deep down. Little boys were not supposed to have malicious thoughts, or challenge authority, or cause real trouble.

Poor Kay Senoff, having to take care for all those sweet little boys who were missing their parents. The trouble was that by Grade Six new forms of nuisance were being hatched, making things even more difficult for her. Kathleen Senoff, who had graduated from Winnipeg Bible Institute, needed every bit of her practical theology to deal with us, as well as the prayers of her supporters for wisdom. Her hair was short, carefully curled, and the patience on face sometimes betrayed a darker mood, perhaps one of exasperation.

Kay and Sam Senoff had been sent by evangelical churches in Western Canada "to go and take care of those poor little missionary kids in Africa." Actually, we didn't really know how busy her days were, buying food for the dining room from the African women who came by with baskets balanced on their heads, planning the meals, and teaching Bible Classes to the Kikuyu women in the lower part of the station.

However, during the days of the Mau Mau it had been considered too dangerous to have the *titchies* go out of the dorm at night, walking down the long green staircase, across the carport, and then out to the corrugated iron shack, the bathroom that we called our *choo*. Instead of going outside, boys would go inside. Two large enamel buckets were used each night, one pee bucket place beside the great, square column, the chimney, in the middle of the hatchery, and another pee bucket in the hallway, close to the rooms where the Grade Five and Six boys slept.

We were never quite able to fill up the bucket in any one night, which was useful because Ma Senoff had to empty it the next morning, but two boys had an appalling thought one day. We all agreed to the plan and encouraged each other to drink as much water on Saturday night as we could possibly manage. The challenge was this: could we fill the pee bucket just to the brim, but not have it overflow? "Full to the brim!" was our boisterous watchword that night. The plan worked, a little too well. We all had to go to the bathroom several times during that Saturday night.

Ma Senoff would wait until Sunday School had begun on Sunday mornings to do her more unpleasant chores but that Sunday she had a very heavy weight to carry.

When we arrived at the dining room at lunch for our special roast beef at 12:00, the door to the dining room was closed. Time passed and we became really hungry and started complaining! Sunday lunch was never this late! Looking in through the glass window in the dining room door we saw the Africans cleaning the green Formica tables where all the deserts had been completely spoiled. Those special Sunday deserts were favorites in an otherwise stagnant menu.

Apple crisp pies, our favorite desert, had been destroyed. Above, from the ceiling, drips kept coming through. Ma Senoff was thoroughly embarrassed and angry, but not as furious as Pa Senoff. We almost lost our privilege to eat lunch, but there was no way to lay specific blame. We never learned the details of how the pee bucket was overturned. Once again, what had started out as a prank ended up hurting us more than anyone else; everyone felt frustrated by the delayed, spoiled meal.

Lunch was finally served at 1:30. I never knew another time when Sunday dinner was served so late. No one ever was specifically blamed, but Giddings, Fish, Sausage, and a dozen others ring leaders were heroes of a very shady nature for a few weeks.

* * *

I had more questions. How could you know what the difference was between breaking rules in study hall (such as playing games), fire works on Halloween Night, actually thieving, and laying a trap for a thief? All four were activities that were "out of bounds", definitely not approved. I think it was about that time, when I was 11 or 12, that I began to meditate on the expression, "a grey area". So, life wasn't just black and white.

Here we were, hearing all those fine Sunday messages and listening to all those chapel talks, but our lives had many places where God still had to do a *big* job.

I'd wonder, "How can you get all that Bible teaching into you and still get into this kind of trouble? I am a Christian, so why do I still do all kinds of bad things? Why do I go along with a group when I know they are going to get into trouble? Why do I use swear words and find it so hard to say words of love and appreciation?"

The hardest words seemed to be, "I'm sorry," and "I love you."

Many times I could not understand my internal conflicts. Complete honesty was not possible; deep down I knew I needed a real change of nature in my heart.

CHAPTER 4

MACKINNON ROAD

*A*t the end of the second term, in April, my father came for me by car and took me home to MacKinnon Road. He was driving his shiny, brand new, grey Peugeot 203 station wagon. I was glad to see him, but my face fell. Why hadn't he bought a Chevrolet? Everyone said that a Chevy was the best and a Ford came next. European cars didn't even register on the list of "Admirable fathers and their fabulous cars." Anything was better than a French Peugeot. The trip from Kijabe to MacKinnon Road took almost a full day, much of it through scrub-brush land and massive, up-side-down looking trees call Baobab trees. Wild game abounded, on either side of the highway, and I lost count of the number of giraffe, gazelle, zebra, ostrich and monkeys seen on the trip.

Our family was living in Officers Quarters, in a house assigned to us by the Prison Department. The British military built MacKinnon Road as an air force base during World War II; the base was to have been dismantled, but fears remained in Whitehall, England, that colonial troubles in Africa might follow. I overheard one of the officers say to my father, "The semi-arid conditions of the coastal strip are ideal for prisons. No one could live for long in the bush even if they did escape. These Mau Mau rebels have to be punished. Did they really think they could fight against the British Crown?" I didn't understand much of his talk but I was thankful for barbed wire, lots and lots of it.

Built to withstand the rigors of a sudden air attack during the World War II, from a possible attack by Italians from Ethiopia, the houses on the disused air base boasted almost indestructible walls. I studied how these houses were built. "Successive layers of cement laid on steel mesh made pre-fabricated walls: those are capable of withstanding a direct hit!" a British sergeant bragged. The word was out that Communism was the world's next major threat. The words, "a direct hit", reminded me of the afternoon practice carried out by *askaris* at First Ravine.

British imagination didn't take into account mosquito dive-bombers. Incredible protection was built into those walls to protect from the outside, from an enemy's bombs, but they could not withstand a quiet, deadly attack from within! British forces might have expected an attack from artillery, but the roof offered no defense at all. It was built with a high peak spanning three central rooms, the idea being to create an updraft on hot days. Unfortunately, mosquitos managed up-drafts perfectly, and had filled every nook and cranny. They multiplied by the hundreds of thousands. On the first night our family moved in, which was about a month before I arrived home from school, mosquitos came dive-bombing, buzzing around Pearl's head. Their raids reminded me of the Battle of Britain; the next morning revealed the damage. Little Pearl's face was swollen. She couldn't even open her eyes because her face was covered with little red welts.

My parents spent the first full day in their new home putting mosquito netting on windows and pumping the house full of powerful mosquito spray, way up into the open rafters. Could a prayer by Moses deliver us from that plague? Gradually Pearl's face cleared up and by the time I came home, the only memory of that horrible night lay in the small brown scabs on her face.

Actually, we occupied two houses. The number of British officers willing to live in that desert were greatly diminished; most British Army men had moved back to England. The houses were small, and the second dwelling served my bedroom, a guest room, and a storage area.

Stepping outside seemed like leaving one furnace only to step into another. At home my mother came out of the kitchen, where she was finishing supper, and brushed away the perspiration with the back of her hand. MacKinnon Road was hotter than hot. The outdoors temperature was boiling in MacKinnon Road and the wood stove made the kitchen even hotter. The British dream of "bombproof houses" was conceived without a person on the committee who understood the meaning of the word "comfort". These were "the ultimate safe houses for living desert conditions – liable to attack". The kitchen, placed at the back of the house, lacked sufficient space in the ceiling to permit the circulation of air.

There was only one reason for us to live in MacKinnon Road, within the harsh conditions of Kenya's coastal dry land, and that was because the Africa Inland Mission had loaned my father as a chaplain for three years. His first assignment placed him in MacKinnon Road where 15,000 Africans were in sentenced to a detention for one or two years.

I felt afraid as he went into those big cells to meet political prisoners each day. When I asked him about this he said, "An African askari stands beside me; no prisoner would think of doing anything to me. One of their own guards me, but more than that we trust in God. He takes care of us, much better than askeris are able to do."

Men in the detention were grouped in cells, divided from one another with strong metal mesh. I pictured those men sleeping on double bunks made of steel, just like the beds in the *hatchery* at RVA. I hoped that men in jail didn't play pranks on one another, or on dad. His job was to talk to them about Jesus. He never owned a gun or carried one; and he never permitted a gun in our house. The idea that some people owned guns really upset him so I didn't tell him that his friend, Wells Devitt, had guns in his home, including the curved one to shoot the buffalo around a tree, the most dangerous game of all.

A few British boys my age lived in near the prison, where the officer's compound was located. We ran from house to house on sandy soil, or walked along the long barbed wire fence behind which Mau Mau lived in big cells. The desert conditions meant that you had to keep drinking water all the time. Adults talked endlessly on three topics: mosquitos, drinking water and Mau Mau, wondering how long the prisoners had to stay in their cells. Once in a while they asked what Kenya would be like after this was all over.

* * *

In spite of the heat I looked forward to being at home even more for the July vacation period. None of my excitement or pain at school was communicated to my parents at home. I spent hours outside where the prickly thorn bushes held many mysteries. Scrub brush, full of thorns and songbirds, surrounded the prison camp. I would ride my new bike three miles in the early morning along the asphalt road, from our house at one end of the prison camp, to the township, on the main highway. Elephants roamed the scrub bush and I was always on the lookout for animals. As I brought the mail home from the Post Office I watched birds of all descriptions. I might stop by the side of the road to count how many weaverbirds entered or left one of the long, thin bird nests made from thousands of bits of woven grass; however, they came and left too quickly to even make a guess.

A new hobby became the talk of our family and led to many conversations with adults. Dad bought me a butterfly net. I'd catch a beautiful specimen, place it in a wide-mouthed bottle with camphoric acid at the bottom, and in a few minutes the butterfly would stop flapping its wings. It was ready to be mounted on the wide insect board that hung in my bedroom. Incredibly, the desert was home to multitudes of exquisite species.

Sometimes I watched vultures fly circling on up-drafts of hot afternoon air, ready to fly down if they spotted a dead animal. Unending days of freedom, they were, with hardly any limits. What a contrast to Kijabe where my main concern was to keep points from being deducted from my point card! RVA meant learning to read, doing sums with four figures on each line and respecting the restrictions and boundaries. At home, where my father labored each day in a prison camp there seemed to be so few boundaries.

Holidays involved endless adventure. Wild animals crossed the road, or walked close to the black tarmac roads. Huge monitor lizards, almost three feet long, ran across our back yard, or through our house. Birds flew everywhere, waking you up early in the morning. Of course, you couldn't go off the tarmac into the bush. The greatest danger was getting scratched by sharp thorns; the fear of a flat tire also kept me on the road. I got a flat tire on my bike one day and had to walk back three miles pushing it in the heat at noon.

All too soon my steel trunk was packed again. My mother stayed up late at night to sew nametags onto each new item of clothing before I left. Again, my trunk was on the pebbly surface of the train station; the approaching train caused my heart to beat wildly. Mom and Pearl were talking to me. Donald, a two year-old bundle of curiosity, was walking along the platform looking at an African's bike. Then he squatted down, examining a slow-moving, green praying mantis. The daily train was going up country. Exactly one day later I would be back in the Hatchery.

"Good by, David," said my mother, kissing me. She gave me a tight hug.

The train pulled away. "You'll be back in just three months!" called my father and then they faded from view.

* * *

Soon it was time for holidays again. Down came my steel trunk from the attic over the *hatchery* and we left for Christmas, dispersing to the four points of the compass. It was my eighth birthday. I was a third of the way through Grade Three and it was Christmas time. The dry undergrowth was void of any green. Vultures squatted lazily on thorn trees and dust hung in the air. This was so different from the lush, exuberant, green highlands at Kijabe, Limuru, and the regions where tea plantations covered the areas a little bit higher than the coffee plantations.

Dorothy, Pearl, Donald and I were together again. We could play all day and sleep until 7:00 in the morning, and no one would take points off if I came to breakfast with scuffed shoes.

On the day of my birthday, mother said, "David, would you watch this cake while I set the dining room table? There is a very naughty little monkey that likes to steal things from our kitchen. He lives just outside our back yard and has the naughtiest little face. He chatters away and tries to come in the door or through a window."

I assured her that I'd be a faithful sentry, but when she came back into the kitchen, five minutes later, she let out a sharp little scream. "Oh, David, What have you done? Look at my lovely cake. How could you have done that? You should know better!"

What could be the matter? A monkey had certainly not come into the room and I was aghast. For five minutes I had been thinking of White Bushbucks and Black Leopards and wondering how that little boy got away from the bad Mau Mau up on the hill, in the village of Lari. Had he climbed a tree, or had he hidden under the corn? Absentmindedly, I was acting out what I thought might have happened to him to save him from death; the thought of his escaping mesmerized me. I had acted it all out with my eyes closed, as if the boy had to escape during the night.

"David, someone put their sharp elbow into the middle of your cake! Look at it! It's ruined!" declared my mother, disappointed. I was horrified; it was true. Someone had destroyed the cake. The enormous dent went down through the cake to the platter at the bottom. I looked at my elbow. How did all that icing get there all over my arm?

It was a clear, pointed lesson. Being absent minded could endanger my future. Mom remade the cake, reduced by one fourth of its original size. A few friends came for the party; afterwards I went out to the back of the property where sharp thorns grew and burrs covered one's socks. I kicked the ground as hard as I could, or dared. How had I been so stupid as to ruin my own birthday cake?

During the holidays Dorothy and I asked a lot of questions. "Daddy, what do you do when you are alone with the Mau Mau men in the prison? Can you tell a man is a Mau Mau just by looking at him? How many love Jesus? Will those men be persecuted and by the other bad men?" I was remembering the horror of the fire and the violence hidden within dark nights.

One morning at breakfast, after we read the Daily Light devotional book, I asked, "Mom, do you think any Mau Mau would ever try to burn our house?"

"Of course not, dear. God takes care of us. He always takes care of his children." She looked to the other end of the table and her eyes met those of my father.

I wasn't sure. If God could took care of us why didn't he take care of those elders and their families? Why were all those houses burned in that village? God wouldn't take special care of us just because we were whites, would He? If not, then why did he let all those 300 people get burned to death?" I didn't ask those questions out loud. Some questions could not be put into words.

There definitely were two worlds: one was the outer world where I conversed with other people; they responded with words and actions. The other world included my thoughts and questions; no one came into it except a few special friends. The questions going around in my head, about the Mau Mau, was part of this inside world. I couldn't tell my father how scared I became thinking about all this at night in the *hatchery*.

*　*　*

Three months later, the semi-arid land sprouted green clothes as the rains came. In just a few days light green leaves exploded silently from tinder dry branches. Clouds of birds played, splashing around in little puddles. Red birds, black birds and brown birds of all kinds sang joyfully all around. I watched a black bird; when the sun shone on its bright black feathers they became iridescent; it moved and the feathers were a dull blue and purple. How could black feathers possess colors hidden inside of other colors? In one tree there were dozens of tiny black birds with red throats. They darted from branch to branch, loud little fights going on with each other; the whole tree seemed alive.

I played with my brother, Donald. He had a new truck and a set of friends all of his own, too; at times he pushed little bugs on the ground. One day a snake, a long Green Mamba, came into the living room while we were having our family time at the end of the day. Mom rushed to the kitchen, coming back with a broom. She knocked the snake on its head and called our African helper. They crushed its skull with those small black eyes.

A neighbor said it was the most dangerous snake we would ever encounter, unless we had a run in with a Black Mamba. This Green Mamba was longer than the broom handle. We looked at its shiny silver green skin, and at its triangular head, which carried its deadly poison. We felt relieved as we buried the snake in the sand in front of our house.

Before going to bed, mom said her prayers for us, "We thank thee Heavenly Father that in Thine loving care Thou dost always keep us from harm, even from this deadly snake." We were proud that mother was so calm in the face of such danger; and glad she knew how to pray at the right time and say the right things in her prayers. When she prayed like that there didn't seem to be the same need to ask bothersome questions.

The next morning Dorothy, Pearl, Don and I went to dig up the Green Mamba in order to examine it, but it wasn't there! We could not figure it out. Last night it was dead, but now it wasn't to be found! One African told us, "The mate comes and takes away the dead snake and buries it somewhere else." Other Africans declared, "A snake never really dies until the sun had gone down on it two times." They also said its mate could come and save it and take it back into the bush. We had so much to learn from Africans.

That event brought back the occasion when mother saw a Puff Adder preparing to pounce on Pearl; she was having her afternoon nap. The snake had fallen from the wooden beam across the house, where the rafters held the roof. It fell to the floor in the center of the girls' room. Pearl was in her crib in the bedroom and the snake was swaying, getting ready to attack my sister who was sleeping after lunch. Mother went out immediately to get help from the house-help and they brought a broom, killing it: two notches on that broom.

* * *

The rains came again; the desert suddenly exploded with color and life. Dad drove us around the outside of the prison camp, creeping along with the headlights from the car casting a dim light. One night the headlights of our car revealed three huge animals standing by the road eating fresh vegetation from the trees. We watched elephants swing their long trunks, pulling down branches, eating from the green leaves that were now easy to reach. We'd be breathless for a minute and then breath slowly, staying silent, relishing the great open regions of Africa. It was so much fun to imagine how that flexible trunk could breathe at the same time as act like a hand and fingers.

The army camp was close by and a British boy and I wandered along the barb wired fence looking in at the enormous trucks, the green-black guns attached to jeeps, and the soldiers on patrol. It was dangerous, impossible, to go in there; there was a war.

More dangerous to little white boys were open pits, a constant source of danger. These were large water reservoirs, intended to provide sufficient water for British personnel. When MacKinnon Road Air Force Base was constructed the thought of children playing near the reservoirs was never included in the risk management; these large outdoor tanks were not covered. Once, just before coming home for holidays, the mother of a boy my age went berserk, crying that unending, unresolvable, terrible scream of pain. The six-year old boy next door had fallen into one of the reservoirs, boasting that he could swim, when in fact he had never been in water before. By the time his friend returned with help, hope had gone. For the entire holiday time a cloud of grief churned through the conversations of British ex-pat families. I thought it remarkable how mom and dad tried to comfort the anguish-stricken mother who finally resolved to return to England.

There was a security, a peace, a rhythm, a bond of love that encircled our house. In spite of the difficulties, the tough assignment in the prison, and the total absence of other missionaries, I sensed that this type of witness was correct for our family. Dad - I called him "Dad" now, as I became more aware of his activities – told of the conversion of whole cells of Mau Mau. In one cell about 100 men came to know Christ. He took a hand-wound gramophone with him, playing songs in Swahili, teaching the men in prison to sing. A couple of Mau Mau men had returned to their homes, having finished their detention, and they wrote to "*Bwana* Phillips", asking for literature to help them grow in their Christian faith.

At this point, dad's work developed further, for now he was working full time in the prison cells, as well as circulating copies of sermons he wrote or articles he encouraged other Christian leaders to write.

* * *

At this point a wealthy uncle on the Phillips side of the family died; dad and mom used some of the money from that inheritance to buy a refrigerator. Ours was one of the first families to possess a technological edge, certainly the only time this ever happened in our whole lives. This refrigerator ran on paraffin. None of the other families could afford one, and so our home became a center of activity for a strange reason.

Milk came daily by the train going to the coast, from Nairobi to Mombasa. Dad would bring the milk home early in the morning, in a 10-gallon milk can. Mom would pour it into many smaller containers. Several families would come for the cool, white, milk that was stored at in our refrigerator. There was always a little extra milk and that went to poor families. Mom didn't have to speak about her love for poor people; we just noticed it. She was always thinking about poor African families, even when we grew tired of Africans standing in line, outside our kitchen, for their quart of milk. She said, "God expects us to help the poor; we can find many ways to be God's means of blessing them." Dad's eyes twinkled when he was happy and these kind acts were even noticed by the Camp Commander, who was very much against the work of the Protestant Chaplain.

* * *

At MacKinnon Road we were getting ready for Christmas. My father had to make one of his regular trips to Mombasa; he prepared with care because the family bank account was extra low, although we didn't know that. We did know that we had no meat for Christmas. Mother always shared generously at this special time of the year.

Halfway along the one-hour long drive to Mombasa, a car passed us going the other way, driving north to Nairobi. The road along that section was stony, with loose stones covering the width of the highway. A stone flew at our windshield; the sudden wallop reminded me of gunshots we heard coming from First Ravine. Instantly, glass lay everywhere in the car; our smashed windshield left the car open to the hot winds.

I waited patiently at each business location while my father did his work. He methodically checked off each task on the little booklet he carried in his shirt pocket. This time, though, the first item was not one he had written down. The day started at the Peugeot garage with a new windshield being installed. This meant two things: the day's schedule had to be re-arranged, making for a late arrival back home, and dad's last bit of money was spent unexpectedly. We would not be returning with food to give away the next day.

At noon dad took me into historic center of Mombasa. On one famous corner stood the imposing Fort Jesus; its tall, majestic, white bulwarks proudly proclaimed the domination of Portuguese traders centuries before. It had been turned into a museum and I marveled that anyone, Arab or Indian, could penetrate those imposing high walls.

It was late afternoon as we started home. It was later than we would normally begin that 60-mile trip. Friends had given us afternoon tea and the visit had gone on longer than normal, so night was falling as our car climbed the steep hill from the coast, leaving tall, green palm trees by the port. When we reached the dry desert area, the dark landscape was a wall of dark scrub brush rushing by.

All of a sudden, the gleaming eyes of a small animal reflected the oncoming lights of our car. It jumped this way and that and then the scared little deer jumped off the road to one side; at the last minute decided the opposite side offered a better route to safety. Our car hit with a thump it as it jumped across the road in front of us. We stopped and our African friend, Fanuel, went back to pick it up. It was one of the smaller animals in the antelope family. We hadn't gone another five miles when the same thing happened again. We arrived at our home, on Christmas Eve with a new windshield in the car, meat for our family and small amounts for other families. All families were going through very hard times that year. For days I wondered about that provision: was it an answer to prayers, or did the two animals "just happen to jump out from the side of the road at the wrong time?"

* * *

My father became passionate about the distribution of Christian literature in East Africa. I sat in the living room of our house one afternoon, listening to him talk with a friend. "Communism is spreading throughout Africa. The only way it can be stopped in Kenya is with the distribution of Christian literature, in many languages."

Such zeal faced almost insurmountable problems. Kenyan society included more than 40 tribes and languages. Some overlapped a bit, but most languages contained different sounds, words and syntax. Swahili, which was widely used, enabled Kenyans of one tribe to speak with the other, while English, not widely used by Kenyans, served as the "language of government".

Dad met an extraordinary man during World War II. Fanuel worked in the British army for years as a translator; he knew nine languages spoken by the people of Kenya and Uganda and spoke English well: a total of ten languages. One of those languages was Arabic, learned while living near the Indian Ocean. I marveled that dad's friend could communicate in so many languages. Fanuel travelled from one market place to another with three metal trunks piled one on top of the other; he loaded them on the back of his black-framed, heavy bicycle. It was the first time I heard the word "colporteur". He often stayed at our home since they had the common desire of distributing Christian literature throughout East Africa.

* * *

Dorothy was eager to climb the tree outside our house. I told her about tricks we did at Green Tree. She tried to climb the lower branches of one tree at the front of our house, but she lost her hold and fell to the ground. A loud little cry followed the initial thud on the ground. She had broken her arm. It was early in the morning and someone called dad from the prison camp and he immediately took her in our car to Mombasa.

In the car Dorothy's head lay on Fanuel's lap. We went to the Mombasa Hospital, and a few days later, she came home with a cast on her left arm. We didn't do any more climbing for a while. At devotions, mommy prayed, "We thank thee, O God that thou hast kept Dorothy safe in this accident. It could have been so much worse. We praise thee for Thy watchful care."

I wanted to be as sincere, as quick to pray as my mother. Mother, with her ready prayers and sincere "Praise the Lord", around the house made home a predictable, loving place.

CHAPTER 5

THE HARDEST PART OF FORGIVENESS

*H*olidays were over and Miss Verity Coder was my new Grade Three teacher. She was strict, on the lookout for cheaters and she knew how to maintain discipline. She had a knack for catching me when I was being naughty. She taught us all our subjects: reading, writing, spelling and penmanship; arithmetic, social studies, and music from America. Like the other women, she wore her hair short, full of cadences and curls. The twinkle in her eye quickly changed to irritation; she had a combined Grade Three and Four classroom; she had her hands full, trying to keep students under control. Her long face was filled with a very wide smile and white teeth, pleasant enough when all was well.

She had difficulty controlling the students at the back of the class at times; unnecessary comments were muttered at the back of the room when her back was turned, as she wrote on the blackboard. I made a smart-ass remark after everyone else had realized it was time to "button down the hatch', to shut up. Others were clever enough to realize that the sky that day showed a tempest blowing up, that she was in a bad mood. I was slow to notice such things; I still had my sails out full when her Nor'easter struck.

Ma Coder asked me to repeat what I had said. I did so, with attitude and my sore knuckles let me know such comments were not acceptable, but I made another smart comment and later missed half an hour of climbing time in Green Tree. It was my first experience of detention. Children under Grade Five did not normally get detention.

An undeclared war broke out. I settled back in my chair, rebellious, delaying the completion of my assignment. Outside of class my small smoldering fire of rebellion was starting to burn. One boy called me a Cranky Canuck and I called him a 'stinking American'." I had no idea where my comment came from and I ducked, but not before he landed a sharp rap on the top of my head. However, I didn't *kwapper*, but kept standing on my feet. Fighting a much bigger boy was a bad idea.

Nobody said that those things shouldn't go in the weekly letter, but you knew instinctively that they were better left unsaid. Ma Coder wouldn't like it if she read my letter home and learned that I told my parents what went on in the dorm. My parents wouldn't like it either. So, it was easier to write, "Dear Mommy and Dad, I am fine. How are you? School is fine, too. I'm climbing Green Tree now, and learning about addition and subtraction. We just learned a new song called, 'She'll be coming 'round the mountain when she comes'. Next week we start on multiplication. I love you, David."

The term passed without having found a resolution to these small outbursts. I made up a number of tasteless jokes, usually using Ma Coder's name in an unpleasant rhyme.

* * *

One day I saw a big swarm of birds coming in over the play area. We were playing in trails carved into the embankment, the thrill being that Dinky toys could go to up and down their own escarpments.

I said to Malcolm, "*Dig* that! All those birds are coming!"

"Those aren't birds," he said. "They're locusts!"

The locust swarm flew past during three days. Before they came everything was green; afterwards, the landscape was a dull, ugly brown. We got sick of killing the insects. The only fun thing to do was tear the back legs off, and holding the hip in between thumb and finger of one hand, squeeze the thigh with the other hand. The leg shot out and the sharp needles on the back of the leg could poke someone really painfully.

Malcolm Collins said that his father, who lived in the desert of North West Kenya, knew when a drought was coming. The drought was about to begin when locusts swarmed.

* * *

When that term came to an end, my point card was filled with little black marks. By now I knew you only got to attend the best party of the term if your point card showed a mark of 7.6 or above, and I barely made it to *Rendezvous*.

Grade Three was almost over and once again the great day of celebration honored the *big guys*. By now the names of senior students were a bit more familiar than a year before because I saw them distinguish themselves on Sports Day, in chapel and other events. What was going to happen to to Wilfred Danielson, David Dibben, Daphne Downing, Judy Rutherford, Stan Barnett and Lois Teasdale? Where did the older students go after spending all those years at RVA? What happened to them?

* * *

There was a special set of deeper life, spiritual meetings in Eldoret known as the Keswick Meetings. These were held in the residence and auditorium of the Eldoret Girls' School, a large British private boarding school with extensive green lawns, attended by the daughters of British and South African settlers. More than four hundred people attended these annual meetings of a one-week duration. My father was the secretary of the Keswick Conference in Kenya and was on a first name basis with so many people.

We enjoyed the trip up country, from McKinnon Road through the unsurpassed countryside. The animal life was abundant; ostriches and giraffe, zebra and antelope came into view and disappeared as the dust rose behind our car. After stopping in Nakuru we posed on the Equator for a family picture.

Bible teaching filled our days at RVA; now, during the holidays we attended Bible Readings or participated in the children's program. Afternoons found us at the swimming pool, jumping in the deep end and splashing each other with shouts of glee.

We arrived at Keswick Conference and I was playing with friends near one of the dorms. It happened to be the dorm where single women were staying. Who should come out of the building but Ma Coder!

Afterwards, dad took me aside, "Miss Coder tells me that you have been quite bad this term. Is that true?" I examined the ground at my feet with focused scientific attention, noting the way that the ants were marching along, pulling tiny loads of cut grass.

"Is it true?" My silence was an unspoken admission. My toe systematically killed any ant unwise enough to come within striking distance. "I want you to say sorry to her during the time that we are here at this Conference."

I tried the only escape that I knew. "Mommy," I said after a tasty meal, "do I have to say sorry to Ma Coder?"

"Say Miss Coder, David! Now, what do you think?" she replied. I didn't know how to respond when people used a second question to answer my inquiry. Adults enjoyed such an advantage when it came to an argument.

Each day I felt more miserable. At the program for children I'd win the memory verse for the day, or the contest for finding Bible references. In terms of Bible knowledge I was in first place, as if that meant anything. If importance was given to putting teaching into practice, then I came last. Obedience and knowledge were altogether different.

Twin sentiments struggled against each other. I felt contrition; I really was sorry that I had made such a big thing out of Ma Coder's name. I was sorry that I had been responsible for the on going little skirmishes in my private war with her. On the other hand, I was not sorry enough to say that I would never do it again. Did God understand those feelings? Many questions could never be uttered.

On the last day of the Conference I went to the women's dorm. "Would you ask Miss Coder to come?" I asked someone. I apologized to her and said that I would not do it again. My sentiments were not completely pure. I didn't know if I might eventually begin another long struggle against her, for one thing.

But, after saying sorry I was amazed at how light I suddenly felt. I seemed to have had an enormous load lifted off. The sensation of asking for forgiveness, saying "Sorry", and being forgiven, was as good as, or better than, having completed the difficult "climbing trails" in Green Tree, our favorite tree between our dorm building and the playing fields. The experience meant more to me than mom or dad could ever know. I found it so hard to genuinely repent, to say I was wrong for dumb comments, for the outbursts of anger and the unnecessary, mean-spirited things I had said about my teacher. There was no one to blame but my own waywardness.

The hardest thing about forgiving, in that experience, was saying I was wrong, that I would not repeat those actions, which I named, and asking her to forgive me. Probably that was the deepest lesson for me from that year's Keswick's deeper life meetings in Eldoret. Beyond the Bible Lessons and the children's program, the word "obedience" had a new meaning.

* * *

At night I lay on my back with my hands under my head. I looked up at the darkness instead of reading books under the covers with my flashlight, risking more points off. Life contained many puzzles. Why was it so difficult to ask forgiveness?

I learned about forgiveness and reconciliation, part of the steady diet at chapel, Church and Sunday School. Why was it hard to put into practice? Again, I told myself that asking for forgiveness was more difficult than all those jumps from branch to branch in Green Tree, chasing each other around the branches like monkeys. Some nights I stayed awake attempting to understand how I could be myself without get into trouble. The thoughts never quite finished forming in my mind.

Once again, the long term stretched beyond me, another 13 weeks at school, followed by a short four weeks at home. I would go to sleep asking another question. Why did time at school go by so slowly, and yet time at home simply sped by?

CHAPTER 6

GREEN TREE

Now Dorothy was starting school and dad drove us to school, rather than take the train. We sang in the car on the long drive to RVA, and the songs took us ever closer to Nairobi and Kijabe, our home for another three months. It was easier to laugh at a little made up ditty than remember the faint sign of tears on mother's face.

It was too painful to remember leaving Pearl, her round little face with the happy smile and bright blond hair worked into two little pony tails, framing her smiling face. Pearl's blond hair was much finer than Dorothy's. Mom commented on how thick Dorothy's hair was. "I hope you never cut your thick, dark hair," mother said. Pearl had looked up at her older sister, "In two years I'll go with you!"

Kijabe's altitude, at 7,200 feet, together with its position on the wind-swept edge of the Rift Valley, meant that classrooms were chilly in the early morning. One of the special treats of arriving early was being able to stand in front of the fireplace, slowly turning around and warming up as hot flames crackled away, sending sparks shooting up the dark chimney. Usually I sat at the back of the class. The Grade Three students sat on one side of the room, next to the fireplace; now, in Grade Four, I sat near the windows.

There was such a variety of capabilities in that classroom of 24 students in the two grades. Teachers wanted academic achievement: a word we heard repeatedly. If we had given teachers a grade, it might have been "too conscientious". Every day we had homework to do at night, including Fridays. On the line for "Faithfulness in giving homework", I would have written, "A + for effort." Everyone always wanted an "A".

* * *

What we boys really admired were qualities related to survival outdoors. One of those who knew how to survive well in the forest was Carl Barnett. The Barnett clan seemed like a skeleton in the mission, holding up the administrative structure, giving shape to policies and decisions; together with a dozen other families, they defined the history of the mission.

Every class had a Barnett: Carol, James, John, Linda, Patricia, Paul, Ted, Elizabeth, Eileen, Charles, or Deborah, at some time in our schooling. They were either brothers and sisters, or cousins. Carl had suffered an unfortunate accident, losing the use of his eye. Carl had trouble keeping up with the rest of the class in those "less important" subjects: math, reading, and writing. For him bird hunting and stone throwing and spotting wildlife ranked higher. No one could throw a stone farther off the edge of cliff than Carl; no one hunted a bird with more caution, excitement or success. The loss of one eye didn't hold him back from playing *nyabes*. He was the champion in each game of marbles.

For example, Carly had the uncanny ability to spot a katydid on a tree. At times during the year the little insects, about two inches long, sang in a choir. The music had one note and each insect mastered the high pitched screech to perfection. Their "songs" were so loud they could keep you awake night and day. Katydids could sing loudly, shouting out, defying anyone to spot them. Their camouflage was amazing. Carly would say, " *Dig* that! Look right there. I'm going to hit it with my *catty*." I couldn't see the insect, and for a full minute I'd gaze at the point he had noticed until I made out the little black wings and head, perfectly merged into the bark of the Black Wattle tree. Carly taught me how to hunt katydids. He saw another one: "wham!" He had hit it dead on. After that, whenever I liked something I said, "I *dig* this," or "*Dig* that!"

Carl might need a new *caddy*; he'd spend a Saturday morning searching the forest for a perfectly forked branch of a tree. Having cut down the branch, he balanced the fork in his hand. If it didn't feel just right he would throw it away and find another. When it felt right he marked off four inches above and below the fork and discarded the rest. Then, using his penknife with care, he made slots around the top of each upper end of the "V".

He cut bicycle inner tubes into long, thin strips of rubber and tied wider, shorter bits them against the wood. The small rubber band went round and round the top of the "V". At times we used patches off old softballs for the leather pouch. The result was a perfectly made *catty*. Stones from his catapult could sail about 100 yards. He was the best shot with a *catty*, as well as with a *nyab*.

Carly had another artistic skill. The stuffed birds that he mounted were just as fine as those in the enchanting panoramic wildlife scenes at the Nairobi Museum where Dr. Leakey worked as he endlessly tried to show that Kenya's ancient soils hid the earliest remains of mankind. We compared the taxidermy skills of Carl and our friends with those of the professionals who mounted realistic scenes of lions, antelope, wildebeest and leopards in realistic, dimly lit surroundings behind great sheets of glass. The result, if RVA had been grading students in this future career, would have easily resulted in an "A".

* * *

There were other survival skills important for youngsters who were growing up in Africa, but none reached the level of climbing trees. Perfecting that skill consumed our free time between 3:30 p.m. and supper at 5:00 p.m. For weeks without end we climbed.

The best place of all was Green Tree, located at the very entrance to the school. Green Tree must have been planted by Providence. It combined the requirements for endless fun: a well-nourished tree offering wild, green exuberance. The lowest branches were easy to grab ahold of. Branches went out in all directions. Even a small boy of eight could get into the tree with ease. We didn't know what kind of tree it was botanically speaking; we just knew it was our kind of tree. Dark green leaves grew at the ends of branches, so the inside of the tree was open, exploding with lurching possibilities from the most timid crawling to the most inane jumps from tree branch to tree branch.

Pa Senoff, our new dorm parent, said he had proof-positive that mankind was going back to the monkeys. He said it in a kind sort of way, followed by a little snorting laugh. He loved to laugh at his own jokes. As a result, we *titchies* thought that he was making an insult of us, but some of the *big guys* kind of liked his dry humor.

When I realized that boys had been climbing that tree for at least a generation of students, and without anyone getting killed, I examined the reckless ways of jumping in the tree more carefully. There were no circuses around Kijabe, but if they were, Green Tree was a perfect place to begin training.

A trail had been established *within* the tree. In fact, three levels of difficulty challenged the strong-of-heart, each trail more risky that the previous one. The most common trail started at one branch and a fellow would leap into the air, certain to grab the next branch several feet beyond his grasp. His legs would follow through and his knees would follow forward, hanging from a third branch. Grabbing it now with his hands, and letting go of his second handhold, he would dive forward to grab a fourth branch. The branches supporting the back of our knees were worn down to a smooth surface. It all required perfect balance to keep from falling ten, or twenty, feet to the ground.

The trail inside the tree was the *"trail of the free and the home of the brave"*. It separated men from the boys. I never saw a man try it, but many of the boys were able to do the trail in less than forty seconds. The first time that I saw a guy do the trail I was left shivering with excitement and with trepidation. I wanted to do the same jumps from branch to branch but feared falling.

The trail could only be done " officially" if there was someone with a watch timing you. Other wise it was for *chickens*. But, you could enjoy Green Tree even if you didn't do the trail. Almost every boy had his own favorite perch in the tree. Some liked to hover right on top, some thirty feet or more off the ground, where they stood on the slender top branches and looked out at the valley, just their heads poking above the leaves. That was a difficult stance; it required perfect balance.

The branches of Green Tree were slender and smooth, straight and solid. They were as hard as steel and unbreakable. It was impossible to break a branch; such was the strength of our favorite perch. I only remember one bad fall, when a guy fell out of the lowest branch. He was about six feet of the ground, trying to get into the tree. He had a white cast on his arm for six weeks. For a while no one was allowed to climb the tree, but then the advice changed to, "Be careful while climbing Green Tree!"

* * *

The brevity of life came to us in a sudden, serious way when Pa DeYoung died in 1957, leaving Edythe DeYoung and her daughters, Jocelyn and Judy, to manage on their own. There were no classes on the day of his funeral, and the little cemetery, below the African Schools and away from the area designated for the new Kijabe Hospital, seemed so cold and forlorn. All the adults had tears in their eyes and everyone gave Edythe long, loving hugs. I could never call her Ma DeYoung after that. There was something brave about her widowhood, living in Africa after the death of the man she loved so much. She was always Mrs. DeYoung to me.

Their home wasn't complete without their father. The day we spent walking to the cemetery, watching the grave be filled with dirt, and coming back up the hill to RVA was one of the saddest, most sobering, I had at school. It seemed like starting to write a story, but never reaching the end, never getting the last paragraph written. Could we ever question the will of God? When someone died prematurely was there ever an answer to the endless questions that came for those in grief?

The special thing about Edythe DeYoung was this: she chose to stay on as a teacher at RVA, even after becoming a widow. She showed how much she loved us; she stayed with her students. Her commitment and resilience spoke, teaching us about suffering without using words. Jocelyn and Judy didn't have a father anymore.

When I was five I watched Rosalie as she breathed her last, the young woman who watched over me when mother went to the dispensary at Kabartonjo to care for the sick who stood in line patiently waiting for medical care. She was so young. And recently, my grandfather, Percy Phillips, had died in England. I didn't know him well, so the impact of his passing away was not so emotional, although I felt sorry for dad who had now lost his father.

The sad trip to the Kijabe Cemetery brought serious thoughts to mind. I realized that being really sorry meant saying you weren't going to do something again. It meant a real change. Then, looking up at the darkness in the night I'd, wonder how many times I had hurt my Heavenly Father. How could I say I wouldn't do bad things again? Some nights I felt close to God. Ma Senoff helped us in our prayers. We prayed for forgiveness for our sins.

Why couldn't everything be as straightforward as a math problem? Math was orderly, just a column of with four numbers on each line. Division was proving to be a little more difficult, but problems always had a correct answer. However, an argument with a dorm parent, which one of the boys lost, made me realize that experiences were much more complicated. I didn't have answers for all the things that kept tumbling around in my head.

Then I was asleep and the sun was streaming in the window again and another day had begun.

CHAPTER 7

MY BEST CHRISTMAS GIFT, EVER!

The next Christmas was memorable for another reason. Grandma Hill, in Winnipeg, had sent a big parcel through the mail. My gift was a special leather belt, with native Canadian Indian designs, red and blue, made from hundreds of tiny beads. It was a fabulous present, one that would make me stand out. Across the back, made out of red beads, were the letters C.A.N.A.D.A. It was my best present; I wondered how Indian people in Canada could sew so many bright colored beads so closely together on a belt.

The belt was so special that it had to be packed on top of my steel trunk; it would only be worn on special occasions. I didn't want anything to damage my special belt. When we arrived at school I proudly wore my new symbol. I didn't mind so much that folk called me *Flappit*. I had my brand new belt on at supper on the first day of the new term.

* * *

The Davis family had asked for and received permission to transfer from the Kijabe Mission Station to Machakos, in the territory of the Kamba people. It was the last term that Ma Davis would be our Home Maker.

So, when we came back to school, our new dorm parents were Sam and Kay Senoff, from Western Canada. A flurry of dust rose from the hill beyond the playing field. A yellow Caterpillar tractor groaned, pushing against the stubborn sod. Pa Senoff was already leaving his mark on the land, creating a new playing field for students.

Sam Senoff's determination showed in his eyes, in his steady gaze; Recently arrived from Canada his sense of purpose was soon put to work, trying to reshape the Rift Valley. His high forehead, short, curly hair and generally tight lips were often covered with sweat and dust as he labored endlessly, after school and every day during vacation. The grassy mound he tried to remove had to be scraped, moved, cajoled, pushed, repositioned and smoothed out. Finally, one year later, it had been transformed into something resembling a full sized playing field. The effort put in by Pa Senoff, Pa Propst and two *big guys* was certainly worth it.

However, the task was enormous and the bulldozer forever seemed to be in bits and pieces, out of commission. It was obvious to all that the Eastern wall of the Great Rift Valley resented a Senoff-sized intrusion against its ancient slopes, no matter how tiny a dent might finally be. The resistance of that land to being removed played a jinx on the gear box hidden in the tenacious, loud, yellow machine that dared to form a level playing area from the side of a hill. I was sure that the task was beyond the limits of the bulldozer imported from America.

The tractor was forever breaking down and spent most of its time resting under the quiet shade of an enormous branch; it was outfitted with yet another clutch and a new set of gears. One of the *big guys* was the resident mechanic. He seemed to live with his feet dancing in the air as his head and arms flailed away inside the bottom of the machine, under the black driver's seat, surrounded by a mass of silver bolts and broken teeth of yet another gear that met its death moving a tiny bit of the Rift Valley.

For a whole year Pa Senoff struggled with the elements but bit by bit the ground gave way. A new playing field took shape where previously a knoll covered with wild flowers stood bravely, daring the never ending wind to bend them over and keep them fixed to the ground. The project added greatly to RVA; all students would use the field for games and recreation, for baseball, track and field, soccer and even marching bands. When it was finished my opinion of Pa Senoff changed radically, for the better. In the future we would play rugby on the field, even though one rocky part resisted the transformation from rock to green sod. That corner of the field always reminded of the Parable of the Four Soils.

* * *

While undertaking the mammoth task of shaping a flat playing field from of a rolling hill, one technical problem resisted a solution. Water had to drain onto both sides of the field. One side hugged the hill, creating a messy little swamp; water would not drain away without expert help from an engineer.

The rainy season dumped water from the hill above onto the field, so it would be unusable for four months unless the run-off water could escape. Pa Propst, the civil engineer on the mission station, and the father of my classmate, Barbara, drew up the solution. The surveying work was done and a long, deep gash cut the playing field, right across center field. A concrete pipe was laid down to empty the rainwater, and then the deep hole was back filled. Grass was planted and the football field was ready.

* * *

God gave Saturdays to boys for play; sometimes we played organized games, while at other times we found odd things to do. On special days, on Saturdays, I wore my beaded belt from Canada. All the other guys could boast about America. I had my prized belt, the best piece of North America around!

The most competitive boys were found on their knees with a marble between their thumb and their first finger. Playing *nyabes,* as the game of marbles was called, demanded total attention and real skill. The purpose was to reach 100 points, or more. The winner from the previous game tossed his marble. Its position formed a new center. He stepped on the marble, forming a tiny concave spot, and then used his hand to draw a circle as wide as the palm of the hand.

The means used to gain points involved smashing the marble of an opponent as far away as possible from the circle. One got a point for each foot between one's own marble and your opponent's, so you paced off the distance between the two marbles, adding your score on the way up to 100 points.

The strategy of the game was to keep your nyabe within the circle. If Carl Barnett's marble was within the circle, he would smash my marble away; his stayed smack in the center, twirling on its axis. He was one of the few who managed a direct hit. Then Carl would pace the distance, one, two, three, adding that number to his increasingly large total.

When Carl had finished counting his paces, and everyone groaned at how far ahead he was, the next player might yell, *Uppies*, which meant he could raise one hand on top of another in order to fire his marble over the *nyab* belonging to another player. The others were on edge, ready to yell *Nix-Uppies*, which meant during that turn the next player could not gain advantage of one hand supporting the other, gaining an inch or two above ground. Occasionally, the winner added the marbles from his opponents to his collection of *nyabs*.

One Christmas, I asked for marbles and received a small bag of marbles that looked like *cat's eyes*. By the end of the term I was down to only one marble. How was it that Carly, with only one good eye, won so many games?

I had played marbles first at the La Verendrye Elementary School in Winnipeg, named for the fur trader and explorer who travelled with his four sons: they were the first Europeans to reach Wyoming and see the Rocky Mountains. However, his name meant nothing to me: I was in a Grade One class for the first three months of school and the snows of Winnipeg arrived. There it was easy to play marbles in the snow and hard to keep one's fingers warm, but playing in the warm, red dirt at Kijabe was so much more fun.

* * *

If it weren't a game of marbles demanding our attention then we would move to the sloped banks. Dinky Toys dominated. The sloping bank, just below Green Tree, provided the perfect location for small cars to zoom up and down the hill, or in and out of little caves. Some *big guys* mastered the art of imitating the sounds of cars and trucks; they could keep this up for hours.

At times like these, on Saturday mornings, I forgot the tummy aches before coming to school. Home was where cinnamon buns and birthday cakes were served. The best of school took place when games of marbles, or dinky toys, or sheer adventure commanded all our efforts. Best of all, I had my new belt.

* * *

The drainage pipe under the new playing field was complete, a huge task. One day, several boys discovered that one could enter the concrete pipe at one end and crawl out the other end, having gone a distance of almost eighty yards on hands and knees. All the boys knew about this adventure. but we kept it a secret from our teachers.

I made my first trip through on a Saturday morning, shivering with fear. If a storm should arise, we would be caught inside and drowned; however, it wasn't the rainy season. Crawling forward into the darkness, I felt black dread; the pipe sloped downward. After 25 yards, the concrete pipe leveled out and there, in the far distance, at the other side of the newly finished soccer field, a tiny spot of light proclaimed freedom, victory, and perhaps a dance of joy for having crawled through the storm pipe.

Bit by bit I wiggled through the pipe that was just high enough to accommodate young boys. The sharp cement bits, which sometimes drew blood on my hands, marked the beginning or end of each section of pipe. These sharp shards demanded concentration and caused me to slow down. Above, tons of red-brown earth formed center field, the middle of the soccer field.

The sharp cement edges biting into my hands were so blasted painful! I kept working cautiously forward towards that round spot of light, which was now becoming larger. I arrived at the end and popped out like a ground hog, and went through the pipe again. I ran back to the dorm, delighted because there could be no "points off"; no dorm parent had ever written a new limitation: "points off for crawling through the culvert."

A thought crossed my mind; no one could imagine every dangerous thing. The Point System, if it was to work, had to have something else besides a list of "Things not to do". Taking points off for everything meant continually adding to the list of "do not do this". Here was this new culvert. I had discovered a central flaw in the Point System, and that gave me a tiny bit of pleasure, but that thought disappeared a half an hour later.

I scrambled up the steep bank, knowing I had discovered something of importance. I ran back to the dorms across the soccer field, across the baseball diamond, across the little road leading down to the hospital and African schools, straight through the parking lot with the flag pole set in the middle, and up the stairs to the Hatchery.

I took my pants off and got ready for lunch. They were covered with damp red dirt at the knees. As I pulled my belt out of the pants I noticed that most of the colorful beads had been scraped off. Those sharp points of concrete inside the pipe extended all the way around. At each joint in the pipe, above my back, a few more beads were destroyed.

My precious Canada belt was spoiled, ruined beyond all recognition! The only thing that remained from its constant encounter of brushing against the top of the sharp concrete spikes inside the culvert was the colored beadwork at the sides, over my hips. Angrily, I yanked the belt out and examined it more closely. It was true! I had ruined my own belt! Having done what I knew would not be approved of (crawling through the pipe), I hurt no one but myself.

I slid my belt back into my clothes locker, right against the back where no one could find it, in the same place where it lay every Sunday to Friday. This time, though, it would not come out to be used again.

* * *

Yes, there were aspects about rules, points, obedience and boundaries that I hadn't thought of yet. The experience of finding out where those boundaries were and how to live within those boundaries was a very painful experience.

I never wore my favorite belt again. Now it was useless. I didn't know if I should throw it away, because it was wrecked, or keep it; my grandmother, Lily Hill sent it to me.

The Point System had its own weak points, but my brushing up against the tight space in the drainage pipe, constantly rubbing against the small sharp concrete spikes at the point where the portions joined together, taught me a lesson. I had brushed up against the Law of Unintended Consequences. Dim coals of rebellion might glow, but who was to blame? There was nobody but myself to accuse for my ruined belt.

CHAPTER 8

TRIPS, GAMES AND LETTERS

One Saturday morning we all tumbled down the steps from the hatchery to the parking lot. The barbed wire had just come down and the resulting empty space seemed to us to be enormous. There, in the middle of a parking lot, jammed into a small cage, was a young leopard. It had set off a trap as it went in to capture the little animal tied to the trigger. The leopard snarled and hissed, setting my hair on end.

The older boys looked on intently, studying the details of how the cage was made. They decided to store away that information for a future date. It came in handy as many small cages were set in the future years; some boys became hunters.

* * *

A month passed by and at breakfast one Saturday morning we were told to brush our teeth quickly and get our beds made. Even the slow moving trucks on the mission station seemed to hurry themselves into action that day. We chugged up the steep dirt road, arriving at the top of the escarpment. We went past small Kikuyu villages and turned into the area where a rouge elephant had gone on a rampage. She had broken off her right tusk at the base while trying to get roots out of the dry ground. Then she had become maddened with pain, for the thick nerve in the center of her broken tusk must have become infected. As she struggled with pain, she had killed several Africans in her frenzy, destroying many huts and *shambas*, or gardens.

Over 120 kids spilled out of the trucks and vans, standing close to the Africans after we raced to the spot where the elephant fell. It was lying on its left side. Such a proud creature at one time, she was now was a pathetic sight. One bullet from an elephant gun had done its work. Because that elephant had become a menace to the African villagers, the DC, the District Commissioner, had granted permission to shoot it. The Africans in those villages had a high regard for the foreigners who, with one blast from their elephant gun, brought a huge animal to a quick, painless end.

Before cutting the elephant into pieces of meat for the people in nearby villages, several old men came forward. The elders of the village were dressed in leather hides, sown front and back at one shoulder. They hobbled forward, using gangly walking sticks. Evidently, their rheumatism was acting up and they wanted the best treatment for this ailment: to lie inside the still warm intestines of an elephant. The huge belly was cut open and the old men's legs and arms received a unique, priceless, medical treatment. Then they stretched out their legs, hobbling off. It was original, rare, holistic health care.

As the job of cutting up the fallen beast began, I was caught between the fascination of a biology class up close, and revulsion at seeing so much blood. Peanut butter and jam sandwiches were being served for RVA students by some of the single lady teachers at a very respectable distance, so I didn't have to watch the bloody scene.

The fresh elephant meat was parceled out to the hundreds of Kikuyu villagers who had gathered. In appreciation for his work of killing the rouge, the African elders cut off a section of the trunk for Herb Downing. He, in turn, donated that delicacy to RVA. At first we didn't fancy the idea of eating elephant trunk. I made up my mind to taste it; it tasted much better than the liver we had been served the previous week! There was only a little bit of elephant trunk for each student. It was the only time I ever ate elephant meat.

A square section of skin was cut off and given to RVA, as well as one of the feet. The rough slab of elephant skin, about six inches in diameter, was nailed to the wall in the RVA laundry. For years, when I went there to get my clean clothes back from the African men who washed our clothes, I rubbed my fingers lightly along the rough hairs of that elephant; tiny hairs were strong as wire. My fingers felt the tiny cracks in that grey skin, contours shaped like a map of some distant world.

I knew that the elephant had to be killed. Nothing else could be done unless someone could make that mighty beast agree to a dental cure, relieving it of the pain caused by infection in its broken tusk. I loved the wild life with its majestic adaptation to the plains, but I didn't like to think about guns, traps and taxidermy. Perhaps the wild, rugged beauty of Kenya presented a false picture. Strong animals ate the weaker ones, and the cheetah, leopards and lions were the most powerful of all.

In our home there was a profound love of the graceful, wild creatures. For the first time an interesting passage from Romans made sense to me. "The whole of creation groaneth and travaileth in pain," went the text, and I began to realize how much more pain and groaning took place in the animal world, the constant struggle of the large cats to survive on the plains. Humans and animals shared the world, and suffering, together.

* * *

I wrote home to my parents about the episode, probably one of the more detailed, interesting letters they received from me. Usually my letters simply stated that everything was fine. I had come to realize that Ma Coder read all my letters because she sometimes made suggestions about what to write. However, this time was different; I wrote about the elephant. While writing I remembered a painful first visit to the dentist and somehow, I felt sorry for the elephant.

Since I was still learning to write bigger words I didn't convey my real thoughts. How unfortunate it was that the pain of a broken tusk could drive an elephant mad, causing it to walk through a *shamba*, destroying the vegetables of an African family, or even killing people! Life seemed unfair for that great beast. I saw a bloated stomach stuck high into the air, and the body being cut with long, sharp *pangas* in the hands of those expert farmers.

* * *

At the same time, a letter came from home to us about a similar experience. A train had smashed into an elephant on the tracks near our home in MacKinnon Road. The black and white picture sent to me showed Don sporting a great smile as he stood on the fallen creature. It lay off to one side of the railway tracks. Don was about five years old. His short blond hair and his bright smile topped off his wide shorts as he stood on the very top of the great belly of the beast. That elephant wasn't a rogue. It had been unfortunate enough to stop dead in its tracks and gaze straight into the oncoming lights of a locomotive.

* * *

An outing took us once a year to Limuru, 20 miles away. Jim and Trixie Hodson supported RVA with their prayers, financial donations and the provision of a wonderful annual picnic for the whole student body.

Their orchard farm included a space large enough for more than 100 students to sit in a circle. The best part of the excursion came when Jim Hodson placed a huge square of chocolate at the center of the circle. All the students from RVA gathered to throw the dice. Two six's earned the chance to carve as much chocolate from that large brown block as possible, but first one had to put kitchen gloves on, which are clumsy because they are used to take hot pans out of a stove. It took several seconds to pull on those impossible, awkward gloves, and, using the thick oven mitts, take up the knife and fork and then begin to chop at the rock-hard chocolate.

Rarely did anyone have sufficient time to balance tiny broken pieces of chocolate and enjoy them because other students kept throwing the dice, intent on taking their turn in the middle. Another set of six's resulted in everyone screaming again with excitement and then another person had their turn. Those Saturdays in Limuru were wonderful.

* * *

Our favorite meal was served for lunch on Sunday: roast beef. Ma Senoff had imported this custom from Canada. Ray made an impression on me as he taught me how to enjoy Sunday noon lunches later on Sunday evenings.

The room we stayed in brought great pride; President Teddy Roosevelt stayed there when he came through Africa in 1909. It was at that time he dedicated Kiambogo building as a boarding school. Roosevelt's hunting expedition became the subject of numerous books in the USA.

Ray had a modern form of "hunting and gathering", much more up my alley than Roosevelt's painful slugging, which had involved trekking through dangerous underbrush. Ray only had to trek through the lunch hall to prepare for a fabulous Sunday evening treat. He was clever enough to take several extra slices of beef in one pocket; into his other pocket he slid two slices of white bread. Sunday evening found him munching on what had to be the world's most enjoyable roast beef sandwich. I learned the same trick, amazed at how delicious food tasted when snuck out of the dining room. The food was served, so it really was ours, but we were not supposed to take food away like this to our dorms.

* * *

Alan Hovingh, the new dorm parent for Westervelt Dorm, had his hands full with boys whose imaginations wandered down many mischievous paths. Once he came back from a holiday to find a fully assembled Model T car in his room. He was not amused, but he was a good-natured man and asked the perpetrators of that trick to take it apart and remove it from his dwelling. Nor was he happy when, on another occasion, his room was full of spume, a massive cloud of shaving cream emptied out of many shaving kits.

Pa Hovingh's days seemed happier for a while when we saw him walking with Ma Barrett, going up the road from Green Tree to her home above the playing field. We whispered to each other the latest gossip about them, when they had been spotted walking together, but nothing came from our fanciful stories or imaginations.

* * *

The highlight of the day took place when the mail came in the afternoon. Letters were written to parents in several countries; in turn, letters and care packages arrived from parents. The biggest thrill of all was to receive a letter and share it with Dot, and later Pearl and Don. Like homing pigeons, whipping around the field and then flapping off quickly into the distance, we circled the porch beside the car park, waiting for a word from home as thoughts took us back to our parents, good food and the next vacation.

Roy Entwistle, Tom Lindquist, or one of the other teachers, would stand on the steps of the Kiambogo building. The mailbag had just come from the Kijabe Township, three miles away. We stood waiting, 120 kids with arms ready to be out- stretched in a jiffy. Some students received letters more often than others. Other students rarely jostled or barged in to that tightly packed group. Perhaps they knew that only the rare letter would come from home. I felt a bit sorry for them. Of course, some parents enjoyed writing their kids while others found it a chore.

I'd rush into the circle. Once a week our names were *always* read out. No matter how small the paper or how meager the news, that little folded over letter was our link with a distant home, our smaller brother whom we missed so much and our family time after supper.

CHAPTER 9

MANYANI PRISON CAMP: THE ULTIMATE FREEDOM

We sensed a new kind of freedom when the barbed wire fence came down. That ugly, spiky wall was intended to protect us from dangerous people; the same need for security lay behind the existence of ancient walls in Palestine, Assyria, Turkey or cities in Europe. Those ancient defenses often combined a wall with a moat. Our RVA protection was a high wall of barbed wire surrounded by a wider outer section, which was composed of pointed bamboo sticks, implanted in the ground at a 45-degree angle.

Pa Senoff and the African askaris had the painful privilege of dismantling the whole thing. The barbed wire had to be rolled up and thrown away. Using protective gloves against the innumerable splinters, they dismantled the sharp bamboo fence, one treacherous stake at a time.

The unkempt, grassy mass under all that rolled up barbed wire provided habitation for mice. As those small, wild creatures lost their protection, we'd say, "*Dig* that, guys! *Severe!* Another family of mice! *Dig* all those little baby mice!"

* * *

I watched all my friends getting their hair cut in the latest style. Ralph Davis and Herb Cook, grade 11 and grade 12 boys, earned their pocket money by cutting hair for the other students in the barbershop. My parents spent one shilling to have my hair cut in the latest fashion, a crew cut. I didn't ask them for permission; they would pay up later.

By now I had learned how to live peacefully in the Hatchery. I was still a *titchie*, an elementary school student. I still hated the *can*, the outside bathrooms. When people called me a *Limey*, I didn't mind so much. Most importantly I was used to the slang and felt part of the school. Everything we enjoyed, or considered worthy, we called *severe*. I was getting better at playing *nyabs*, and I almost won a game once, but Carly was *most severe*; he won that game, too.

* * *

The hot, scorching sun beat down on the plains that term. Wild life was hard put to find a usable drinking hole. All the ponds were drying up. Kenya was agonizing through one of its periodic droughts but in December 1955 the drought was just beginning.

It was the end of term and the train took us home for Christmas. The train steward awakened me at 4:30 in order to get off at the Manyani Station at 5:00 am. The train took us home for Christmas and it stopped at the Manyani Prison Camp. This was a detention camp for 15,000 Mau Mau detainees, located 120 miles from Mombasa, and six miles south of Voi. Our new home was located just across the highway from the renowned Tsavo National Game Park. Dad was the Protestant Prison Chaplain.

Dad and mom arrived by car, the sky still dark. With a crew cut I suddenly felt more grown up and I reached up to kiss my mother. She put her hand to her mouth, "Oh, no! David! What did they do to your hair?" She couldn't get over the crew cut. "I hope it will grow out. My, won't everyone be disappointed in you! How did it happen?" She made such a noise about my hair cut.

Squirming against the back seat, a small struggle took place inside. Should I tell the whole truth, or could I cover it up by a little fib? "All the guys are having it done," I said. "It's the new style. I walked into the barber shop and this is how I came out." I could have said that I asked to have it done. I had opted for half-truth, a fib. It was easier to try to blame others than to take the blame oneself.

When we got home the smell of hot cinnamon buns met us, and I knew she had been up until late the previous evening getting them ready.

* * *

A British Sergeant winked at me at the Mess Hall when I wandered in with some of the British kids. Mananyi Detention Camp was not the same as MacKinnon Road. There was more of a temporary sense here; some Mau Mau detainees had already been released and returned to their homes. Those who were "soft core" went back to their families after a shorter period of detention. The "hard core" men would have to stay in prison longer.

After breakfast, a gigantic praying mantis crawled ever so slowly as it edged imperceptibly towards to its prey. Spindly, its long legs moving with minute precision, it performed a beautiful intriguing dance, marching towards its prey. Suddenly it reached out and death came, a minute struggle, an image of what took place in the Tsavo National Game Reserve every day; larger beasts devoured the smaller ones. Dad said he would take us to see the animals several times during the holiday month over Christmas.

I wondered where my home was. Was it where my parents lived? They had just moved from MacKinnon Road to Manyani. I loved MacKinnon Road, but we would never again return. The Hatchery certainly wasn't my home, even if I did spend nine months there each year. I decided that home was wherever my parents chose to live and work. In the enchantment of getting to know my new surroundings, with a game park on one side and rocky hills close by, I never told mom or dad what really happened at school was really like.

* * *

One of the Army blokes, Dusty, a Captain, taught me to play Checkers and he always beat me. After a while he taught me how to play chess, but he always told me how many moves I had to make a safe turn.

Then *Dusty* would say to me, "David, you're going to lose this game in three moves." I had the agonizing knowledge of a coming blistering attack; unlike the praying mantis, he was kind enough to tell me of the approaching disaster. The praying mantis kept its small, pointed hands together until the last second, but *Dusty*, my adult opponent, rubbed his hands together, leaning over the chessboard, and then he'd follow up his statement with three quick moves, pouncing with glee.

* * *

Dad rotated between hundreds of cells, usually holding an evangelistic service for one hour in a cell, then meeting with individuals for prayer. The temperature in those corrugated iron buildings approximated the temperature at the surface of the sun.

One afternoon he took us to Tsavo National Game Reserve, just across the road. The car snaked through dry vegetation, low brush, mid-sized trees and towering baobab trees, heading for the famous slab of rock overlooking a watering hole. An African sat in the passenger seat, showing the way.

After driving a short way into the enormous reserve, we arrived at a small stone hill where there were known to be animals on the other side that came to drink from the lake in the late afternoon. We climbed the steep rock, still hot under our hands. Then, we held our breath.

Below us, fourteen elephants entered and left the muddy water. One would go in and spray itself. And it would start singing in its shower. Another answered its call. One was a baby elephant, oddly different because of its smaller head; it playfully rubbed up against its mother's front legs. The elephants took naturally to the water, their tall trunks splashing dirty, red water into the air and then covering their backs with brown-reddish slime. The little tip of flesh at the end of their trunks whiffed the breeze, enjoying their afternoon dip in the lake. However the lake, which was large in the rainy season, had now shrunk to the size of what they must have thought to be a tiny puddle. I felt free to just lie on the rock and look down at the great party going on below us.

The drought was becoming much worse and everyday people talked about the effects on the animals close to us, in the bush. Some adults thought the animals might even invade the area where the officers lived, in their search for water.

* * *

I'd never been swimming before, and so I wore a plastic buoy around my waist the first time that I jumped in the water. The plastic slipped off and I was left thrashing in the water. I was so afraid I pounded the water wildly. I suppose that the others in the pool thought that I was just playing. They were also shouting and pushing, shoving each other under the water and they paid no attention to me. For a jiffy I thought I would drown. Using every bit of self-control, I stopped for a second then moved one arm slowly. I moved slowly towards the edge of the pool. Once more and now I was moving in a bit of a wobbly line. My heart was pounding with fear, but I was determined to swim so I launched out from the edge of the pool just a bit, and then grabbed the edge again. After a few times I found a confidence and a new sense of appreciation of the water. The swimming pool at the officer's mess became most welcome in that heat at Manyani Prison Camp.

* * *

It seemed that elephants could smell water at the swimming pool at the officer's club where we played. One morning, about a week before Christmas, the fence of the swimming pool was broken down. Everyone could hear the loud swearing of the Army Major, whose voice could have become the stuff of champions in the World's Loudest Shouting Contest. He examined elephant dung covering the blue tiles around the pool. He was incensed, and vowed to make the fence stronger so no more animals would break through and drink the precious water supply in the swimming pool.

* * *

The next morning mom asked me what I thought of the elephant I had seen in the window, looking in at us.

"What are you talking about?" I asked.

"Why the elephant I showed you, the one that was just outside, not even three feet from us last night." She sounded exasperated.

"No, I didn't see any elephant last night." I wondered what dream she was talking about. I certainly hadn't seen an elephant last night, especially one looking in our window.

"Why, David, I called you after you went to bed. An elephant was only a few feet outside the living room window. You came and stood with me and didn't say anything and then you went back to bed."

I felt so disappointed. That was the first time I had been sleep walking, and I'd missed such an exciting evening. Problems were compounding for me; now I would have to deal with being absent minded as well as being a sleepwalker.

* * *

We heard about "character" so much at school and on Christmas Eve I faced one of my first real tests, not an examination like Ma Coder gave, on a sheet of paper, but in real life. It was time for the Christmas party for the kids whose dads served in the army. The British Army gave toys appropriate for each age group. Little kiddies got smaller presents while bigger ones received presents more to the abilities of their age. I had just turned ten, two-days before. The little kiddies got their gift, being called up by name, one by one. Then came the fives and sixes. The sevens, eights and nines came next, first boys and then girls. Dorothy, Pearl and Donald had each received little gifts from the Officers.

The 10, 11 and 12 year old boys were next, and then the girls of that age group. I had been left out, but I knew there was a wonderful tool set waiting for me, just like the ones my new friends were beginning to use on loose nuts and bolts in the Mess Hall.

It was just that my name had been overlooked. I was standing at the back of the room in which all the moms and dads sat with their children. Finally, all the gifts were given out and only one gift was left. It was a red and white wooden horse, a toy horse on the end of a pole. It was the toy that had been handed out to 4 and 5 year-old boys.

Walking to the front of the room to receive my British Army Christmas gift, knowing I had been left out of the list for the coveted tool boxes, I felt a mixture of emotions: anger, disgust and perhaps the desire to make a nasty comment. Instead, as I accepted the gift, saying "Thank you, sir", I realized that someone had made a mistake while buying these gifts. I composed myself and ran back to my family jumping on the floor as if I were a five year old. People laughed and cheered, but I felt so disappointed.

Dad said, "I'm proud of you, David." I knew he felt my pang of disappointment, too. I could see it his eyes. However, his kind words engendered a moment of tenderness; suddenly, I wanted to tell him about the many adventures at RVA: hikes up the hills, sports days, Halloween parties, and songs boys listened to on their radios. I hesitated, waited while the noise in the party died down, but didn't know how to start. I couldn't find the words to begin so I kept silent.

* * *

Knowing that they were able to push through the feeble barriers built around the swimming pool, and confident that they would be welcome once more, the elephants returned.

However, they were not prepared for the reception they faced at the swimming pool. Inside the mess hall the British men zealously guarded the cleanliness of the blue ceramic tiles around their pool and had no intention of changing any more broken tiles. The elephants were chased away with loud noise and with car lights shining on them.

In addition to this reception party for the elephants, preparations for a real reception were taking place. Christmas was upon us and a senior military man from England was to arrive the next day, paying a visit to Kenya, his purpose being the inspection of Manyani Detention Camp. Early next year he would return to Britain with a report on the success of the Army's fight against the Mau Mau. This visit had been planned for more than a year and our Major General had started to prepare for the arrival of his visitor as soon as he learned about it.

Mother told us it was the Major General's desire to show real Kenyan hospitality, which in this case meant serving fresh pineapples. Consequently, the back yard next to ours was out of bounds to everyone; hundreds of pineapples received generous doses of precious water every day. Our neighbor, the Major General, was going to give the best impression possible to his senior official; his idea was to provide freshly grown pineapples at a wildly extravagant party. Good British discipline would shine through during the drought; all it took was ingenuity and "The Party at the Edge of Tsavo National Game Reserve" would be commented on in London for months to come.

The elephants, unable to break into the Prison Camp at the west end of the compound, circled to the west and then around to the north, out of sight of the beer party which was now in full swing at the mess hall. The noise from the officer's party resounded long into the desert night. Of course, elephants have a wonderful nose for sweets, and they must have found this a most enchanting Christmas Eve treat.

At mid-night, as Christmas day came, the Major General returned to his house. He was just in time to see the last of his scrumptious pineapples being appreciated by a joyful herd of thirsty, hungry elephants, quite satisfied – "Thank you very much!" - by this free food. He had returned home from the mess hall only to discover that elephants had broken through, what was to them, the flimsy little fence at the back of his yard. The animals had enjoyed their own party, hundreds of ripe pineapples, and they hadn't even been sent an invitation! So much for building a picket fence where wild animals roamed.

Our neighbor was more than livid; a strange color of purple spread from his gills to his fin. The wicked thieves (he used much worse language than this) had come only 12 hours before his important visitor was to arrive.

The next morning, Christmas day, the man reminded me of a rouge animal, at least of what I imagined the rouge would have been like. His anger had no limits, cussing and thrashing about, walking disjointedly along the long, dusty street in front of our house, swearing even more, calling down curses on those wicked animals that had the gall to eat his precious pineapples just one day before he needed to them. Mom called us indoors to protect us from more bad words.

* * *

For Christmas dad was in charge of the Christmas program for Protestant families on the army staff. The Roman Catholic families had just finished their mass in the Mess Hall the previous night before the beer drinking had begun.

Over 100 copies of the faithful Golden Bells that dad used were placed in a pile on a table at the back and it was my job to give one to each adult coming for the Christmas program. These hymnbooks were useful for people from Britain because many of the favorite songs sung in Anglican, Methodist, Congregational and Baptist churches were included;

they were often used for home meetings and evangelistic sing songs. I was glad to welcome the folk at the door, handing them a copy of the Golden Bells as they came for the Protestant service. It seemed that so few of the men could smile. I could not understand how they could come to a Christmas service and hardly sing, barely participating in the glad news that Christmas brought. A couple of the army men, entered with their children, one hand resting on the wife's shoulder, in front of them. Several paused to rub their hand across the short hair on top of my head; they knew my mother's distress at the American style of crew cuts.

Mom said, "Merry Christmas to you, too. And, oh it's growing out! It will soon be all right! David's hair will soon be right!"

Her comment made me withdraw; I wanted to tell to my parents all about the events at RVA but the golden opportunity slipped away. My parent's questions came, "How was school?" followed by an automatic answer, "Oh, just fine."

* * *

Christmas night the animals came back again and dad ran to his car. He was not going to have another elephant that close to our house again. For my part, I was not going to lose sight of such a wonderful animal.

"Stay back in the house!" he demanded. I refused, rushing around to the passenger's side of the car. Dad drove forward slowly, blinking his lights on high beam, honking his horn and chasing off the big elephant that had drifted to our house. The elephant was very close to the bonnet of our car, as dad would call the hood of a car. It stared at the car and flapped its great ears back and forth many times, a sign of distress or anger. It stepped forward and then backwards. Then it slowly turned, annoyed at the fuss, and wandered back into the direction of the Major General's house.

* * *

Two days later we drove to Mzima Springs, a natural pool where melting water from Mount Kilimanjaro springs joyfully and endlessly from the ground. Hippos yawned at the surface and then dipped back below the surface to browse on the plants growing in the water. We watched the hippos and left our picnic lunch on a table; in an instant the monkeys that had been jumping from branch to branch above us were eating our bananas.

I could hardly wait to get back to RVA. So many of my classmates had stories to tell about wild animals and usually I was the one listening. This time, in the January term, I would be able to tell my story: the swimming pool in the Manyani Detention Camp had become the drinking hole of choice for a herd of elephants.

In addition, I had a whole new vocabulary to use, thanks to the loud voice of the Major General, whose voice seemed to reach to the ends of the officers' street, if not all the way to nearby Voi. Those words were not slang; these were real men's words.

* * *

Three months later, we were back home at Manyani Prison Camp.

Something was curious about living at a boarding school and then at a Prison Camp. At RVA we had rules, especially ones against going out of bounds, and there were prizes given to those who were the best behaved.

On the other hand, living at Manyani, there seemed to be no rules when I was on holidays. I could go anywhere, except into the jail, so I spent time at the Mess Hall, at the swimming pool, and riding my bike up and down the roads. There were no rules about going into the Tsavo Game Reserve, which lay at the edge of our property. I rode my bike down the roads and into the Game Reserve where wild creatures roamed, admiring the birds and adding many new specimens to my butterfly collection.

By far the best time of the day as a family was after supper. Dad never seemed to run out of adventure books. Supper was always delicious. Each of us took turns choosing the next book for Family Night. Every evening, seven nights a week, was Family Night; dad would lean back a little bit in his chair, rubbing one shin with the other foot, as he read chapter after chapter out loud, with wonderful expression.

Mom sat on one end of the couch, her head bobbing up and down as she accompanied the story and either mended socks, or sewed name tags onto clothes to be taken to the RVA dorms. When she had finished those chores she managed fine embroidery, which all of us learned, but because it was obviously a technique perfected by women I never blurted out at school, "Hey, guys, did you know that I did this fabulous embroidery project at home over the Christmas holidays?"

One week it was Don's turn to choose his book to be read out loud and he said that he wanted to go to school with us, "Soon I can go to school, too!" Sometimes we siblings almost fought about the next book that dad was going to read to us.

I had had the part of one of the three wise men in the choir presentation at RVA, just before holidays. It was a solo, one verse, in front of all parents and students. I felt a new confidence. Singing, music, mirth, and home life: these were the warm qualities that we looked forward to as much as the hot cinnamon buns and the fresh bread that mother made for us to greet us when we came home.

Cinnamon buns kept on coming out of the oven, and every night we heard another few chapters read to us from storybooks. And every night we always resisted going to bed. "Just read us another chapter...pleeease," became our final plea before the inevitable.

"Time for bed, children!" came the same answer, every night.

* * *

Occasionally dad took us on a very special outing and one of these was to Malindi, a port about sixty miles up the coast from Mombasa. The people of that area were largely Muslim and the tribal customs were different from those of other Kenyans, "up country". The scenery along the beaches captivated me; huge rollers boiled in with seething foam glistening in the sparkling sun.

Along the costal road men and women, bare to their waists, walked in the hot sun. Their skin shone with oil spread as a sign of beauty. Women balanced large water pots, often just 5-gallon paint cans, with one hand and held the little hands of their beautiful children with the other hand.

We stopped halfway to Malindi in a village called Lamu to see the ruins of an ancient Portuguese fort. The ruins were in the midst of a palm plantation and palms were waving their hands to heaven in the eternal wind. Some trees grew towards the ocean and then changed to an upright position. The men who climbed those palms were grateful for the easier footing the leaning posture provided.

The remains of the fort were scattered under the shadows of the palms. Soldiers and sailors built the fort four hundred years earlier; now archaeological excavations were under way. Around the site were the exposed foundations of the town hall, the residences and the walls of an ancient Catholic church. While we were discovering the ancient site, Don was brilliantly using his pent up energy after having been in the Peugeot car for several hours. He jumped over the low walls.

Dad called out, in a very urgent voice, "Donald! Stop jumping! Right beside those walls are the wells that the Portuguese used for obtaining their drinking water. We don't want to have to pull you out of one of those wells!"

I went over to the closest of the wells. It reached way down into the black earth. A long way down, there was a little reflection of light, which made me shudder. I couldn't imagine my brother falling down one of those wells. I didn't say this out loud, but I knew from the intense feeling right then how much I loved the little blond guy who was my brother. He shared our room at home. He had his own set of Mecano building supplies but he shared it with me.

Something stuck in my throat; I wanted to say, "Don, don't fall down the well! I want you to share our fun and to do so many things together. I never want to lose you! It would be the end of everything if you fell down a well!" But there was no need to say it. He hadn't fallen down a well and, anyway, how could you say such a *grimy* statement out loud. *Grimy* was the current slang word at the dorms for anything that was so full of sentiment that it made you feel uncomfortable. Survival at RVA in Grade Five made you repress all the *grimy* things that might come.

You couldn't survive RVA if you didn't bite your upper lip very, very hard.

CHAPTER 10

VISITORS WITH UNIQUE GIFTS

The mission station at Kijabe was one of the largest evangelical missionary communities in the world. A large concentration of Christian workers was needed for the nine schools, the printing press, the new hospital and a nurses' training program.

Missionaries seemed to be constantly arriving and leaving, their passports being American, British, Canadian and South African. and several others as well. Mostly, they came from the States, almost all career missionaries. There were over a hundred missionaries in 1957 and almost 175 six years later.

Since this was a mission station the Bible had to be the staple diet for each day. Along with the steady diet of white bread and potatoes came the vitamins of Christian teaching.

We were up at 6:00 a.m. and at breakfast by 6:30. Bible readings came from Daily Light. Before chapel started at 8:00 a.m., we were to have had our personal devotions. Chapel lasted 20 minutes. Classes began five minutes later. Sometime during the day there was a Bible class. At the evening supper table another Bible reading from the Daily Light set us in the right mood for study hall, at the end of which the more wide-awake students listened to one last devotional thought from the teacher on duty that particular night. The hour before "lights-out" was best concluded with personal prayers.

The whole program complemented the Memory Program; red ribbons lined with an increasingly long collection of little awards, each indicating another chapter or song learned by heart. Of course, by now everyone had the two initial awards on the red ribbons. Written on one small scroll were the words, "The 39 Books of the Old Testament", and on another small scroll, "The 27 Books of the New Testament". I received awards for that assignment early on; the order of the books of the Bible was one of the easier assignments.

The whole spiritual program of our school was intended to arrive at one destination, to drive rebellion *out* of little boys, but I suspected that it could result in the opposite, driving some *into* insurrection, open or not.

* * *

There were constant streams of relatives and guests who arrived from the United States to visit these missionaries and we could spot visitors a mile away. They always spent at least part of their time on the small knoll beside the bell at the north end of Kiambogo, close to the basketball court; the view was excellent for photos. Holding expensive cameras they would try to capture the whole, stupendous view of the Rift Valley, which included a 180 degree panorama. Not satisfied with just one mountain in the valley, they wanted the landscape, impossible unless one had a wide-angle lens. After five minutes of swinging in first one direction and then another, and then trying to decide what was the best choice that their 55-mm camera would take in, they'd shoot a picture. Then the process would start all over. We had several little wicked expressions for these fly-through visitors. Hadn't Jesus said, "Go ye into the all the world and take pictures?"

Church, or the main worship experience, was scheduled for Sunday afternoons at 4:00 p.m. Many missionaries attended the African service in the lower section of the mission station in the morning and then heard a sermon in English in the afternoon. Before Jubilee Hall was built, the entire missionary community met in the Butterworth Library, situated on the main floor at the south end of Kiambogo, under the Girls' Dorm. Chairs were laid out in a semi-circle around the square room. The huge green tables used for studying were moved into one corner.

At times we tried to crowd close to the bookshelves in order to have "alternative reading matter", especially if the preacher happened to be Ted Teasdale that afternoon. He had a great grasp of the Scriptures and knew the relationship between the Old Testament and the New Testament like few people did; however, his voice might put me to sleep. I tried to understand how African Christians, men who were in preparation for work in little rural villages, could listen to foreigners for hours. The Bible School was down at the very bottom of the mission property, where the "out of bounds" began. When Ted preached, the shelves of the library made a slightly-louder-than-silent rustling sound.

At other times, the preacher that afternoon might be Jim Wilson. We would crowd as close to the platform as possible. Jim was a teacher at the Technical High School; his strong points were carpentry, machine lathes and geometry. He wasn't much of an expositor, but somewhere along the line, he discovered that he could blend magic and the Bible. Perhaps he had spent too much time studying the confrontation between Moses and the magicians in Pharaoh's court. At any rate, we longed to see more of his tricks. At times it wasn't easy to understand the relation between his magic and the interpretations he developed about the Christian life, but the church service was certainly much more captivating. And it was impossible to forget.

"What do you think it meant for the children of Israel to come out of Egypt?" he asked. We knew that he was setting himself, and us, up for another trick.

"First of all, God had to call those two men, Moses and Aaron, out of the desert." Suddenly, a blue ball, a red flag and a white handkerchief appeared from a black hat.

"God can do miracles, you see. He just took those Israelites out of Egypt. And then what happened to the Egyptians?" We knew that the objects had to disappear.

"Well, God sent a great cloud," he waved a red kerchief, "and he sent those soldiers down to the bottom of the sea." The kerchief was removed and not one of those objects remained. We all roared, just for only a second. Then we stopped dead in our tracks. You weren't supposed "to laugh out loud in Church".

One quick glance showed that Clara Barrett and Mr. Teasdale were busy reading their Bibles, their heads pointed towards their laps. A small red patch was climbing up Herb Downing's forehead. Herb Downing was the respected principal of the school. His brother, Kenneth, was the Station Superintendent, the SS. Not everyone on Kijabe station thought tricks used to embellish a sermon were the best ways to spend a Sunday afternoon worship service. However, the Bible really did talk about tricks in Pharaoh's court, so nothing was said against Jim Wilson's sermons.

We knew that something was going to appear from nowhere. It did. On the back of the David Ness's shoulder there had appeared, as if by the hand of God in the desert, a small pigeon. We stared in wonder! Where had that bird come from? "So you see, God provided manna and birds and all kinds of wonderful things in the desert. And of course their shoes didn't wear out, either."

He had just set himself up for another trick. We loved it. We knew it wasn't real expository preaching, but it was impossible to forget his sermons. Jim Wilson was just getting going. The sermon went on through clouds, fire and water. He left us without any doubt. God was the most fabulous worker of miracles in all creation. God was more than just any old magician. He really opened up the Red Sea and made birds come from nowhere. If Wilson could make a bird appear like that, just think of what God could do!

At the time, we were so awed by the audacity of his magician's skills and the novel interpretations of the Bible, that we forgot the rest of the Bible story. What had God done to the magicians in Egypt? Jim Wilson never told us about them! We did, however, have a magnificent introduction to the Exodus. For days in the dorm, while we were playing the endless Monopoly games, and while we were waiting for our partners to take their turns at going around "Go", or get out of "Jail", we'd imitate the sermon.

Only something was missing. We couldn't make birds appear from nowhere. No one could copy the fabulous tricks we had seen. Pa Wilson's boys were spared from most of our "tricks". We did it out of consideration for the interesting spiritual lessons we received when it was their father's turn to "preach".

Thus we learned Exodus, but before that we had to learn Genesis.

* * *

What an excellent introduction came to us for Jacob in the book of Genesis! One day an enormous man arrived in the church building. He was different, just oozing leadership qualities. He stood beside the bell, at the north end of Kiambogo building, overlooking the valley. He sized up the panoramic scope of the challenge in an instant.

He wasn't one of those missionaries who stood on a spot for long, trying to figure out how to capture a visual 180-degrees in scope, first pointing the camera this way and then that. Jim Voth didn't need five minutes to take a good picture. He took his first camera, took one snap, then moved the camera thirty degrees, took another, and repeated process six times. It was all done in a flash.

Then he accepted another camera from his tall, skinny friend that had a convex, tiny, little stomach, and took six more pictures. One set of prints came out in black and white and the other set were colored slides. Pronto. He would put them together to make a panoramic vista. He was the type of guy one could learn from really fast. You could see right away that he was a "man's man".

Jim Voth had been a gangster, in fact a gang leader, in Chicago and the Lord had touched his life. Then he went into radio business. With his 350- pound weight, we felt, he could throw his voice halfway to the Rocky Mountains at least. He stood up to speak. "I guess you are wondering about my weight. Well, you should have seen my size before the Lord got a hold of me."

We looked at each other quickly, eyes open to new possibilities. We all laughed. His weight was the most obvious thing on the platform. John Stauffacher whispered to David Downing, "He must have needed two chairs to sit in."

Jim went on, "Of course when I came on the plane they weighed me and made me pay for three seats of normal passengers." We laughed again. True or not, (and it was true, I was convinced) we were captivated. "I was like Jacob," he said. He had us transfixed as he told us the details of the gang wars in Chicago and the long process by which he had come into God's light.

For a long time afterwards I associated Jacob in the Old Testament with a very large girth. God had somehow got a hold of that great belt and made a stubborn man walk in a new direction. If God managed to transform both Jacob and our speaker, then surely He could do it with me.

I also had a great respect for the strength of angels after hearing that story because I imagined an angel wrestling with Jim Voth. After all, Jacob had wrestled all night with an angel; his hip was out of joint and received the name, "Israel". God wrestled with Jim Voth, too, and look at the difference; he was now an evangelist.

* * *

Fortunately, missionaries needed a steady spiritual diet, not the special ice-cream-and-chocolate-cake variety of exciting stories. Ed Arensen became a regular teacher, often bringing us significant messages. His captivating Bible explanations influenced me a lot. Someone circulated the story, true or not, that he preached twice, once in his home to a mirror on the door of his closet, and then at worship time. I marveled at the dedication of anyone who could go through the same sermon twice in one afternoon.

* * *

Perhaps the oddest way of learning the Old Testament characters was learning to suffer with Job. One visitor had a strange spiritual gift, "the gift of a long breath." I mentally gave him the nickname, *The Machine Gun*.

Most preachers had a similar gift, speaking for a long time. However, this guest was different. He had been working on the book of Job and had discovered a new way to preach, so he was going to relate Job's trials "really fast". We sat forward on our elbows, so to speak. One of the boys whispered quietly, "Sounds like he is going to tackle all the disasters of the Ancient World in one breath!"

At the back of the room several books were immediately tucked into their respective shelves and we waited for what would come next. He took one gigantic breath and let it out slowly through expanded cheeks. Then he took another breath that was even larger. At the third breath, we were all with him, breathing deeply, our lungs full.

He opened his mouth, starting at the first verse. We had our Bibles open in a flash, determined to catch him in case he messed up a single word. Nope, he had King James, down to the commas, memorized perfectly. By the time that he got to the fourteenth verse we wondered if he could keep on swimming to the other side of the pool.

The *Machine Gun* kept on. Disaster after disaster kept attacking Job. It was worse than some of the shooting in World War II. Strangely, Job never even paused for breath when he decided to praise the Almighty instead of curse Him.

Our preacher managed to quote the entire twenty-two verses without stopping for air. When he finished, he came up for air and his face shone a light purple tone. We felt as if we had seen a diver at Mombasa swim to the reef and back under water, never coming up for oxygen.

His audience all came up for air at the same second, for while he had been slowly exhaling we had been gradually holding our breath as well, several times. I wanted to cheer, but in church you never let your emotions show. While he preached his message on Job, I tried holding my breath and reading from the Bible to myself. I'd only get to the eighth or ninth verse. Determined to not be so far out distanced I tried to repeat his performance, and of course couldn't manage it. I lost the whole point of what he said in the message, but for years I remembered the effort of trying to swim under 22 verses and come up at the far side of the passage without coming up in the middle for air.

* * *

Our introduction to the newly developing science of Missiology came about when Eugene Nida spoke to us. At that time he had only learned about 20 languages. We wanted him to say a few words in each one; he didn't do that, but he explained Bible translation. He gave several illustrations of the complexities involved in finding correct words in the vernacular of tribal peoples to translate a Hebrew or Greek word. One classmate responded, "When I grow up I want to be a Bible translator."

I went through the afflictions of Job. How could one translate the Bible for Eskimos? What would they think of a lamb, or a camel, or an ox when they had never seen such creatures? Could you say that Job had all his sea-lions killed? That didn't seem to make sense. Yet, if they couldn't think about a lamb and what sacrifice meant, then how could they understand the great sweep of sacrifices referred to in the Bible? Eugene Nida helped by adding another dimension to the work our parents carried out in villages and towns. We could only wonder at the complexities of languages in Central America. How might all those languages in India receive the Bible in a way that they could understand it for themselves?

For some reason it wasn't hard to remember stories we heard on hot summer afternoons. The effects of all those Sunday messages were both positive and negative. Positively, we learned our Bibles from front to back and front again. Negatively, we often associated Biblical teaching with men who taught us those specific passages of the Bible.

For several years there were students in chapel who tried holding their breath. While boring messages were given, we'd mark the watch and signal with our hands in silent messages to each other, "*Rubot* just came up after 2 min and 3 secs." *Rubot* was one of the champions at holding air during chapel. I never got much beyond a minute.

* * *

Chapel services were limited to the regular teachers that we had. At one point Pa Senoff was to do a series on Genesis. He got to the fourth chapter and decided that a little joke was in order. He said, "Did you ever hear about the minnow that was beside the whale? He said to the shark, "Am I my brother's keeper?" Pa Sam Senoff burst into laughter at his own joke. He laughed so hard that he couldn't remember what he was preaching about.

We had no idea what the joke was meant to be. He couldn't find either Cain or Able in the wilderness that followed. We started to laugh, and he thought we had just caught onto his joke, so he laughed some more. Then we laughed even harder because we knew that we had fooled him and that he was enjoying his joke while trying to remember the main point of his chapel talk.

Chapel was out early that day, which was a wonder. We loved it when he told his own jokes, laughed at them, and then lost the thread of his thoughts. He never would do that in science, chemistry or physics classes though. He found his way around all those strange colored glasses in the lab, but his chapels were not that easy to follow.

CHAPTER 11

MA REED, LIVINGSTONES, AND THE COW TROUGH

Three steel trunks being loaded into dad's grey Peugeot 203 for the trip to school for a new term and Dorothy sat in the back seat with Pearl, who was starting Grade One. Pearl's disposition was so cheerful, bright and alert, so ready to learn. A sudden impulse came to me to tell about dorm life, how horrible it was sometimes. Pearl's innocent face seemed so sweet and I didn't want to pull her down on her first day at *swot*. Once at school, Pearl had found out for herself how horrible it could be when people made fun of her brace on her leg. She got nasty nicknames, some of which were actually cruel.

Dorothy and Pearl sat at the girls' side of the dining room. I saw them every day, but didn't have much to do with each of them since we were in different dorms and separate classes. We would share letters and news from home, though, and there were days when, after I had received a letter from our distant home, I felt like being kinder to Pearl, maybe to everyone in my class, not just Pearl and Dorothy.

It wasn't just letters that improved my disposition. "Teachers make so much of a difference!" I thought, leaning back in my seat, enjoying the story about the ancient kings of Egypt. "Ina Reed brings us exciting stories and takes us to places in the world we knew nothing about. She teaches stuff we didn't even know about before; I enjoy it so much." I looked at Ma Reed as she sat at her desk. She wore the same shape of glasses as Kay Senoff, accentuating her ready smile. Her endless enthusiasm came through in her broad smile and straight posture. Her hair was slightly longer than that of other teachers; her words and attitudes overflowed from a deep well of inner resources.

She taught Grades Five and Six in one classroom, first attending to Fifth Graders, then giving them work while she juggled the other group. I was in Grade Five and she had several Grade Six students at the board; three boys were against three girls in an addition contest. Our class sat next to the windows. Schoolbooks were piled on neatly organized shelves, carefully arranged between bookends.

She insisted that we work on our penmanship and urged us to round out our letters so that ours looked the way she wrote. Penmanship actually was a class in our curriculum. I didn't improve that much, but her constant encouragement stayed with me, a silent voice in my memory, always reminding me in her rich voice, "David, you can do better!"

What was it that made one want to obey Ma Reed? What was it that made us able to try things that previously seemed too hard? Why didn't students want to fool around in her class? The Grade Six class math class was over and now they had homework. Ma Reed turned her attention to us. She explained science, math and reading and little bubbles of excitement welled up with every new discovery. Could she even make me enjoy spelling? At the end of the morning, after recess and reading, she reached for her big reading book, and then, while we were captivated, she would take us to far off lands.

There wasn't a sound in the classroom. David Campbell, Ray Davis, Diane Dilworth, Danny Stauffacher, *Peanut*, *Fish*, and Jon Salseth: all of us listened. Then she had us to go the blackboard for "math drill".

One day Ma Reed said that she had a new project for us. She explained the Memory Program. She hung up a bright red ribbon for each person attached to a little blue nametag. She went through a long list, including verses, hymns and chapters of the Bible; she wanted each of us to memorize them all. The longest chapter we had to memorize was Romans 8 and the longest Psalm was 103. Everyone was encouraged to come to class a little bit early, just before class, to repeat the passages we had just learned by heart.

The challenge was real and exciting. She would come each day to school early and listen to us recite and she wrote down the date beside the verses learned. Patricia Marsh, Andrea Propst and Diane Dilworth were well on their way to getting to their second red ribbons and mine was only half full. I became discouraged but Ma Reed called me aside and said, "You have a good mind for memorizing. What's the next set of verses you want to learn by heart: the Beatitudes?" Ma Reed called me to her desk again at the end of the day, "I know that you can do this. You have a really good mind, if you just get down to the job. And, you know, I think that boys' brains in this class are just as good as those of the girls! Now, don't get discouraged!"

Ruth Schuitt, a new girl in the class, memorized the Bible as well any of the girls. The initial enthusiasm among boys for memorization was a sprint, slowing to a walk and then plodding like a hike on Saturday mornings. On the other hand, the four girls in our class rushed ahead, sprinting, out-classing us, adding more awards on their red ribbons.

I left the classroom and ran down the hill, ready to jump up into the strong branches of Green Tree. Somehow, Ina Reed had inspired me to start memorizing hymns, psalms, individual verses and whole chapters of the Bible. My red ribbon was like the desert where we lived: green shoots came only occasionally; I cringed when my ribbon had the fewest awards, but her quiet encouragement and determination inspired me. For the first time I found myself really enjoying every subject at school. She was one of the most loving teachers I had, an answer to the prayers of many parents who wanted their children to get the best possible marks. Besides taking us to her home, she introduced us to science, and social studies, people in far off lands. I groaned through math, which seemed to go so slowly and then relished stories of distant lands, which went by all too quickly.

* * *

Sports Day, at the end of every term, three times a year, was our great delight, falling on a Friday. Each student acquired a life-long identity; either a Livingstone or a Stanley. Livingstones never doubted their superiority, while Stanleys bragged on and on about having won more Sports Days.

Muriel Perrott had created the two-house system two decades before. The British system of houses in boarding schools in England fostered competition. After all, something was needed as a healthy diversion from endless creative pranks. She chose the names of two famous explorers of Africa for the two "Houses".

The London Missionary Society had sent fearless David Livingstone, a Scottish Congregationalist, to Africa as a doctor. Later, he gave up mission work in favor of exploration and he disappeared for six years.

Henry Morton Stanley, an intrepid journalist for the *New York Herald*, went to Africa to find Livingstone on the shores of Lake Tanganyika in 1869. His adventures equaled those of Livingstone, and hundreds of miles from any town or city Stanley caught up to the man he was trying to locate. We were taught those famous words, "Dr. Livingstone, I presume."

The real story was that Livingston was *with* Stanley, not *against* him, but the finer points of history didn't matter. Who cared about those details? If you were designated as a "Livingstone" you forever would be against those who called themselves "Stanley".

That friendly humor of two white men meeting in the African bush disappeared each Sports Day. It really was Livingstones *against* Stanleys. For us, David Livingstone was the real hero, the explorer who opened up so much of Africa and whose remains lie buried in the great Westminster Chapel in London, England. For the students who were our opposition, H. L. Stanley was the real hero, having been able to track down a white Englishman in the center of Africa, making Livingstone famous and leaving Stanley rich.

* * *

We shouted, yelled and cheered as the total for sports events brought out the temporary animosity, and perhaps temporary insanity, at the end of every thirteen-week term. My sister Dorothy found her name on the list of students in Stanley House; I was a Livingstone. Even siblings, separated at each meal, and living in dorms where we could never see one another, now had to compete against each other.

Activities included every single student, from Grade One right through Grade Twelve. Competitions included long jumps, short jumps, high jumps and races of 50 yards, 100 yards, 440 yards, 880 yards, one mile and long distance. Pole-vaulting followed baseball. Girls' and boys' teams both played soccer. Basketball and volleyball became the high points of the day. The various ages competed against each other. Along the parking lot the students in high school staffed tents. The sales from hot dogs and hamburgers were counted up at the end of the day with profits going to Senior Safari, the absolute highlight of the whole RVA experience.

Senior Safari was the day in which the Grade 12 class snuck away from the rest of the school. They would be gone for a week. The entire school participated, buying hot dogs, hamburgers or mouth-watering "hot chapatis".

* * *

Two of my special friends were going on Senior Safari and I knew I would miss them. Helen Devitt, my first friend when I came to school, four years earlier, would be leaving Kijabe. Each Sports Day the *big guys* distinguished themselves: Lois Danielson, Richard Boda and Naomi Downing were three of my heroes, but I rarely had any interaction with them. Paul Barnett, who occasionally said a kind word to me, was going to America. Next year it would be David Downing's turn. Each year a few of the older students became my heroes.

The rhythm of *swot* was clear: advancing each year to the next grade and finally leaving. You made friends and then lost them. You could not keep a friend for life. RVA was in Africa; most students returned to America. It was always that way at RVA.

* * *

Except today, on Sports Day, everyone's efforts were needed, even the youngest children. You rejoiced in your friends-for-a-day were and shouted against your enemies-for-a-day. No one could avoid the excitement. At the end the points were added up and a great cheer would go up from the Livingstones and a sudden groan from the Stanleys, if the Livingstones won, as we would exclaim, "Shelley cheated on the high jump", or "You guys wouldn't have won if we had Charles Trout with us. He's back in the USA for a year. You watch out next term!" It seemed that the Livingstones won more often than the Stanley, but Dorothy said I was biased. "Actually, we win more often!"

* * *

I was so proud of the Bible I took to school after having received it as a Christmas gift. Its front and back covers were made of olive wood from Jerusalem. At the bottom of the front cover the word Jerusalem was written in black ink in very fancy Old English writing. The Bible had pictures of scenes from the Bible printed in color. I felt guilty that I was often looking at those pictures when I was supposed to be listening how to learn to avoid temptations.

One day it was announced in chapel that there would be a Baptism Class. Ma Reed talked to us more and I wanted to be part of the event. I started attending the special classes held after Sunday School each Sunday morning. At one point the teachers began to tell us how we could avoid temptations. Now, there was a big subject!

Baptism classes included studies on temptations, so I paid attention, especially, to those. How could one avoid temptations? They kept saying that no temptation, - not the temptations to swear (which was getting a real hold on me), or fight, or get angry, or steal - that none of those temptations were so strong that we had to give in. I didn't understand all the reasons given, even when I followed along in my little Bible. It was easier to study at the 20 colored pictures of Bible stories spaced through the book than to learn how to put the verses into practice.

* * *

One day, about three weeks before the day set for the Baptism, we were in the study hall. We trotted down the steps from the up stairs rooms down into the dining hall. Grade 5 and 6 boys stayed in four smaller rooms upstairs, no longer in the Hatchery, since, like little birds, we had supposedly broken the shells around us and could act more independently, needing less supervision from dorm parents. Since the baptism was coming up soon, we were to be more serious about what it meant to be a real Christian.

Grade five boys stayed in the far end of the Kiambogo dorm where rooms were reserved for four students to each room. *Fish* and *Giddings* and *Peanut* and I shared a room with a magnificent view of the spacious valley. The valley changed colors during the day, projecting colors: purple, blue, brown and yellow hues. The sun moved across the sky and the season rolled around. We never tired of gazing at Kedong Plains below, imagining that we were close up to the animals.

For study hall we had to take just the books that we needed for that nightly two-hour torture. The clock was supposed to tick towards 9:00 p.m., but something made it slow down each weekday night. By chance, though, we found out how to make it move faster. We passed little papers back and forth, silently, decoding numbers.

"K9, H8, I3"

Back came the other shots. "B1, B2, B3"

Oh no! My friend had just discovered my battleship! Two more shots and I would be in trouble, since I hadn't discovered any of his ships yet. We silently played Battleships, using checkered math paper. We hid submarines, frigates and battleships on our paper, in "our square" at the top, and then took three shots at the concealed ships that our partner hid, filling up the "opponent's square" at the bottom of the page. The daily two hours of study hall sped by so much faster when we could play such games, of course, making sure we were not detected.

However, the Law of Consequences caught up to me. In spelling the next day I missed my mark, coming in at the end of my class. The enormous challenge of sneaking up on imaginary submarines was far more exciting than the real world of English, math and history.

* * *

The day for the baptism finally came. Pa Teasdale was responsible for baptisms. We marched down to the African section of the mission station; we students gathered around a cow trough in the mid-morning sun. I was nervous; my knees were shaking a bit. There were about a dozen of us; most of the students in the little group being baptized studied in Ma Reed's classroom.

Just before the baptism Danny Schellenberg turned around, "Do you know your verse you are going to quote as your life verse?" I didn't know what to say. I instantly forgot all the memory verses that I had been working on in the Memory Program. Fortunately, I did remember John 3:16.

One by one, our turns came to be baptized, and now, Danny took a step forward, climbed over the top of the cow trough and down the steps inside. He was asked if he believed that Jesus is the Son of God, and he responded in a loud "Yes," and gave the same answer to other questions as well. He walked up the four steps, his face dripping and one of the teachers handed him a dry white dry towel.

Then it was my turn. I walked up the first step, then the next three steps, over the top of the cow trough-turned-into-a-baptistery, and I answered "Yes" to all the questions. I repeated John 3:16 from memory and was baptized with that verse as my profession of the Christian faith. It wasn't a bad choice for a life verse; it was handy to have learned Scripture since I was five years old and a bit disconcerting to realize that my mind went blank at the most awkward time. Pa Teasdale lowered me below the water quickly and just as quickly I was on my feet, sputtering a bit because some water got into my nose. I took the white towel offered to me. Trying to breathe properly I forgot for a minute that I had been immersed in a cow trough, which was used by the cows on the mission station as their drinking hole.

It wasn't the first time I realized that my mind had a way of giving out in the oddest way. Was it just plain fear or something much more serious? The baptism would have been perfect except for my embarrassment as I slid below the waters, embarrassment at almost having been the only one without a memory verse. So now I had to pay attention for various reasons: not remembering things, being absent-minded and sleepwalking. Because I had missed that elephant due to sleepwalking, I decided my "danger list" needed attention in three areas: memory and paying attention, and putting Submarine games away.

Perhaps, though, Ma Reed's classes, the weekly Sunday School studies and the constant devotions, at breakfast and supper, had begun to rob off. Could the sudden urge of temptation really be overcome with God's help?

Pearl and Dorothy were never as badly behaved as I was, of that I was sure. They had friends in the dorms that were much better for them than my friends. Liz Allen often talked with Pearl. I saw Dorothy a dozen others in the class with Clara Barrett.

* * *

One day a special letter came. The news in mother's letter changed our lives.

"Dear David and Dorothy and Pearl," mom wrote, "We are going to move from Manyani. Dad has a new job and we are looking for a house in Limuru."

Limuru! Why, that was just 20 miles away! Limuru was close by, only halfway to Nairobi! If we couldn't live on the mission station, like the Hollenbeck, Arensen, Barnett, Propst, Downing, Giddings and Cook's families, then at least we would be closer to home.

Manyani was a full day's ride away by car; Limuru was only an hour away. Consequently, home would be closer to school.

PART TWO
KEDONG DORM

CHAPTER 12

KARIBUNI COTTAGE

Spell bound, I stared out of the car windows as we drove down the long driveway to Karibuni Cottage, our new home in Limuru. *Karibuini*, the Swahili word for "Welcome", is what a person would say to a guest coming to ones' home. That word, the name of our home, was painted on a white board with black letters and it stood beside the driveway. A tall, dark-green hedge marked the edge of the property along the picturesque country lane, connecting A Route to D Route, the two main roads from Limuru to Nairobi.

I was speechless upon arriving in this small green paradise for the first time. The lane down to our house was lined with jacaranda trees, and their branches, meeting overhead, formed a long, green canopy down the slightly sloping hill. As long as two football fields end-to-end, the lane welcomed us with vibrant various shades of vibrant purple hydrangea, and many other flowers.

On the other side of the driveway, vegetable gardens soaked up the sun. Fruit trees shaded the property line. Where the driveway met the manicured grass lawns, a charming wooden arch supported well-trimmed green vines. A cedar tree, so tall it seemed to touch the clouds, kept its outlook post at the center of the lawn in front of the house. It was on the far side of this huge, sturdy tree that our car came to a stop; we were parked on a manicured lawn in front of our new home.

I gazed in awe at the bungalow in front of us. It boasted a newly painted red corrugated iron roof resting on a cut-stone, ranch-style house. It wasn't really a "ranch" house at all. The house had started out in life as a single room, but increasing prosperity brought the owner the means to expand his dream house one section at a time. Since the process of enlargement had happened more than once one could see how the house had evolved with ever increasing modernity. The house sat comfortably on the brim of a gently sloping hill. The largest room was the living room, with a broad, stone fire place and a piano. The couch was blue, mom's favorite color. Four bright-red cement steps lead down into the dining room. Standing on the top of those steps and looking out the large glass window at night, one could see the distant lights of Nairobi, twenty miles away.

We were close enough to European civilization, belonging to the white settler community, whose families lived among well watered gardens, resembling far-off England. Yet, at the same time we were close to the Kikuyu village, just 500 yards away, to hear the sounds of drums at night, to know that Kenyan proximity meant we were neighbors to men and women with deeply held African sentiments.

Throughout the property, surrounding the home, flowerbeds and vegetable gardens proclaimed previous years of creative and constant care. The explosion of flowers in the well cared for gardens made us aware of their ability to create a sense of peace.

The house was just what mother and dad needed for their work. Mom's office was tucked into one corner of our dining room. We heard her, even late at night, typing manuscripts. She was good at languages, and could carry a conversation about almost anything in Swahili, Kamba, Kipsigis and Nandi. She didn't know the other languages, though, and these demanded equal care in preparing documents for the printing presses: Luo and Kikuyu. Her work in literature production entailed coping the first draft of Sunday School lessons and sending these copies to church leaders, asking for corrections or modifications. Writers in distant places corrected the manuscripts, or suggested modifications; then she typed another draft, once again in six copies. When everything was correct, the final draft was sent for publication at the AIM Press in Kijabe. She kept up a constant correspondence with friends and supporters in Canada. She typed quickly and efficiently; letters had to be mailed at the Post Office in Limuru every day.

Dad's office was located outside the house, attached to the kitchen, where our African servant worked. When visitors came to the house, dad was able to step outside his office to greet them as they stepped off the lush green grass onto the open patio beside the kitchen and office area.

There were three bedrooms, a huge one for mom and dad, a larger one for Pearl and Dorothy and the smaller one where Don and I slept.

Mother's love affair with flowers blossomed here at *Karibuni Cottage*. Below the house, just off the dining rooms steps, a rose garden bloomed all year. Beside it, on either side of the rose garden, large cedar trees welcomed eagles who made their nests in the top branches. Between the tall trees a weeping willow swooped down from above with long, graceful, supple branches; it constantly sprouted little red flowers.

At different times of the year various flowers filled the flower beds: gladioli, nasturtiums, honey suckle, geraniums, crown of thorns, pansy, fox glove, ferns, bougainvillea, poinsettias, snap dragons, chrysanthemums and patience.

Below us, going down to a small creek about 300 yards down the hill, lay a small copse, a little planted wattle forest full of maturing trees. The bark in wattle trees possessed the tannic acid that leather merchants needed to tan hides. To the west a cultivated pyrethrum field sprouted millions of small white flowers, harvested to produce insecticides. A chicken farm lay to the east, beyond the tall trees which looked like a forest.

From one edge of our property we looked out across 175 miles on a cloudless day, gazing at the double-humped profile of Mount Kilimanjaro. We were always anxious to show our visitors that view of the great African mountain, a pearl of great discovery.

So, *Karibuni Cottage* was half British and half African. In England, houses acquired their identity with an individualized name. Here, in Limuru, British settlers chose Swahili words, now integrated into their everyday vocabulary, to give an individual identity. Further, if they couldn't own a castle, they certainly could bedeck their cottages with flowers.

* * *

Each morning I had to pump water from an underground cistern; it spurted into a small tank on top of the red corrugated roof. Rainwater, which was captured from each roof during the rainy season, made its way into seven 1000-gallon metal tanks. One tank was located at the corner of each building. A tap at the bottom of each tank had to be turned off carefully after being used, mindful not to lose a drop. These tanks provided water all year, both for drinking and washing. Between the wet months of the monsoon came several months in which not a drop would fall from the clear blue skies. Pumping the water took a full 20 minutes and the small hand pump wore my muscles out on each arm several times before that squeaky job was over for the morning. I had the wrong motives, of course, for pumping the water, since I hoped that my thin biceps would grow. I longed to hear the words in the dorm, "*Flappit*, look how your arms are getting big muscles!"

I'd pump as fast as I could and then run into the bathroom to see if my muscles had grown any larger, and then promise myself that I'd pump even more furiously the next day. Never mind, one day, after all the pumping, I'd get some muscles on my upper arm. Maybe I'd be as strong as Tim Udd, or Sausage, or any one of the other guys. Of course, I shut the bathroom door tight so that neither Dorothy nor Pearl would catch me anxiously awaiting the results of that morning's effort.

We soon made ourselves at home. Pearl and Dorothy placed hundreds of books in a large bookcase. Donald and I had little room for books because there was space in our bedroom only for two single beds and a chest of drawers.

Vacation time at Karibuni Cottage was like living in dreamland. A large lawn at the back of the house needed cutting regularly. That lawn, more than an acre in size, afforded us an ideal place to ride bikes. The small level area in the wide expanse of grass served as a badminton and tourniquet court. We played for hours on end, biking, flying kites, reading, making tree houses and enjoying the sheer beauty of the greenery. Dad bought some rabbits and I fed them greens from the garden, forgetting to feed them more often than not. There were chickens in the coop. We could take hikes down the property to the bottom of the hill.

Dad's radio picked up the Voice of Kenya, the VOK, from Nairobi, as well as the BBC in far-away London. I looked forward each day to listening to the news at noon.

On rainy days we read books, played the piano or listened to a collection of 78 recordings, donated to mother. We would play our favorites over and over again. I became familiar with classical music, especially that of Bach, Beethoven, Brahms and Mozart. *On the Jericho Road* was one of the best Negro spirituals because the voice of the bass singer went almost down to the far notes on the piano.

I'd try to imitate him, going down one minute and then finding my voice was an octave higher the next minute. I was becoming disgusted with my voice. I tried to keep it low, but all of a sudden it would surprise me. I asked dad to use his razor. The number of cuts on my face kept me in the bathroom for a lot longer than the few seconds I needed to cut a few bits of stubble and I often had tiny blobs of toilet paper to wipe away the blood.

* * *

Since Limuru was half way between the printing press at Kijabe and the secular printing outfits in Nairobi, dad went to both locations to coordinate the printing in the Literature department that he had helped to start for the Africa Inland Mission.

He almost always looked stressed after returning from Kijabe. "Look at how many printing mistakes there are in this book!" he'd exclaim. "We've just got to have the Herb Cook make his typists do a better job on the proof reading! This job wasn't done thoroughly!" He was reading a book in Swahili, Kipsigis or some other language. Dad had a very high opinion of books that were correctly, and thoroughly, printed. He said so, repeatedly, in his best British accent. On one occasion he arrived home fuming. He didn't say a thing about his trip to Kijabe. He had gone to get the final copy of a book that an African friend had written. Dad saved his frustration until we had gone to bed; we could hear his voice, which was louder and shriller than I could ever remember.

"Hazel, dear, this is just the limit! There are 45 mistakes in the book, and I haven't even got half way through!" Dad's favorite word was "thorough". He was teaching us, with his best British accent, to be "thorough" in life. He didn't have a very high opinion of printers, be they Africans or Americans, if weren't thorough in their proof reading.

When they didn't do their best, it was "just the limit." RVA had its property limit, beyond which no student could go. Dad had his limits, too, demanding perfection in Christian literature going to the churches, Sunday Schools, or the *Matangazo* magazine, which he edited. Since the printing presses at the mission weren't doing a "thorough" job, dad began giving some of his contracts to printers in Nairobi. He certainly believed in competition, explaining that people in monopolies ended up becoming lazy, if they didn't have to compete. A lack of competition permitted laziness to set in, he believed, "and then people don't have to do things thoroughly!"

The printing jobs in Nairobi went to Mr. Patel. His Indian name, his Hindu religious preferences and African staff fostered a healthy competition with the AIM Press at Kijabe. Our weekly trips to Nairobi were fun. Dad would make a thorough list in his black notebook, wrap his wide rubber band around the notebook, as if to keep his annotations, written in small English boarding school style, from falling out on the floor somewhere, put the notebook into his shirt pocket and open the garage doors.

* * *

Our garage was just off to one side of the wooden archway. Two wide green doors, sagging a bit in the middle, were kept shut with a bright new metal lock. The room beside the garage was our workshop, full of hammers, chisels and saws.

Above the car a spacious attic served as an ideal storage space for cardboard boxes, wrapping paper, string, old cases and trunks that had been used in the move from Manyani. Smaller cardboard boxes were stored and then used to ship Christian literature. Dad and his faithful African helper sent books to cities and towns in Kenya, Uganda and Tanganyika.

When it was time to go to Nairobi, there were little fights to see who would sit near the windows. Don, the youngest, sat by the window seat most of the time. It took only an hour to arrive in Nairobi; it was the most pleasant trip possible and I loved the long hills racing down into the lower altitudes from the uplands.

Going to Nairobi we passed the greenest regions possible. British settlers had proven that the grass really was greener on the other side of the ocean. Tea plantations covered the hills with verdant bushes, apparently meant to resemble a carpet. We passed private farms, horse ranches with white picket fences, banana plantations, a tea factory, *shambas*, or gardens, of Africans, several villages and long rows of planted trees beside the road.

Everything tumbled over itself in the enjoyment of rolling down the hill to the plains. The road dropped 2,000 feet in 20 miles. At times, mist hid the tops of the trees, or the steep valleys were hidden behind the quiet kitten's footsteps of the fog that came and went without a sound.

An hour later we arrived in Nairobi, and dad stood in line at the Lloyds Bank. Mr. Singh, at the cashier desk, counted money so rapidly I couldn't keep up as his fingers flipped through the bills. At lunchtime we'd lay out a picnic meal. Dad would run a little straight line thoroughly through each item on his "To do" list. Dorothy poured hot tea out of a thermos. Pearl would be reading a book and Don was running after another majestic butterfly with long blue tails on its wings. I'd admire the bougainvillea bushes that shaded our car from the afternoon sun, or I'd be sprawled out on a carpet on the ground looking at the sky.

* * *

At other times, we took a special trip in to Nairobi. Just outside of the city the Nairobi Game Reserve enclosed lions contentedly sleeping on their backs in the shade of an acacia tree surrounded by their families, the pride of their lives.

Giraffe lunched on the top branches of the acacia trees. Gazelles used their necks like pumps, bending down to eat the grasses and lifting their heads to see who was passing by their grazing field this time. I never could understand how a giraffe could reach around the sharp thorns in the acacia tree, bite and then swallow spikes as strong as nails.

I found myself becoming strangely fond of animals, trees, birds, eagles and flowers. My butterfly collection, begun in MacKinnon Road and Manyani, gained many new specimens, but not nearly as many as when we lived in the dry south-eastern areas.

* * *

We made trips on a regular basis, on weekdays and on Sundays as well, except that on Sundays we dressed in our best clothes. I had a grey suit and a little black bow tie. Dad was helping start a new church, a Baptist church, since dad didn't appreciate the preaching at the nearby Anglican Church on "D" Route; its rector didn't deal with the text "thoroughly". Dad has been ordained as a Baptist minister at his home area in England, in Dorking, Surrey. His family came from a long Anglican Church tradition; one uncle had become Methodist. Dad, the one who went the furthest from his home roots, had become a Baptist minister.

The new church in Nairobi met first in the offices of the Saint John's Ambulance, which offered courses in life saving as one of their educational ventures. I always thought that was a fine place to start a Baptist church in an office, where "Life-saving" courses were offered to people willing to jump in and save those who had almost lost their lives from too much water.

As the holidays came and went, the fast-growing congregation met in the much larger meeting hall at the Arboretum. Trees and bushes brought from locations all over the world were cultivated there. Later, the Baptist church relocated to a permanent location, beside the Mayfield Guest House. It became known for excellent African leadership.

* * *

While cleaning the ball bearings on my bike for the fourth time one week, I wondered what I would be when I grew up. I knew from experience that I could never make a living as a carpenter. That was proven by my recent second-rate job when building a tree house in the avocado tree.

Well, perhaps I could be a chef in a kitchen. I decided to give it a go. For some strange reason I had the idea I could be a better cook than the African staff that gave us our unchanging fare at RVA. Dad, mother and Don went to Nairobi; I decided to stay home to make a cake.

I found the recipe book. The first item called for two cups of milk. Easy! Milk was kept in the fridge, just inside the front door. After having mixed in a number of ingredients, I tasted the mix, just as I had seen mother when making cinnamon batter. My cake mix tasted bitter, unlike hers.

"Come and try this, Dot," I urged.

She tried it. "Ugh! You've put something in that shouldn't be there."

How could she be so foolish? I checked and rechecked the recipe. I had followed the instructions exactly and I was confident in my budding abilities, unrecognized by the world at large. However, nothing would improve the horrible taste of the mix in the bowl.

No amount of sugar or spice, added in liberal quantities, improved the stuff. I knew that something had gone badly wrong. I was about to cook the cake, but I feared that the future results would be bad for my health.

Well, like the ancient kings, I needed a taster to detect mortal poisons. We had our own kitten. In fact, at times we had more than one cat. "Here, Kitty, Kitty," I called concerned for my future reputation. "Here's something delicious for you!" Kitty was unsuspecting; she brushed herself against my leg and I gave her the mix that I was afraid to eat and afraid to throw away in case mother found it. Relieved when nothing happened to the little grey creature, I said, "See that wasn't so bad."

Five minutes later, Kitty headed for the flowerbed. First, she gave a little yelping noise; I had never heard a cat make that noise before. She tried to cough, then rolled over in pain, rubbing her back against the red earth in the ground.

When Mother arrived back, later in the day she said, "What did you do all day?" Pearl and Dorothy were reading, as usual. I said, "I tried to make a cake, but it didn't work out. Sorry."

Mother went in to get her milk from the fridge. She searched, then asked, "Has anyone seen my sour milk? I was going to make some cottage cheese tonight." Sour Milk! Why didn't anyone tell me that was what the problem was? For more than one day I thought that we had lost our kitten; Dorothy and Pearl could be so uncooperative.

* * *

The Fomegelli family, Italians, lived in a house across the other side of D Route, close to the Experimental Ape Farm, where the Leakey family was learning about primates. The three Fomegelli kids often came over to our house. One day we played "Kick the Can" and I hid in the best place, the attic of our garage. I ducked under some cardboard boxes in the darkest corner. I'd wait until all the other players had been caught. Then, out of nowhere I'd come and kick the can, and everyone would go away safely. With the prisoners free, I would be a hero.

Becky Fomegelli, who didn't seem to like me, would be forced to admit how smart I was and maybe she would even talk to me. Becky came to the edge of the attic several times to see if I was there or not. I could see her, but she couldn't see me because it was so dark in the attic space above the car. Finally, she got tired of trying to find the last player.

"I'm going home!" she declared, disappointed. I had been so smart that I was dumb. No body wanted to play the game anymore. I had ruined the game for everyone. After that Becky wouldn't talk to me at all.

* * *

There were lots of moles in the garden where the sweet potatoes grew. Moles had a tastier time with our sweet potatoes than our cat had with my wonderful cake mix. Every day a fresh pile of dirt indicated the growing multiplication of new members in that vexatious family. For a long time, mom and dad paid a half a shilling for every mole that was caught. I admired the way the ingenious Kikuyu could make a trap to catch those pesky little creatures.

The Africans were so clever, setting a small, round, hollow bit of wood in the ground. Through the middle of the trap, a long strip of bark from the wattle tree was connected to a branch stuck in the ground above the trap. They told me that if they used a metal can, instead of natural wood, the animals could smell the human scent and wouldn't run through the trap, but if they used their trap with the wattle tree spring, then the trap worked. A little rounded twig was set on the surface sticking up out of the fluffy, green leaves. You could hear it when the trap went off, trapping the neck of the mole in the hidden obstacle six inches under the ground. For a while, we had almost an industry of rounded twigs on the top of the dark green leaves that made up our large sweet potato field.

Our little orchard was full of peach trees. There was also an avocado tree, which was a perfect place to set up my tree house. The skills that I'd lacked at the age of seven had not improved, but I tried anyway. I hauled several boards up the tree and set them against the niche in the tree that provided the greatest support. A little platform with some degree of stability provided hours of literally direct contact with the nature around me. Hundreds of birds flew around us. At times I tried to imitate their calls but that just scared them off.

* * *

Mother and dad not only believed that we should help the poor. They actually did it, making me very proud of them. While other people might discuss "why" the Africans were poor, mother talked with them, concerned about the life story behind each widow and orphan. She learned about this family or that one and remembered the names of ever so many children. Mom and dad knew widows and the orphans were unlikely to get the food they needed to live. Men had run off to Nairobi; husbands sat in jail, and sickness and accidents had taken the lives of some fathers.

There was a short, dynamic little lady, Hannah, the mother of six youngsters, who helped us in our home. Earlier, God had blessed her with a fine Christian husband. She laughed when the children came and wept when she lost her husband. Hannah became our maid, but not a normal helper in the home. She and our mother were partners in Christian ministry, one, a white lady, supported by Elim Chapel in Winnipeg, and People's Church in Toronto.

Hannah's contribution in the partnership was priceless. She knew almost everyone in the village nearby. More than four hundred families lived in little thatched huts. These Kikuyu homes were known for wattle sticks pointing into the sky, ritually protecting a house from evil spirits, night and day. Hannah's house didn't need a stick because she didn't believe in the evil spirits; instead, she trusted in the Almighty. One day, when she was down to her last morsel, Hannah prayed for food to give to her children and that day she passed by our house. She read the name, "*Karibuni Cottage*, Welcome!" That day she went home at noon with enough money to feed her family. Hannah and mother had now become real friends. They talked about everything and prayed together.

Each morning Hannah arrived at our home at 7:45. A few minutes later, several other women arrived. They spoke with in Swahili; Hannah explained which of the ladies were the neediest. She had real wisdom and learned the personal circumstances of each African mother. She spoke with authority and grace. After several more minutes, mother and Hannah would decide which of the women would work that day. They arrived carrying their little ones on their backs, tucked in a long, colorful cloth suspended around the forehead. The little ones swayed in the sun, often sleeping, tucked lovingly on the backs of their mothers. All morning 12 widows worked side by side, clearing the garden, planting seeds, cultivating the land and watering the ground. They sang together and could hear one another speak across wide fields on our little rented farm. At the harvest time the women who had done the hard work for months kept the fruit of the harvest, mother's creative way of multiplying blessings for the poor.

At noon payments were made for a full day's work, although they had only worked four hours. In effect, the women were getting twice the hourly salary. Of course, it wasn't much, but that money fed 60¬80 people every day, including the children of the widows. I was so proud of mom and dad for productive work and generosity shown to needy women.

* * *

Sometimes Grandma Hill would send parcels from Winnipeg; she was a widow and also loved widows in Africa. Grandpa Hill, mother's dad, had his life snuffed out by a drunk driver one night in Winnipeg; he was crossing the street to the plant where he worked as a night watchman. Aunt Ruth and Aunt Helen, my mother's sisters, would have found items on sale at Eatons. Little shirts and dresses always appeared in the parcels; flannelette nightgowns and shoes came for children. Children walked up and down D Route in clothing that came from Eatons and The Bay.

* * *

My questions seemed a bit more grown up after we moved to Limuru. Contrasting aspects of life confronted me: the poverty of African villagers, experiments involving apes at the Richard Leakey Primate Research Institute a half a mile away and the splendid golf course close by, where white settlers dined at the club house and then watched splendid horses gallop around the race track.

One question led to another. Why did the African families have such big families? Why didn't they just stop having children? Why did they all live in a crowded little village? Wouldn't they be better off if they lived more scattered out? They didn't have very much land, but they had such big families. What would happen two generations later when there would be too many people for the available land? If each family plot had to be divided between the sons when a landowner died, then in a few generations there would only be a small area of land for each family. If not enough land was passed down from father to son what would happen to the African families in the future?

Take the little Kikuyu village near us. There were almost 1,500 or 2,000 people in a relatively small space. Their village space, with tiny round huts filled with smoke from the fires for cooking supper, were so different from that of Mr. Eden, whom we knew in Limuru. Mr. Eden was a white settler who had more farmland than several Kikuyu villages put together. Mr. Eden's mother taught us piano and singing lessons; they lived quite close by and during vacation time, mom and dad wanted us to take music lessons. Mrs. Eden Senior taught in her living room and a huge, clean carpet with large, upholstered chairs surrounding her impressive grand piano. The house honored ornate British traditions; entering that mansion was like taking a breath of Europe.

Mother was never one for philosophical talk about poverty and riches. She just told us basic facts about the Eden family. "They are so unhappy, my dears, even though they have all that land. Why, Mr. Eden's wife just got up and left him one day. She went back to England, to London, with the kids. Now look at that huge farm. There he lives with his mother, as he did before being married. He doesn't have a thing: family, wife or children. Isn't it just terrible how his wife just went away? We invited him to come to watch the Moody Bible Film we showed in our house, but he wouldn't come."

Mother left us guessing. She never said "affair, or adultery, or extra-marital cases". We had to fill in the details in our imagination. Sex was not a common topic for discussion. Mr. Eden may have lost his wife but he still had the large acreage; sixty women from the village worked picking tea leaves. Another twenty Africans took care of his cattle, and the pyrethrum fields needed at least another forty women. These women threw little yellow blossoms into the open yellow cloth on their backs. So it wasn't exactly right that Mr. Eden had nothing. He supported 120 families, ten times as many as my parents could help.

So there you had it. The Eden family had lots of land. The Adams family, who also lived close by, had less land; they were also rich. We were not as rich as either the Adams or the Edens. The Africans had much less than we had. We were in between. A small farm of about 6 acres was not much. I didn't even know if you could say we "had" six acres since we didn't own the land.

Was life always going to be out of balance? Mr. Eden, a white settler with no family to take care of, owned more than an entire village in which almost 2,000 people lived. At times I wondered about my future in a land in which the number of Africans was so much greater than that of the white settlers.

I was reluctant to talk about these things with my father. I knew how strongly he felt as a result of the actions taken by the Mau Mau to get rid of people like the Eden family. In fact, dad was writing a book, *From Mau Mau to Christ*. When we read the book, we understood why he rarely spoke about the atrocities committed a few years earlier. From his conversations in the prisons of MacKinnon Road and Manyani he had learned so much about witch doctors, the Mau Mau oaths and the sacrifices of animals.

* * *

Here, in Limuru, several worlds lived side-by-side. The Kikuyu village had its own culture, including customs for boys aged 12, witch doctors and demands upon their future. Beside the Kikuyu village was the sign for the Richard Leakey Primate Research Institute. The next property was our destination for music lessons; Mr. Eden and his mother occupied the largest English house around. The British farmers shared their golf course, the horse racing track and Brackenhurst Hotel.

Who would control things in the future? If the Kikuyu men didn't like the wages received from the Bata School Factory in Limuru, just four miles away, could the workers force the factory owners to pay higher wages? I had just heard the word "strike" for the first time. It took me a long time to think through these new ideas and each new idea created another set of questions.

What about the Mau Mau? I had come back to them again. Hadn't they been trying to get their land back? They said it was their land, because the land around a village belonged to everyone in that village. "No," the British said, "the land belongs to individual white families. The land was empty when we arrived. The railway was pushed through from Mombasa to Kampala, and all this empty land was here for us to claim."

Who was right? Who was wrong? Independence from Britain will have to come, that's what dad was saying. Then after Independence who would be in charge? Would war begin all over again? Would we have barbed wire around our school again? I couldn't help wondering at the tremendous conflict that was coming in the future. The Africans didn't have enough land and their families were far too numerous.

* * *

When Kikuyu people fell sick they went to the witch doctor. He was the most feared man in the village. And when anyone died we heard the wails begin at sun down and go on all night. Sometimes, the screaming was almost unbearable because it was so sad. When a chief died one night the wailing was extra-loud. Why did they weep and wail like that all night yet British people took death with only a few tears?

* * *

The time had come to go back to school, to *swot*, and that involved all European boys and girls. We were not the only ones staying at boarding schools. The Prince of Wales School, the Duke of York, and several others served the educational needs of white kids in Kenya. There were said to be only a few thousand white families in Kenya whereas more than 7,000,000 Africans in at least 40 languages were growing at a very fast rate.

Preparing for any boarding school meant sewing name tags onto clothing, towels, sheets, blankets and jackets. Anything that would go through the laundry at boarding school required a name tag. At the time, name tags were a growth industry in Nairobi where Asian merchants attended the needs of the white settler population.

A new term had begun and September marked the beginning of a new school year. Don was six now and he began *swot* so now there were four trunks to pack into the car. Each night, while dad read books out loud, mom sewed on name tags on Don's new clothes. His name had to be on everything: socks, shirts, underwear and pants. Dad read another book while we stretched out on the carpet in front of the fireplace. Cedar logs crackled loudly, punctuating our last evening at home.

The next morning arrived and it was time to go. After breakfast and good-byes, we managed to heave two large steel trunks onto the roof rack, and the other two into the back of the station wagon. We waved good-bye to mother, standing at the base of the small stone stairs beside the kitchen. She wiped away her tears with the corner of her blue apron. All four of her children were now going to RVA. Dad's Peugeot went slowly through the wooden arch, taking us back to school.

Don was starting Grade One. On the way to school, just as we got to the top of the escarpment, Dorothy turned to him, "Don, you have to learn to tie your shoes!"

Don said casually, "Yea, I'll learn sometime," and he chuckled. He had the full confidence of a six-year old combined with an easy resilience and a captivating, casual sense of humor. Those qualities would enable him to get along with others while away from home, even if the experiences in the dorm would stretch him to the limit.

"No, but you have to learn right now!" Dot was the responsible one; her excellent sense of timing was preparing him for the experience of standing at "Inspection" each morning. Don was at one of his "teachable moments." Sitting on the back seat of the car Dot showed Don how to fold this lace over that one. These were actions his little fingers had to master; he could not put it off. While dad drove to school, Dot taught him how to tie his shoes.

The car driver in Kenya sits on the right hand side and drives on the left-hand side of the road. I was in the front seat of the car, on the left, in the passenger's seat; when we came to the top of the escarpment I looked over the precipice. Far away, three thousand feet below, the Rift Valley was already shimmering in the heat of the day. At one hairpin bend, gruesome because of many unfortunate deaths, the rusted hulks of six or eight cars lay scattered down a steep cliff in a hodge-podge, willy-nilly manner. Life had been taken away unexpectedly when drivers went over the precipice, unable to make that sharp turn.

I looked back to the back seat. Dot was helping Don survive the first day of *swot;* he learned quickly. My first day at RVA came back so clearly in my mind; I remembered how I got my nickname. Looking at Don, I already knew what his nickname would be. He would not be able to escape. He was my younger brother so he would be called *Titch Flappit*. RVA possessed an unchangeable code.

"You're going to be called, *Titch Flappit,* Little Flappit," I said. "Now, I'll help make things easier for you. Get to the dining room early for breakfast. I'm in the older group; at breakfast I'll bring you out several pieces of toast, covered with strawberry jam."

Soggy toast needed an explanation early on in his school career. It was toasted over coals in a brazier, then piled one piece on top of another until hundreds of slices of toast were taken from the kitchen to the serving window of the dining room. "It's soggy, it's white toast, usually burned in one place and not even toasted in another, but it will do! And I'll get you toast, passing it on to you at the door. Don't let prefects see me doing that, though, other wise I'll get points off."

"What does that mean, 'get points off," he asked. The car kept winding down the escarpment with dad at the wheel. "You'll find out at the dorm," I answered. "If you do bad stuff, points come off your point card. You will do good stuff but don't ever expect points to go back onto your card. Each term you feel like the path is downhill."

Dot took over, explaining how the point cards worked. She gave him a better explanation then concluded, "That's why you have to do your shoe laces up. You don't want to get points off at inspection."

"See, I did it!" Don said victoriously, showing his shoe, with a tie that was loose, threatening to come undone, all on its own. A triumphant little smile and impish grin filled his face. His was the face that would get out of trouble any time, just by smiling broadly. If Ma Senoff came looking for a culprit Don would only need to grin a bit and then she would have to go looking for the guilty party somewhere else.

Coming adventures, and coming hurts: he was in for it all. I was so fond of him. It wasn't possible to protect him from the coming hurts in dorm life. He'd have to struggle all by himself in those dorms where all the Grade One *titchies* were starting. He was almost six and I longed to be able to tell him how to survive the cruel events that one lived through in the *titchie* dorm. I also knew that in no time, he'd know how easy it was to step "out of bounds". He was going to stay in the KLD Dorm. The tracks were close by. He'd be tempted to be in the forest all the time, or walk along the railway tracks on the top of the mission.

We were almost at the dirt road that jutted off the highway, the entrance to Rift Valley Academy. I looked out over the valley to the almost-eternal mountain with the deep round rim, enfolding the volcano, that deep mysterious crater. I had tears in my eyes and a smile on my face. Maybe, in years to come, Don would laugh at adventures he was going to experience. I had a few of my own to tell already. There was a side to Dorm life that I disliked: sudden hurts, a sharp tongue that could cut a wide patch open down inside of you, the older boys who might twist your arm until you said, "Uncle". I bit my lip. It would never do to arrive at school with tearstains on your cheeks. You might even get a worse nickname. Anyway, by the age of 12 you would never cry again.

So, I smiled at him in the car. Don had learned how to tie his shoes. And for her skill in teaching him to tie his shoes in such an unlikely place Dorothy had gained a new name in my vocabulary. From now one, whether mom liked it or not, I was going to call her Dot.

CHAPTER 13

PA HOLLENBECK AND BAND PRACTICE

Mother and dad must have been proud of their children, with all four of us being away from home together. Don had his new dorm; I was part of Kedong Dorm, and the Hollenbeck family looked after my new home.

Pa Hollenbeck was our new *dorm father* in the Seventh and Eighth Grade dorm. Everything about the man seemed jolly, starting at his waist and moving up to his laugh. Sometimes his rolling laugh caused the belt of his pants to shake up and down in time with mirth that spread across his face.

Best of all, he was a band specialist, able to play any and all instruments, from trumpet to clarinet. Our best trumpet player at school was his son, Bob Hollenbeck. Bob, *Titch Hollenbeck*, often sat beside me in band class. He played his trumpet, licking his lower lip a couple times, then his upper lip. His fingers lovingly caressed the trumpet's three valves and pushed them down slowly, as if by some stroke of misfortune one of them might have become rusted since the previous day. He blew a clear trumpet note, a liquid vibrating sound that sometimes sent shivers of joy down my back. Bob obviously took after his father. Both father and son were specialists in music and I envied them.

I tried to imitate Bob by licking my lower lip twice, then my upper lip and then push down on the valves on my cornet. There must have been a reason that my instrument didn't ever produce a bright, round, wholesome ring that came to him naturally. Was it because my cornet was slightly defective? After all, it had two bumps; someone had dropped it once. The real reason was that Bob possessed skill, so I pondered, "How does a person get skills in life? Are you just born with them? If you don't have skills to play, like *Titch Hollenbeck*, can you become skilled just by working hard? Do you get good grades in every subject just by studying enough, or is there more to it?"

* * *

Band practice had its ups and downs, often for the better, but I after one term I still didn't get the rhythm of some of the songs. Ten months later, when things didn't improve, Pa Hollenbeck said, "Are you having difficulty with the timing on this piece?"

I had come in again on the wrong note and he was clearly frustrated; I was mad at myself. A bright red flooded my face, more painful than an unwelcome sunburn on my back. I determined to count more carefully, "One and two, three, four, one and two, three, four and one, two and three, four."

Shortly afterwards I made another mistake; the band came to a halt, one more time. "I think that you should look at the timing more carefully," he suggested, frustration showing through. His voice, which was usually encouraging, showed irritation this time. Humiliated by my lack of timing on second trumpet and angry with myself for not being able to count the beats and half-beats correctly I determined to tap my foot in time with his regular beat.

* * *

Almost all the grade seven boys had put their minds to playing the trumpet or French horn or trombone. Pa Hollenbeck had us firmly in his tow. The band classes were held in the newly built Jubilee Hall with its great soaring roof, towering high enough to strain the back of the neck. The sound of the clarinets hitting wobbly notes bounced off the corrugated tin roof magnifying that elementary principle, "Keep on practicing!"

Band practice was held in a semi-circle. Pa Hollenbeck needed a Second Trumpet to complete his band. He had given me a cornet with shinny valves and the bright bell.

"You need to practice more, *Flappit!*" he said, encouraging me. I made a commitment to myself. I would use the free time after school, between 3:00 and 5:00 p.m., to improve my skills on the cornet.

* * *

Things didn't get any better after I moved to Ma and Pa Hollenbeck's dorm. They found that fine balance, being open to the boys, but being firm at the same time. They would even let us go out of bounds, for example, if you had shown "an improvement in your attitude." That was how Peanut and Giddings, Fish, Roger Crimson and I had been able to go on our bubble gum hike.

The students were going to go down to the Kedong Plains for a trip one Saturday. They would see animals, the impossible hope being that of spotting a leopard, the wiliest of the big cats. Since not everybody could go in the best truck, only those who were the "best behaved" were allowed to go in the open backed lorry. "Spoiled brats" I said, referring to a number of the guys who had the highest marks. Pa Hollenbeck didn't let me get away with it. He *benched* two of us. Crimson and I were the worst, since we had talked back to him.

"Don't you sass with me," he said, his face suddenly a darker color, but we sassed him right back. We were not going down to the plains; we'd lost our coveted Saturday trip.

Roger's father was an excellent pilot. He could land his small Mission Aviation Fellowship, MAF, Cessna on shorter runways than any bush pilot. Roger had picked up a lot of his father's skills in aviation already. When the school had all gone off on the trip down to the plains, Roger and I gathered all the desks in the study hall and made them into a huge single table. Then we folded scores of papers making tiny planes of all sorts and sizes. We got up on the massive table, standing on the "airport" we had made. His planes were all marked "R", for Roger, and mine were all marked "P", for Phillips. We had a contest to see who could keep the greatest number of planes in the air. There were several varieties to the game, too. "This is better than going on that trip," exclaimed Roger.

"Sure is! Aren't you glad that you got punished! Haven't had so much fun for ages," I said as I launched planes as fast as I could throw my arm. One of the paper planes circled back behind us. There in the door to the room was Pa Hollenbeck, watching us. He was just patiently waiting there, his belly slightly larger than his belt, waiting for the instant, the inevitable second, when we would notice him. He shook his balding head and we were absolutely crushed. He had heard us, our comments, and he looked us straight in the eye.

Because of his patience and attention to me in band, I viewed him as one of the better teachers. I really did not want to hurt him.

He'd forgotten his binoculars and had returned for them to take them on the trip. We were caught. He knew what we were like, what we were really like. The Law of Consequences had caught up with me. I could get around the Point System at times, but timing needed to implement the rules of life took a lot of practice.

* * *

After almost a year of band I still had not mastered the timing. It wasn't a surprise that I didn't get to beat on the big wonderful, bass drum, or the other drums.

There were a whole little squad of drummers who had special lessons. The snare drums were the best; snappy, loud and commanding attention, they made me imagine the wily revolutionaries, those brave fighters who fought against the red-breasted British soldiers when the War of Independence began in Boston. Pa Hollenbeck even gave special classes for those agile drummers. He delighted in teaching people music. Kenton Fish was a budding soloist. Ray Davis played on the piano, and our Young People's Meetings on Sunday nights played host to new combinations, duets, trios and quartets with boys, or girls, or both boys and girls.

The spark of fire began in my chest. I quit band class in anger and frustration one day, and thought of doing the same thing with piano; mom wanted to me master the piano. It was boring going up the scales and down the scales, and up the scales and down the scales, time after time. Why couldn't you just get on with playing something interesting? A half an hour a day wasted going up and down the keyboard! Another destructive little flame was licked up the sides, beginning to burn, evidence of my rebellious nature.

* * *

At RVA my questions had involved thoughts about games, going out of bounds, hot beef dinners on Sunday for lunch, and how I might win in a game of *nyabes* against Carly Barnett. But now, the first hormones of puberty were upon me and new thoughts filled my mind and imagination. Hormones were beginning to kick in; we learned about sex, some knowledge coming from stories told to each other and some from the books we read. Some of these books were even found in Ma Barrett's library.

Pa Hollenbeck was direct, open and very helpful. Before going to town one time he said, "I'm taking all you Grade Seven and Grade Eight guys to Nairobi. Now, let me tell you what happens if you ever get together with a prostitute." His description of permanent sickness and disability left me with no desire to ever go down that path, and I was thankful for his frank talk. It was a talk never to be forgotten.

* * *

Jim Hollenbeck was a real *dorm father*, taking time to talk with us afterwards, personally, not condemning us; he continually encouraged improvement in our attitudes. His kind instruction to us after he had caught me red-handed flying paper planes perhaps motivated me more than any other gesture that term.

I realized how easy it was to lie, to cover up one's true intentions with a half-truth when he gave us the chance to walk out of bounds, to walk out to the highway and back. Partially free, determined to do whatever we wanted to, we had marched way out of bounds, strutting down to the Plains and limping back past the Kijabe township, covered with sunburn, laden down with too much chewing gum stuffed into our t-shirts. I knew Pa Hollenbeck was right; I was in the wrong. I was angry about my own stubbornness, and even more frustrated that, having started band with one instrument, I had not kept at it.

CHAPTER 14

THE TOOL CUPBOARD, DEBAGGING AND THE FIRE

*M*y worst class was spelling and my Junior High teacher was determined to help me improve. Gladys Bellinger did her best through math and World History to instill both precision in logic and knowledge of world events. Her not-so-hidden agenda was to help me improve my attitude. She was well equipped for the task, having endured the rigors of Nebraska State Teacher's College.

One day I was supposed to be writing out words that I had misspelled. Since I had a dismal average in this class, I would be writing out words, ten times each, long after everyone else was on to their reading and geography homework. One day she returned a page to me and asked me write each misspelled word 20 times. Up until then the penalty had been 10 times for each word. Repetition was supposed to take over where she left off.

I had to do something creative so I tried several different contraptions. The most successful involved placing five ballpoint pens between two cardboard slabs, setting them in a straight line. Then, when I wrote one word, I would actually be writing five words because four more pens traced the same lines. My invention would cut down my punishment by 80%. Ma Bellinger caught onto my trick the first time I tried it. I had to use pens with different colors and, once again, she didn't like my attitude. She was frustrated with me and I was even more disconcerted, having had my good invention rendered ineffective, and continually making the same mistakes in spelling.

* * *

Gladys Bellinger had been born with the strength of character to take on students who were 12 or 13 years of age. For me, her resolve to keep unruly students under control started at the top of her head, with the naturally wavy salt and pepper hair, her steely eyes that could spot a misdemeanor a blackboard away from the back of the room and her steady jaw. She did not tolerate disobedience.

One day Ma Bellinger caught me reading Ernest Hemingway. No one was allowed to read at the end of her class; the last ten minutes were set aside for doing homework. However, since I chose to do my homework during study hall in the evenings, I pretended to do math while reading *For Whom the Bells Toll*. How an existential novel had ever passed Clara Barrett's eyes, I never knew, but Hemingway made his way to the fiction shelf.

I sat in the back row in the Junior High classroom since I had the timing of my teacher figured out. I could read a half a page while she walked down the aisle away from me and

I placed my novel under my math book as she walked toward the back of the room. While she would turn her back again I had another 30 seconds more in my novel.

Ma Bellinger caught me when she turned around unexpectedly. She was aghast! Hemingway had gained a welcome space in the library and he was tossed into the dustbin of disapproved books in history. She didn't need teacher's school to help her decide on an adequate punishment for a recalcitrant student. I needed isolation; such antics could be spread, sort of like a flu bug.

* * *

Beside our classroom, underneath the south end of the porch, she found a suitable place. The tool cupboard was full of tools, used to keep lawns trim and cut cedar hedges around the school yard. I entered with my nose up in the air and said a sarcastic, "Thank you, Miss Bellinger." Naturally, it wasn't a thank-you at all, but another sassy comment. African employees had hung a tiny broken mirror inside; I spent a long time examining my worsening acne. After I got used to the darkness I examined other things, too.

An hour later she came to get me. "Are you sorry?" she asked.

"No." I answered, truthfully.

"Do you want to stay in here another hour?"

"Sure!"

I stayed in another hour and found I had much to learn. Could I figure out which one of the African staff used the garden shears? What clues had he left? When was the last time he used the shears? I examined the clippings, now a dull, dry green, and decided to become a detective in real life. I found dozens of things to examine in there. Besides, Math class was over and history class had begun. This was better than hearing about President Andrew Jackson, or learning about the deliberate slaughter of Indians in the westward push to establish new territories, which later became new states.

Ma Bellinger returned. "Are you ready to come out?"

"If you're ready to have me."

"Don't get sassy. You're going to get into trouble. David, you have a real attitude problem!"

"Only when I want to."

"What are you doing in here? Why do you want to stay in here?"

"I'm examining all these tools. It's interesting. This pick balances back and forth; it takes only three seconds. Do you think it would be a safer tool if the handle was longer?" or..."

Her face showed a red-hot anger. I was hauled back to the classroom. The Point Card that hung over my bed got several black marks that day.

The Bible Classes she gave combined both mathematical precision as well as a good grasp of history, that of this world and the next. For a whole term we made notes on the Moses' tabernacle in the wilderness. How she knew what each color of the curtain meant in heavenly language, and the nature of symbolism of each article in the furniture of the tabernacle, I could never understand. Her steady determination to instill Bible principles almost checked the agitation in my spirit. She did her best; I knew she had good intentions.

* * *

A dim fire had been raging for a long time somewhere down inside of me. I didn't recognize the explosive power of rebellion until it was a full raging fire; it was capable of undoing the good that my parents and teachers had tried to teach me. Emotions were like dry timber, able to burst out as flames of anger, sparked by critical comments from dorm mates, or because of my own foolishness.

* * *

My worst moment came in October 1958. The cruelest event was to be *de-bagged*. We wore baggy shorts, inherited unfortunately as baggage from British colonial rule. These shorts were called *bags*; they came down to one's knees, and used twice as much khaki material as was necessary. Since dad was British, and since he wanted me to enjoy a double inheritance from his culture, my clothes really were bags. I hated that uniform.

To get *de-bagged* meant being tricked into going into the forest below the school, out of bounds. The *big guys*, perhaps Grade 10's or 11's, would pull a guy's *bags* off, their strong arms preventing the smaller guy from escaping. Of course, the *bags* would be neatly found on your bed in your dorm. The bewildering trick was how to make it back to the dorm dressed only in underwear. Since staff member's houses were scattered about and since girls walked everywhere around the school property being *de-bagged* was debasing, painful, something to be feared.

The most humiliating thing was the sense of powerlessness and a loss of self-respect. It happened rarely. Usually the *bags* were given back in the forest. I heard the word and feared the act.

* * *

One Sunday at noon several guys whispered in my ear. "Hey, *Flappit*, do you want to see something *severe*? We have a little leopard; it's caught in a trap!" They had me at my weak points, my interest in wild animals and wanting to be on the inside of an in group.

"Promise not to tell anyone? The trap is out of bounds! Come on!" they urged. This was new for me, being accepted into the company of the *big guys*. I hesitated but saw it as a way to make up for a broken watch. Here was a great bit of news and I would get in on it first, before any of my friends, before *Crimson*, even! I went along with them.

At the far end of the playing field, out of sight of all the dorms and houses, they grabbed me. "*De-bag* him," they yelled together.

"Don't you dare!" I wrestled, not willing to give up. I fought really hard and I almost got away but they caught me again. Two guys held my arms; two others held my feet. I tried kicking anyone or anything that came near, preferably a nose or a mouth. Another fellow unloosened my belt and took my pants off. I was now only in my socks and shoes and underwear. I used every bit of my best bad language against them that I had learned. They laughed, coughing with bursts of laughter.

My face was purple with frustration, fear and humiliation when a bell rang.

It was the bell heard all over the station. It was always rung slowly, deliberately, to wake us up, or to call people for special events. But now it was going as if it had a mind of its own. There was only one reason to ring that bell like that. A fire was burning.

* * *

"Fire! Fire!" the five guys yelled, looking at each other and then at me.

"Wow, that's *severe*! Just when we were de-bagging him! That's the fire bell, you guys," shouted one of the guys who held me on the ground. The thick forest hid almost everything, but black smoke rising into the sky had appeared. Smoke was fuming, boiling upwards, growing aggressively against the blue sky. The fire bell kept telling everyone on the station. It was the urgent call for help; that included everyone on the station.

The *big guys* ran up the forest path, across the winding road at the far end of the soccer field, and up towards the fire. At the edge of the field they dropped my khaki shorts, where I found them. No one would be looking at the soccer field while flames were gathering strength, so I was saved from one fear, only to be confronted with something so much worse. By the time I had my shorts on and my belt buckled up an angry, swirling, black cloud filled the sky. My five 'friends' had crossed the road, climbed the steep embankment, which was the far end of the soccer field, and were half way across center field. I followed far behind, running as fast as I could, heading up the hill towards the smoke.

* * *

We were not the only ones running in the direction of the smoke. The Stevenson's Dorm, where my sisters stayed, was burning down. By the time I arrived, out of breath, I saw how badly Stevenson Dorm had been damaged. Flames were lapping all sides of the two-story building. Dorothy and Pearl outside the building stood with other girls, all of them tearful, crying, watching their possessions go up in flames. The young girls lived on the top floor and the Giddings family lived on the main floor. My friend was Roland Giddings; his parents, Bob and Dorothy were losing all their personal things, being consumed in an inferno of smothering flame and smoke.

Someone called out that all the girls were safe, but there was a fear that the walls of the dorm would fall over and out onto the bystanders. No fire equipment could fight those hot flames and now the whole school, teachers and students, stood awe-struck, talking in little groups of four or five, circulating, get further details. Some asked how it got started. People stood at the back of the building, which was on a dirt hill looking into the windows of the second floor, and then walked down the slight incline around to the front.

Then the loud bangs began. Those explosions were caused by barrels belching open in the unbearable heat. A single lady missionary had left and she had stored her belongings in an upstairs, back room. The fire consumed her barrels, her belongings; she lost everything. A 21-gun salute would have proclaimed victory; this was a total loss.

Everything lay blackened and grimy under the soot that billowed around. The north wall of the dorm had now lost its wooden supports due to the intense inferno that had gutted the main floor; the beams holding the upper floor sagged and gave way and then the blaze crackled even more as wax floors exploded with intense heat. The wall began to lean outwards, more and more, as if it were personally responsible for the loss felt by the Giddings family and the 20 or so girls. Anyone could follow the slow destruction of the wall, that process of death.

Some hadn't noticed the danger of a high walling falling on them, couldn't see the imminent harm. *Titch Hollenbeck*, using his loud, trumpet-like voice, as well as several of the other more responsible guys, dived into the clumps of little kids who were looking up at the grey, black billowing clouds of destruction. "Get back! Get back quickly," he yelled. Their quick act of mercy may have saved some students from harm.

As if tired with its life, having stood so firmly for years, holding up its share of the weight, the wall, now exhausted, began to shudder. It leaned like a falling soldier, shot through the shoulder. The peak of the wall, which had held the roof, started to fall and then the whole wall gave way, taking with it half burning beams still stuck in its side. They were like burning spears piercing the belly of a great soldier. A cloud of red-brown dust spat heavenward as the wall smashed into the ground with a violent jolt. Like a great hero in a battle, the wall had fallen. Stevenson's Dorm lay in ruins. Its foundations were nothing but ashes and hot coals. Dorothy Giddings, who was a dorm parent to the younger girls, supervisor of the laundry, had lost her home.

A short while later the afternoon church service was held. We were in shock, amazed that Robert Giddings, whose turn it was to speak that afternoon, could preach. He said nothing about his tribulation; he was like Job, able to bless the Lord at all times. At RVA we were taught to accept all the events of life, both good and bad, as coming from the hand of God. I had already heard that lesson in the life of Job; the story was to be told as quickly as possible, taking emotion out, accepting disasters in life.

* * *

The elementary girls faced impossible pressures, for they were away from home and now had lost their dorm and all their personal possessions, little treasures that made their home a place of comfort. A dozen others were crying along with Dorothy and Pearl. Girls wept with their arms around each other, and I saw Pearl and Dorothy were safe so I hadn't lost them.

There had been more danger for Pearl since she had a brace on her leg, but she got out of the building in time. Only after intense loss was it possible to realize the value of familiar things. The teachers doubled up, opening their homes for the homeless kids. Mrs. Boda, Mrs. De Young and others provided a temporary space for the girls, sharing in their loss, helping until permanent quarters were found.

* * *

I was in a cold fury. I had nearly been de-bagged, in fact I had been. I'd been taken in by a dirty, miserable, trick. The fire inside was a rebellion, as dangerous in its own way as the fire was to the building that had just burned down. However, this was a fire that others couldn't see. I began to want to run away, to quit school. "I'll be OK with a Grade Eight education," I boasted. "I'll run away and no one will find me. Grade Eight is all you need in life." Roger was my best friend now; he told me, "You can't run away. Think!"

My half-serious plan was to get down to the docks in Mombasa. I remembered all the ships that came in to port. I kept returning to the Mombasa port in daydreams. The long quay, softly lapping water, ships moored with long, strong ropes, wild ocean waves and gulls gliding over the tall masts called me away from school, from math and spelling. I'd find a means of revenge, of expressing my rebellion. "You don't really need more than Grade Eight in life, you know." I half wanted to act out the book *Men Against the Sea*.

We were walking up past Jubilee Hall, past the enormous eucalyptus tree that always gave off such a sweet aroma. Roger declared, "I'm going to get a good education and be a pilot." I knew he would become a pilot, like his dad.

"Why don't you start Boy's Brigade," suggested Pa Entwistle. He was one of the kindest teachers. I admired his kids, Daniel and David, remembering them as the best-behaved kids. Boy's Brigade was probably what I needed. Already 23 guys had joined and they were learning the skills to live and thrive in the outdoors.

"Naw...I'm going to do other things, better things," I replied. I was grateful that Pa Entwistle took an interest in me. In fact, it took only a few kind words to postpone my run-away plans. However, I had no money, so that was also an important obstacle.

* * *

The Tool Cupboard, Debagging And The Fire

Advertising brought a new type of pleasure onto the scene. Pez was a new candy and it came in a tiny packet, unloaded into a small plastic dispenser. The clever campaign made dispensers come in various colors. The small candies broke down slowly, if you sucked them instead of biting them; each color signaled a different fruit taste. The best part of a class was to eat a Pez candy without being caught. The worst part was getting caught and having the Pez dispenser taken away until the end of the day.

The time for Keswick Convention arrived once more. We made our way up country to Eldoret, stopping the car to straddle the equator, one foot in the Northern hemisphere and one in the Southern. As before, the meetings took place at the Eldoret Girls' School. Dad advertised the event, answering the correspondence and attending to 101 details.

I knew I'd never be able to catch dad's attention in the midst of all those arrangements. Mom and dad were not ignorant of the fact that I was having problems; actually report cards came to our home, the most painful and the most anxiety-producing part of the whole term. When the report card had come the previous holidays, there had been a strange stillness in the house. I expected an explosion. Instead there was a regular supper. I went to my room and heard Dorothy talking to Pearl, in a quiet voice in the hall outside my room, "David's report card came and mom says it's a very bad one with lots of black marks against him." I learned that night that I was about to be expelled.

"What do you think will happen?" asked Pearl in a half whisper that my ears were not supposed to pick up. Her question was mine, too. There had been no big explosion. I was grounded but not for the school antics. I was grounded at home when I broke the lock of the garage door open to take my bike, going to the horse races. Dad hated horse races. He always used the same illustration, referring to the man in the butcher shop. "Look, he lost three fortunes on gambling on the horses. Isn't that the limit?"

There it was: a moral lesson every time we saw that sad-looking man who cut up the meat for all the folk who came to buy cuts of meat. I didn't know that dad had also received three inheritances, and that he had put them to better use, purchasing printing presses for Kijabe station, presses that were now producing hundreds, no, thousands, of books for Africans learning to read, learning about Jesus Christ.

At Keswick Convention I expected dad to be angry with me. Instead, he took me for a walk to the area of the swimming pool. It was the best part of the sprawling complex that made up the Eldoret Girls' School. "What's the matter, David," he asked, putting his hand on my shoulder. "What's getting you into trouble? Why?"

I wondered how to explain what *de-bagging* was. Should I start by telling him about the rhubarb that I couldn't stomach? What about arm-twisting? "The boys are so mean." I began, knowing that the love of my father was more permanent than that of any dorm parent. It didn't matter how dedicated the dorm parents were who came from America. Instead of going into detail I mentioned only a few things that had happened. Nothing came out about my idea to run away, to start working on the Mombasa docks. The episode about de-bagging was left out, as were a hundred other events.

"I want to pray for you", dad said. He put his hand on my shoulder and prayed. I hadn't felt that loved for so long. How could you run away from home, or school, when a parent took time out of the frighteningly intensive load, preparing a conference, to pray with you and talk with you? He took the whole afternoon off, walking around the school grounds with me.

I didn't confess that the previous year I had gone to a movie down town Eldoret, something that would have upset him a lot, so I left it unsaid. I also didn't tell him how the previous year at the conference I had gone with two of my friends; the three of us had slipped a unpaid-for book into our pockets. Two of us got away without being caught, but the third guy got caught. The Indian merchant threatened like mad. "I will call the Police!"

We all imitated African and Indian accents. We could tell a story, switching back and forth between accents: American, Southern USA, African and Indian. Those stories were saved up for the dorm, though. You could never tell them to your dad. I cried as dad prayed for me, this time tears of real repentance. I was sorry; clearly I was beginning to make a mess of my life.

CHAPTER 15

COALS OF FIRE

Special meals were served when Christmas holidays arrived. Celebrating the end of Don's first term in First Grade was special, too. We had gifts at Christmas and extra cinnamon buns fresh from the woodstove. During the holidays we told our parents about the past term. I told them that I was still having a rough time, mostly with the teachers. Mom and dad looked at each other with that knowing look, and I didn't know what was coming, possibly a reprimand or some kind of discipline.

Instead, I received a special gift, a watch, which covered both my birthday and Christmas. It was a real treasure and I prized the gift. No doubt my parents were not only proud about Don starting school, but also a little worried about my *attitude*. I had heard my teachers speak to me a number of times about my attitude recently. If dad thought a watch would help me see the RVA world differently, he was completely right. I wanted to be back at school to boast about my Christmas gift.

* * *

Before the January term began, the Annual AIM Conference was held at Kijabe. Our family stayed in one of the rooms upstairs in the Kiambogo building, a room I had stayed in the previous school year.

This was the first time I realized that tensions existed between various mission families. Morning meetings centered on the Bible while afternoons were dedicated to "mission business." Assignments of new missionaries, re-assignments of returning families from furlough periods and the management of mission properties dominated the agenda. Some people had begun to discuss the place of Africans in the structure of the parallel organization, Africa Inland Church, or AIC.

When I asked to sit in on the "business meetings" Dad suggested that I leave, because, as he said, "There are different ideas about what we should be doing while we live in Limuru." Until then I had little or no idea of politics between adults.

* * *

Five days later I was wearing my brand new watch when dad dropped us off for another 13 weeks at school. The best gift of all time, even better than the leather-beaded belt from Canada, was wrapped around my wrist. Classmates would soon be trading exciting adventures from the last five weeks. In no time my trunk was unpacked, once again, everything put away. I was so proud of my new watch. Leaving my dorm I walked onto the long porch, close to the dining room door. In a few minutes we would charge through, gathering around the supper tables, ready for the first meal of the new term.

Two *big guys* had picked on me before. I hadn't forgiven them for leaving me in the forest half dressed. They seemed to enjoy being tough, making smaller guys feel afraid.

One of the worst things that they could do to *titchies* was lift them off the floor, hooking the belt onto a coat hook right beside the dining room door. A *titchie* hanging from a coat hook, his belt imprisoning the waist and leaving him flailing in the air was a pitiful sight. It was impossible to get off the hook by yourself, so someone needed to take mercy and lift a little guy down. Two of the guys waiting for supper had threatened me once and I said something mean. Pushing me around a circle seemed more fun, since I was now almost too big to hang on the coat hook.

"Look, *Flappit* is back!" A circle of about six or eight guys formed quickly and I was pushed back and forth like a big basketball. If I tried to escape from the circle, a foot shot out, ready to trip me up. I went around the circle, back and forth, from side to side. Someone pushed me on my shoulder and I slammed into the other side of the circle, where I was shoved again in the direction of another boy. A crazy pattern of cheers and hooting erupted. At first I enjoyed the pushing and entered in with good humor. It was fun to be the center of attention before supper on the first night of the new term.

One of the boys had very strong biceps and a slight sneer on his face. I made a nasty comment about his muscles, which had held me on the floor of the forest. He gave me a push, sparked by anger. I used language that was not becoming of a missionary kid and now the pushing was suddenly violent. Someone tripped me, just as I arrived on that side of the circle. I fell, a really hard jolt. My face and arm smashed into the floor.

Supper bell went just then and everyone went inside for the meal. I got up off the floor. During grace for the meal I looked at my brand new watch, less than three weeks old. It was broken, useless, from the hard fall on the floor. A little curse came out, under my breath, while the blessing was being said.

My seat was at the end of a table that had been where I first sat so many years before. I was so angry from the pushing, the tripping, and the nasty punch on my arm that a dim red haze covered my eyes. My shattered watch was a jolt that lasted longer than my sore arm. Three hours after arriving at school my present was useless. I was devastated.

* * *

I couldn't blame anyone. If I did, I'd get plastered. I leaned back in my chair against the wall, which was against the rules. The wall was built of cut stone, painted a dull green. There was a slight bulge on the wall beneath the paint.

A hidden memory came back from three years before. Some rhubarb pie had been served at that meal. It was green and should have been allowed to grow for another full season before being picked! You had to eat your dessert, even if you didn't like the food, but that day, a couple of years ago, I got rid of the dessert really fast.

At that meal I had taken the rhubarb pie, the part I couldn't eat without gagging, and scooped it into my spoon. I waited until someone cracked a joke; everyone at the table was laughing, then I placed the spoon behind my chair. My thumb was on the edge of the spoon to serve as a lever. In one split second, splattered rhubarb covered a very small section of the wall behind my chair. The stuff was so sticky that it remained on the wall, never even dripping off. The rhubarb dried out, just another bump on the rough wall made of cut stones and since it was near a corner, no one noticed it.

Now, feeling that same place on the wall with my left hand I rubbed my fingers over the new coat of light green paint that covered the little bulge of dried rhubarb that had covered the wall three years previously. The fresh coat of paint covered over my disgusting act. Only I knew what had happened. There was no need to wonder if my previous little fit of rebellion would ever be discovered. Many acts of rebellion could be covered over.

* * *

Perhaps repeated feelings of mutiny were like an accumulation of old dried rhubarb covering painful emotions, shielding the heart from past pains. Perhaps a person could conceal frustrations by growing a tougher skin. At any rate, I couldn't knock the *big guys* around even I wanted to hang one of *them* from the coat hooks.

Could a person cover up rebellion without facing the results, or did these agitated feelings cause worse results? Did the Law of Consequences always catch a person out? And, why was rebellion wrong, anyway if the *big guys* broke your watch on the very first afternoon back at school?

I swore under my breath and didn't say anything at the first supper, back at school. After supper I marched to the dorm room, fury burning inside. It was not a good start to the term, and the next several days were spent in feeding the furnace of those hard feelings. There was a tight circle of response and counter-response, of my angering others and their punishment against me, followed by my own further resentment.

* * *

One physical education class, the captain of our team was sick. Consequently there was only one good pitcher. Ted Honer, our Physical Education teacher, decided magnanimously to do the pitching for both teams. "That way it will be equal for both teams," he said.

I played second base. The other team had Tim Udd, who was a real slugger. We had Danny Schellenberg, who made up for Udd. Their team was up to bat. Ray Davis rounded the bases and was on third. *Fish* made it to second, without Ray getting home for the winning run. Then *Campbell* batted and got to first. I held *Fish* on second, hoping that the next strike would be the third; their side would be out. Pa Honer pitched the ball slowly and Jon Arenson hit a weak ball.

The ball bounced once and Pa Honer caught it in his glove. If he threw it fast, getting it to first plate before Ray got to home plate it would be three down. The game would still be a tie and we might win it. Recess would soon be over and I looked forward to being on the winning team.

Ted Honer took all the time in the world, waiting as Arenson ran towards first. He tossed the ball towards first, but the other side got their run. Ray had run up the score for their side and they still had three runners on base. Ted Honer couldn't even throw the ball fast enough to get a guy out at first!

I booed from second. Pa Honer looked at me, frowning, but I was incensed. He ran towards me but I tore off, reaching center field. He ran some more and I looked around. He ran after me, chasing me. The game had come to a standstill while three perplexed runners waited to get batted in. I stayed just outside of the reach of our physical education teacher, but still he came on. I reached the soccer goal at the far end, more than 100 yards away. I ran off the playing field and into the forest "Off Limits, Out of bounds", standing near the place where I had been de-bagged.

* * *

Phys-ed class ended and Ted Honer reported me to the Principal, Pa Downing, right away. Actually, Ted was really a very nice guy. He was slow in some ways, but it was part of his gentle personality. I later came to appreciate him as a fine missionary. On that particular morning his throw to first base was too slow; my sassy mouth was too fast.

I slunk back alone to Kiambogo building for the rest of the morning classes, walking slowly across the soccer field, kicking every tiny stone in the way. My timing was worse was that of Pa Honer! He was slow and cautious. I was quick, reckless and angry. I knew what was coming: a conference with the principal. When enrollment began to grow the small office area downstairs was expanded for additional staff. We Junior High boys lived at Kedong Dorm and my old bedroom was now Pa Downing's office.

Of course, the lecture I received was deserved; I already had several strikes against me, so to speak. I'd said bad words to Ted Honer, sassing and demeaning him. Worse yet, a few days before a teacher had found a nasty note I had written, full of bad words. The worst part was that Pa Downing and Pa Honer didn't have to tell me. I knew it for myself: I definitely had an attitude problem.

CHAPTER 16

THE VIEW FROM MOUNT LONGONOT

One Saturday we were awake early, our day for a special picnic. Everybody was going to Mount Longonot. We showed up in casual clothes for the great outing and piled into trucks. Just past the point at which the train crossed the highway, down on the plains, where our little adventure had taken place, a dirt trail led to the base of the volcano. We tumbled out of the truck, holding for an instant onto the wooden back so as to not lose balance as we jumped to the ground. Brown dust still rose up from the track; balding tires had left smooth tracks.

The base of the volcano soared upwards in a gentle slant, apparently an easy climb. Shouts of anticipation came from several. Some already knew the trail so they were soon gone from view. Sandwiches and cookies and canteens came in boxes, brought up by a designated team.

Reaching the narrow, circular rim of the prehistoric crater, we looked down into the crater we had seen every day, always observing it from afar. Inside, at the base of a steep stone cliff, a forest grew on the flat plain. The bottom of the volcano looked flat. I didn't know what to expect. We gazed at the mountain each day, but to actually look down into the unexplored volcano was to appreciate the power, the majesty of nature in a direct, uninhibited way. We were only tiny dots spaced out along a gigantic, circular rim.

We called out, shouting, trying to hear any echo across that massive pit in the earth. Silence met our best efforts. It was hard to believe that the enormous cavity in the belly of the earth had been formed as uncontrollable power exploded upwards, flames and lava leaving this permanent scar lying 20 miles in each direction, filling the plains.

* * *

The crater was nearly circular, about five miles around. Towards the top there was a sharp little peak, triangular, proud, a silent symbol of assertive power. Below us, towards the huge hole, there was a 50-degree slope. About three hundred feet below that slope the volcano's sides became a sheer drop, absolutely perpendicular. I looked for a way down but saw none. There was a fair amount of danger to the trip, but only if one got off the trail. I didn't want any horseplay.

The trail wound around the gaping hole. At one point on the north side of the volcano there was a smaller volcano resulting from another outflow of ancient, wild fury. It was a baby crater, if there was such a thing. On the south side a huge mass of black lava sloped downwards gradually. It had flowed at its own speed to a point several miles away, and then dropped off suddenly to the valley floor.

Apparently, there had been many explosions during the active period of this volcano. One was the sudden eruption, leaving the massive crater. That blast had been strong enough to toss tiny black shards as far away as our section of the distant valley, some fifteen miles away. We often came across these sharp, black shards; they were as sharp as arrows intentionally made by ancient tribesmen.

A second type of volcanic activity was the regular flow of lava, slipping downwards, slowly filling up the valley. This slower flow must have taken eons to complete.

* * *

From the top of the mountain we saw vast areas of the Rift Valley that were unseen before. Another volcano, even larger, lay to the South. Amazingly, Mount Longonot wasn't nearly as large as Mount Suswa. To the north lay Lake Naivasha, its pink shores marking the presence of millions of flamingos.

Each location provided a new perspective of the valley, the plains, the great Kijabe ledge and ravines carved by erosion over countless ages. As we watched the scene, the clouds moved overhead. Shadows of clouds were a great brush that constantly dipped into the palate, finding new shades of colors. Nothing changed in the shapes of the land, but suddenly the tones in the picture changed. An artist could understand the change of hues, imagining them as different parts of the pallet. An artist, like Phil Lasse, could see those details, capturing different angles, understanding perspective, putting it into a work of art.

* * *

I looked at two of the teachers who had accompanied us on this trip up Mount Longonot. Since they had arrived lots of things had begun to change at the school. One, Phil Lasse, was an artist. The other was our English teacher, Trumbull Simmons. Trumbull, or Ted Senior left Belgium Congo when the movement for independence degenerated into an all-out ugly war. Thousands of Africans were killed, mere pawns between the soldiers and the new guerilla movement.

After leaving Congo, hundreds of other missionary and settler families found refuge in Kenya or Uganda. The Simmons family left Kivu Province in Congo, together with many other AIM families. Ted was an expert in English literature and Mary held credentials in French. Together they were a welcome addition, beefing up the teaching staff at RVA. Ted Junior and Cindy, his sister, now in high school, were the children of Trumbull and Mary; the Simmons lived up the hill on the mission station.

Pa Simmons was the one who had everything under control today: the lunches, the trucks for transportation and the permission for us to go this far out of bounds - legally. Trumbell Simmons, Pa Simmons as we called him, was ever-so-slightly balding. Tall and lanky, more agile in his mind even than he was in his feet, he constantly inspired us to do better. Having studied at Haverford College and then at Harvard University, in the Graduate School of Education, he seemed to walk on a cloud of excellence, attempting to lift us up to the loftiest heights of the English language.

He could joke endlessly, imitate Italian accents, quote poetry for hours, and make kids feel at home in their open house when Ma and Pa Simmons invited us for board games and served us hot coffee cake. He was clean shaven and his penetrating eyes missed nothing. His purpose was to teach English so that every student would be an overcomer on that coming day of doom: the SAT tests. To this end he wrote ten new words on the black board every Monday morning; on Friday we had to use those words in a sentence, showing our ability to spell and use the new vocabulary correctly. For all of us Harvard meant only one thing: excellence.

* * *

Talking to Pa Simmons at the top of Mount Longonot was our other new teacher. Phil Lasse was leaning on the steel metal drum that was placed just under the very peak of the mountain. The drum was scratched with hundreds of names, each one proclaiming the proud achievement of some long forgotten "explorer". Phil, with a nicely cut brown beard, had just the slightest bulge around his belt. His eyes constantly took in details, the most alert eyes one could find. He captured a scene and left another unpainted picture on the extensive image bank of his creative mind. As an artist, a lover of nature and a sharp observer of the Scriptures, Phil Lasse was gifted with a unique way of drawing in young people. Some people gravitated to music or poetry; Phil's emotions took in both the emotions of students as well as the features of landscapes and African animals.

Among the *big guys* this year were Don Hoover, John Skoda, Howard Anderson, Alice Propst, Marcy Propst and Ruth Ann Downing. I admired them for many reasons, principally because they had been wise enough to achieve the rank of "seniors"; now they had almost completed their time at *swot*, never having been suspended or expelled. That was sufficient for anyone to be my hero.

Suspension, or being expelled, was my worst fear, but it was easy to put that out of my mind when hiking around the rim of a volcano. I was thrilled that my sister, Pearl, made it all the way to the top, in spite of the handicap of a metal brace on her right leg.

Going on this hike was *severe*, even if there was no *choo*, and even if the older *dames*, showed me up. Some of those girls climbed better than I could. Anyway, I made it along the narrow path, laughing and singing, like the others, and didn't *kwapper*, although I did almost stumble once when looking back over my shoulder. We used slang without even knowing it was slang. For me the whole English-speaking world spoke that way; I had no idea that we spoke with an East African English accent, or with strange words.

We paused for a rest. From the top of a mountain one could look at things differently. I found answers to some of the questions in my mind. Immediately, though, others began to form, raising problems about even more difficult, troubling issues, but this was not the time to think about political problems between African colonies and Europe.

* * *

Pa Simmons was calling everyone from their observation points because lunch was being served. Then it was time to start back to RVA. While on the top of the mountain, the sun had reached the top of its journey.

My mind focused on peanut butter and jam sandwiches. RVA was just a tiny glimmer of light reflecting the sun's perpendicular rays, the buildings being distant, almost insignificant specks on the distant forested, green slopes of the Rift Valley. From this vantage point, the crater filled our entire outlook and the school was just a dot. From there, however, the same buildings were our complete security, filling up our whole life, while the crater, here, was just a distant mass on the horizon. It was amazing how one could see things differently just by obtaining a new angle.

Phil Lasse could make a picture out of it. No doubt, Pa Simmons would ask us to write another one of his essays.

Walking back down Mount Longonot, riding back to RVA in the open truck, I sucked in the late afternoon air. Someone began to sing, "She'll be coming round the mountain", and we all joined in, singing one American folk song after another. The wind of the road filled our faces; the distant freedom along the shores of America called to us across generations. Long-dead songwriters still left the mark of their creativity on our lives, just as the long extinct volcano left its mark forever on the landscape. Each song cast its own variety of colors and emotions, just as the passing clouds had done along the valley.

CHAPTER 17

THE COMOLLI FAMILY DISASTER

*R*ambunctious must have been their middle name. The Comolli family lived in Nairobi and, like us, they went to boarding schools. Several expensive private boarding schools in the Nairobi area provided British education and the three Comolli children studied at the three most expensive institutions. Our parents were always concerned about reaching others for Christ, be they Africans or Europeans so inviting Italian teenagers to stay with us for the holidays was a new approach, one I had not seen before.

* * *

"Now, children," wrote mother, "when you come home in the holidays you will have to double up in your rooms. Dad and I decided to invite the Comolli children stay with us for the summer holidays. You remember Mr. Comolli, the Italian manager at the car dealership? The parents want to visit the grandparents in Italy and will be gone for six months. We'll work out the details when you get home. Love, Mother."

While helping other people was one of my parents' joys in life, I did not think that piling three kids into our home was going to be a good idea, so I had my doubts.

The Comolli parents got on the plane for Italy. Like a good Catholic, Mrs. Comolli had a little silver cross hanging on a silver chain around her neck. She was Latin to the core of her soul, forever using her arms, expressing opinions with wide, vivid, generous movements. Her gestures even showed where commas, periods and question marks should punctuate her talk. Those hands and emotions would have made a good Pentecostal of her.

The father, a little bit more subdued, was also completely Italian in his outlook, especially in his love affair of fast cars. Italian feelings of exuberance filled his face, unlike dad's colonial British lack of emotion, expressed by a stiff, upper lip.

The British DC's, or the District Commissioners, were the descendants of the military experts, who had won World War II across Africa. Ousted from Ethiopia by the British, Italians never could forgive the Brits for taking that choice bit of Africa away from them. During the 1950's the British extended their influence in East Africa a little more so Mr. Comolli had acquired his distaste for anything British.

I sometimes wondered if mom and dad's effort to take in the three Comolli children had to do with dad fighting his own in-born prejudice against Italy. Or, perhaps, it was his effort to win a Roman Catholic family to Protestantism. On the other hand, why did an Italian family consent to have a Protestant family take their children in for five weeks? Perhaps they were low on European friendships at that time in their lives. However, the fit was theoretically perfect with their three children almost matching our family's ages. As always, the devil lay in the details.

Mavis Comolli was 15 years old and had inherited her mother's joys of enthusiastic expressions. She was already accomplished in using her hands often and fittingly. After all, she was determined to take care of her two brothers. Anthony, or Tony, 16 and a half, was a carbon copy of his father. Michael, the younger brother, was eleven.

"Welcome," we all said as they arrived. "Karibuni Cottage!" They unpacked their bags from the car, looking around the grounds with excitement, glad to see such a large garden with so many places to play hide and seek and to ride their bikes. Like us, they were only too happy be finished boarding school. We settled in for summer holidays, which were almost five weeks long. During that time we'd live in close quarters.

My parents had no idea about accommodating themselves to the needs of an Italian family, so it didn't take long for slight differences in life styles and opinions to come into the open.

* * *

Mom and dad weren't ones with opinions about religious matters. We had family devotions, religiously, each morning after breakfast and at night, before we'd go to bed. Our first morning was a sign post on the road of things to come.

"Do we have to sit through this Bible reading? Mr. Phillips, your first prayer was so long! At home we just say a few words and then dig into the food. And, now it's time for more prayers after breakfast?" Mavis said it with gusto and a wave of her hand. Her hand started near the Bible and almost took her right out the window, the window being the closest part of our house to Nairobi.

Dad answered slowly, "Yes, in *our* house we take time for the Scriptures." He said it in his finest English accent, accentuating each "S" sound like a little whistle. His reply contained the slightest element of reproof. Was he saying, "Why doesn't your father take time for this important spiritual exercise first thing in the morning", or "While you are with us I want you to learn good Protestant traditions"?

Mavis, Tony, and their little brother, Michael, sat back, their arms crossed tightly and their heads bowed. I doubted that they were praying, though.

The day passed, supper had come and gone, and minutes after we started our family evening, which spanned a story, singing songs and prayers, Mavis asked, "How much longer is this boring story going to go on?" The scene was being set for an uproar. Her idea of fun was talking about nail polish and lip stick, both of which were new to our home.

* * *

Had Mr. Comolli ever gathered his little family after supper for the reading of an adventure book, like the one we were reading? *Heidi* was one of Pearl's favorite books. Most likely Mr. Comolli took Tony and Michael to admire the engine of a sports car. That was what a car dealer should do with his boys in the evenings.

It was not long before things became exciting, much more exciting than summer holidays had ever been. "Have you ever taken everything on your bike apart?" Tony asked me. He seemed so much older than me, knowing how to do anything and everything.

"No," I answered, only too eager to learn how to do that. I found parts in my bike that I never knew existed. Little springs and ball bearings lay all over a large cardboard in the garage, no two parts of my bike touching each other. They lay in neat rows; the frame stood alone. I called, "Dad, come from your office to see my progress in mechanics!" Perhaps this was an opening for some adult career. I wiped a bit of grease off my fingers.

Dad looked down at Tony and said, "I *was* going to use that lovely cardboard box to send out Sunday School materials to Kapsabet." The way he said it sounded a trifle judgmental. His "s" sounds whistled. Was he also surprised, admiring someone who could do something he couldn't, disconnect all the parts and put them back together again?

Kapsabet was a small town near Eldoret. Had Tony even heard of it? If he had, he wouldn't have cared one bit for dad's books being sent there. Tony's dad would have thought of Kapsabet as a point along the car race, the marvelous East African Safari that brought sports enthusiasts each year from every corner of the world to examine how much punishment a car could take on Kenya's muddy roads and still stay in one piece.

That was another thing Tony and I had in common, not just bikes and ball bearings.

Tony taught me about the East African Safari, pointing out the techniques of the drivers as they sped around dusty bends, or how the co-pilot assisted the driver, or how the teams worked together, each person contributing a key part to the success of the race. He doubted that dad would let him drive our Peugeot in Limuru. We poured over names, the past victors, the makes of cars and the larger-than-life drama created each year by the rally. Tony knew the names of the winners of the Rally from each year and he made me jealous by the amount of knowledge that poured out of him.

* * *

There was another thing that dad needed to know. Mr. Comolli had never told Tony that horse racing was wrong; quite the opposite was the case because Tony wanted to me to see racing horses up close. The next day I began to understand stables and horse feed, bridles and saddles. Tony knew so much more about the world than I did, aspects of life that I never even knew existed. I had never been allowed near the racing horses.

Tony was also an excellent shot with a slingshot, or a *catty*, as we would call it at RVA. We went down to the dam, about two miles down the road, and he took out his *caddy*, his slingshot. Pulling back on the rubber bands, aiming high in the air and adjusting his calculations a couple of times, he squared his jaw, drew a bead on and let go at one of the two ducks far away, bobbing in the water.

There was no way a stone could go that far, but it went up and up into the air and then I lost sight of it and waited. Suddenly one of the ducks slumped down. Its head lay lifeless in the water. Tony had an excellent arm and a sure eye. He had killed a duck right across the dam. The chance was probably one in a million. The duck was floating in the water where we couldn't reach it; we didn't have a boat and we didn't want to trespass on yet another farmer's property.

I couldn't wait to race home. We tore up the back lane and down to our house by the back of the Anglican Seminary "Dad, guess what," I exclaimed at lunch. "Tony shot a duck from right across the dam! It just went... bingo! The stone was right on target!" Dad's look told me how disappointed he was that Tony was fast becoming my hero.

* * *

On Sunday, there was a mild argument. Mavis wanted to go to a Roman Catholic Church in Nairobi. Tony didn't care about church at all and Michael was quiet during the entire argument. I don't think that the Comolli and Phillips families had worked out these details in advance. Mavis was used to a large sanctuary, which was where her parents always attended. We worshipped in a small business office, in what was now called the

Baptist Church of Nairobi. Mavis could not worship in a place called St. John's Ambulance and she let everyone know that. Why, her arms would hit every wall.

Mother spoke sweetly as if her smile could solve a centuries-long religious conflict that at times had enveloped great swaths of Europe in wars that lasted decades. "No, dear. When you are in *our* house we'll go to *our* church." We four were to stay home from church that Sunday, which was an absolute first. There was not room in the car for nine people. Mom and dad would ride in the front and the three Comolli kids would sit in the back seat.

There was no room for arguing. Obviously they could do little about it all. However, their grumbling indicated that the Comolli kids weren't really ready to worship God, either spirit or in truth, that morning. The three returned silently, refusing to comment on the music, prayers or singing at the newly inaugurated Baptist church.

* * *

The scope of Tony's skills left me with my mouth open. I never knew how many useful things that could be done with those tools in our tool shop. For one thing, our tree house grew by several boards and it was now almost a real miniature house.

The experience of living with a Protestant family was hardest on Mavis. She didn't appreciate her folks having left them alone in Africa. She liked staying for five long weeks even less when the people were staid, unemotional, British Anglo Saxons. Further, her choice of recreational activities didn't match those of my sisters. She was about four years older than Dorothy and wanted to talk with boys, lots of them.

For example, Mavis didn't want to stay in her bedroom, reading one book after another. She preferred a badminton court. She heard that boys hung around Tigoni Corner, but dad wasn't about to take here there, even when he filled up the car with petrol. Consequently our favorite pastime was visiting the Fomegelli family, who were lapsed Roman Catholics and also Italian. We went with Tony, Mavis and Michael, enjoying an endless round of Monopoly, Raid and playing cards.

Of course, mom was against all card games, so even these visits created a fuss.

* * *

I was learning more from Tony. Our bikes were cleansed of every possible speck of dirt. The ball bearings were carefully installed three or four times a week. Tony said he was going to be a mechanic, so I suddenly became interested in that profession, too.

Tony and I wandered further and rode out bikes to Limuru Township, a new development of stores and offices, garages for cars and professional services. The growth in Limuru was taking place opposite the Bata Shoe Factory, up the hill on the other side of the railway. In these new stores Tony examined long hunting knives, leather boots, guns and bits and bridles. None of these had ever been made as purchases by dad.

* * *

Storm clouds bigger than those brought by the monsoons were growing inside our house even as the sky outside was as blue as Chinese fine china. By the second week the winds in our house told of stronger gusts to come. Then the Comolli kids became a bit more defiant.

"Difficult, my dears, they are just a little bit difficult. We'll just have to pray about it," was mother's gracious handling of the worsening scene. She tried playing some hymns at our evening devotions, but she wasn't very good at the piano, and nothing had been resolved at all about prayer times. Mavis snickered while listening to mother try to play and sing. Dorothy and Pearl looked at each other with wide eyes.

A few bad words were said in dad's presence. I never knew so many bad words existed in Swahili or Kikuyu, the languages spoken around us. When these words were all strung together, the effect was startling, a little bit exciting, a little bit evil. I wondered where Tony picked up all those bad words.

Mavis increasingly felt boxed in. Unlike Tony and Michael, she had to share a bedroom. Dorothy and Pearl tried their best to share everything with Mavis. Tony and Michael occupied our bedroom. Don and I moved into the sun porch so mother lost her sewing space; the sun porch was her favorite place for sitting to sew as she looked out over the rose garden.

The second Sunday of vacation saw us going to the Baptist Church, leaving our three visitors at home.

* * *

A week later the protests became louder and longer. Mavis and Tony didn't feel comfortable wasting the evening with "family time". Reading books was for school time! Who wanted books to be read on holidays?

They demanded to listen to loud music on the radio. During the day, the "Top Ten" came over the Kenya Broadcasting Service. They sang songs they heard, rocking to Elvis Presley, imitating other singers. Rock and Roll came to our house in an extraordinary way. Mother and dad thought all that was "worldly", and told them so. During the day, the radio was turned down low as Tony listened to the radio, his ear glued to golden-brown set made in Germany. He sat in the blue chair next to the bright red-brown wooden cabinet that dad had asked one of the Mau Mau ex-detainees to build. Tony could look out of the dining room window and see Nairobi. His thoughts, like his parents, were far away.

* * *

One night Donald and I were put to bed early. We went to the sun porch and climbed beneath the sheets. It was Friday night and we were almost asleep when the most awful screaming broke out. "I never asked to come to this terrible house," sobbed Mavis with a great wave of her hand. Her gesture took in our entire establishment. "I didn't want to come here and I don't want to stay here!" Mavis tossed her head with the smart short hair recently cut at a saloon in Nairobi.

Mother was getting ready for bed and her long hair, almost always done up in braids, was hanging down to her waist. Mavis insisted that she was not going to waste her holidays staying with us. "I need more freedom!" She wanted to talk with boys during the holidays and felt too cooped up in our house with all our rules and regulations.

Responding calmly, mother said, "While you are at *our* house you need to obey us. Besides, your mother and father don't want you to spend time with boys they don't know."

"I'm not going to stay here!" Mavis shouted.

Dorothy and Pearl, dressed in their night gowns, watched helplessly while standing in the doorway of their bedroom. The screaming got louder; Mavis' face became really red. The fray got thicker and Mavis pulled mother's hair, using words that hadn't been said in our house before.

Dad came running in from the office. "Now what's going on here? Mavis, stop it, instantly!" His "s's" were a clearly hisses, meaning, "Mavis, leave Mrs. Phillips alone!"

But Mavis wasn't finished and her rage hadn't yet reached the point of explosion. Dorothy gave a little scream and ran to release her mother who was being physically handled by the expressive, emotional hands of a distraught teenager, a guest in our home.

* * *

The next day, Saturday, our car dropped Tony, Mavis and Michael off at their boarding schools. They would finish their holidays there; they wouldn't be at *our* house.

There was a collective sigh of relief around our house. Don and I got our own beds back. We no longer had to sleep on temporary camp cots. Pearl and Dot could read to their hearts' content after getting dishes done in the morning. Mother and dad were free to get their work done as normal.

In a way, I felt sorry for Mavis and Tony and their little brother, Michael. Didn't their parents really care for them? What happened to your home when your parents left you, instead of you leaving your parents?

I thought to myself, "Mavis is going to get into bad trouble." She was rebellious, her attitude was showing, and she had clearly overstepped her limits.

Yet, I had new skills in the carpentry shop and in the bike department. I was anxious to take my bike to school. However, dad said I would have to wait for that.

CHAPTER 18

IN THE TWINKLING OF AN EYE

Now that the Comolli children were gone we settled down to a quieter holiday time. Dad and mom's collection of books meant every room in the house had some reading material. I took out one of the books to read, *In the Twinkling of an Eye*.

It was a novel written in the 1930's and had as its basis the futuristic situation of a young man who knew that Christ was coming back. He did not get ready for this situation and so, when the Rapture came, he was left as a non-Christian in a world of suffering, persecution and calamity. I read the book in almost one sitting, spell bound by never-ending action in a world that had no more Christians. The worst part of the book had to do with the Anti-Christ, a figure dedicated to violence, corruption, ultimate control and international evil. The Anti-Christ was taking over the world and the hero (or anti hero) of this book was constantly grieving that "he had not been ready."

* * *

Dad wanted me to go into Nairobi with him to the printing shop. I admired Mr. Singh's black beard, woven over and over itself and with ends disappearing into his turban. I couldn't imagine how his turban could be wrapped so tightly around his hair. It was against his religion to cut his hair, and since his hair didn't believe in stopping its growth, there was always more and more hair to wrap under that great bulging turban.

While I was busy thinking about black hair, enormous mustaches woven into his beard and his red turban, dad was busy evangelizing the men in the office. I suppose that dad had talked to them several times before. Maybe these Indian men would become Christians if he explained the Gospel to them one more time.

Dad was ready for Christ's coming. Why, you could see that just from the way he used his time. While he talked to men who spoke Indian languages about Christ, I thought about what a pain it would be to have to do all that hair up every morning.

We had lunch. I poured the sizzling hot tea from the thermos. Dad took a short rest while I read a book. A few flies buzzed around our car and I tried to shoo them away. Before going home in the early afternoon dad had just one more thing to do. His list was all stroked off, "done thoroughly". We would get home early today.

* * *

Dad went around the corner and down a half a block to a bookstore on Government Road. I knew the store and the street well, as I'd been there many times. Then, five minutes later, I sat in the car on the angle parking protecting our car against the street vandalism. I saw him come around the corner, walking towards the car. I looked away for just an instant to the Chevrolet parked beside us, a new model that I had been admiring. Then when I looked back to where he was coming towards me.

Dad was gone!

I couldn't believe my eyes. Why, It was impossible! There he was one second and the next he was gone!

Christ had come back! I wasn't really a Christian after all! So my doubts were really a sign that I hadn't really been saved! You couldn't be a good Christian and have all those questions and doubts. I'd recently learned bad words from Tony Comolli, another bad sign. Moreover, I felt really repentant for having sneaked off to the racetrack to see just one race. But there it was, Christ had come back in the twinkling of an eye.

* * *

All the scenes in the book I had just read came back. If Christ had returned, then violence I had read about in the novel was going to break out before the day was over! I had no home, no money and I was only fourteen years old. Worse yet, I didn't even know how to drive! How would I get back to Limuru?

The minutes ticked by. Dad had disappeared, gone for good. An even worse thought ran through my mind. If he was gone, then mother and Dot, Pearl and Don were gone and all the kids at RVA had disappeared, too! All the kids at RVA were gone too. It was the first time that I felt real affection for every one of my classmates. After all, I'd just lost them all!

But, how could this be? I remembered so clearly the night I became a Christian. I was in Kabartonjo. Just five years old, I had been looking at the stars. The previous day I had heard a talk by an African evangelist about God knowing the names of all the stars. I wanted God to know my name too, to have my name written in "God's big Book" in heaven. I had asked Jesus to come into my heart and I could still remember the wonderful sensation of a clean heart. If that had really happened in the past then how could I not be a Christian now? It was easy to see: people could lose their salvation!

I was in a sweat. Still there was no sign of him. Five long minutes soon became thirty minutes of torture. I was sweating, not because of the sun. Another horrible thought crossed my mind: I didn't know how to sell dad's car to get money so I could survive and I would face seven years of *Great Tribulation*. The theology behind the book, *In the Twinkling of an Eye* hit me like a blow to my solar plexus: I had not been ready!

Thoughts of desperation came. I would have to find Hughes, the car dealer dad did business with. I'd have to ask how much our car was worth. But how could I sell a car that wasn't even mine? How would I begin talking to the manager? "I wasn't ready when Christ came back and now I have to sell my father's car. How much money will you give me for my dad's car?" Nothing in that opening sentence would make sense.

* * *

Just then, dad strolled out of the bank at the corner. His work was done. He'd now finished for the day. I'd never been so glad to see him in my life. "What kept you so long?" I asked, as casually as my voice would manage.

"Oh, just a little money matter that I had to resolve."

I never told him about my terrible fear of the Rapture and his having been taken while I was left behind. I certainly didn't breathe a word about my plans to sell his car, the only way to get money for the next seven years. I knew that the Beast would never let me get away with working since I didn't have a bright "666" painted on my forehead. These were things better left unsaid.

* * *

Unfortunately, my pride was still with me. I wanted to get a nice tan. Pearl and I were more fair-skinned while Dot and Don could get a fairly good tan. I decided to use a long Sunday afternoon rest time for a really good suntan. All the guys at Westervelt Dorm, the dorm for high school students from Grades Nine to Twelve, were used to lying out in the sun from 1:00 p.m. until 3:00 p.m. in the afternoon, then everyone got under the cold shower, cooling off in time for the worship service at 4.00 p.m. at Jubilee Hall.

I'd had a long hike the previous day to the hill behind the school, up to the Bamboo Forest where the Mau Mau had hidden so successfully from the King's African Rifles. In the "good ol' days", as we called them, Art Davis, Mike Malloy and Jonathan Hildebrant had discovered a trail to the Bamboo Forest high in the Uplands. Thick lumps of bamboo were so impenetrable that a fugitive would be safe only a few feet from a soldier, which had made the Mau Mau even more real in our active imaginations.

We had tramped down from the hike, exhausted. That next Sunday afternoon, I lay down in the sun with my back soaking up everything the sun had to offer, warmth as well as ultra violet and infrared rays. It felt so good to sleep in the hot sun light. I'd just think about the Comolli kids and my recent experience of nearly being left in the Great Tribulation for a few minutes. After all, our teachers believed in the Pre-Tribulation return of Christ; I had no idea about any other interpretation of the events in the book, the narrative that had given me great tribulation of the soul.

When I awoke my back was sore. It was 3:30. I had slept more than two hours in deadly equatorial rays. The cold shower was a little comfort. During the church service I didn't dare let my back touch the back of the chair. Even the chair felt hot. By the time Young People's meeting came, at 7:00 that night, the pain was worse.

* * *

By Monday morning, my back on fire! I could hardly study in the classes in the morning. After lunch, during library period, my back demanded relief every three seconds, but when I touched it, my skin seemed even hotter. I couldn't sit still and Ma Barrett came over to see why I was wiggling around in my chair. "Oh, It will be OK, it is just a little sore," I said. She thought I had a mosquito bite.

The flame was unbearable, spreading up to my scalp and down to the edge of my shorts. I left the library without asking for permission, went to the bathroom and almost cried in pain, pealing my shirt off. Then I put it back again and stumbled through the rest of the day. I decided never to get a suntan again in my life. Just then I remembered the Vitamin E cream that mother had included with the things in my trunk. It was from Eaton's, in Winnipeg. "You just might need this someday. Perhaps you'll get a scratch from a tree or something." Mother never knew how she rescued the day.

After spreading the soothing cream over my back, I put my shirt back on over a very, very red back.

* * *

I was once again being hurt by my pride. Why did I want to get such a tan? Just because all the others had tan-able skin? My stubborn pride was my own worst enemy.

Even after I had gone through my Great Tribulation I wasn't ready to admit that the thing that got in my way more than anything else, more than the guys who were mean to me, more than my teachers, was my own stubborn pride.

PART THREE

WESTERVELT DORM

CHAPTER 19

NICKNAMES AND CHANGING BOUNDARIES

Once someone got a nickname, he owned it for life. "Mother," I said, "you should hear this story about *Skunk*. You know what he did? He started to..." We were recounting some of the adventures that we had had at school on one of our first mornings at home on holidays.

"What an awful name!" she cut in, as she passed me the hot toast. "Can't they think of nice names at school?"

"O.K., forget about Skunk. Let's say his name is *Perfume*. Now, you should hear this story about *Perfume*..."

Somehow the story just wasn't the same. Jim would forever be *Skunk*. It didn't matter that he didn't smell bad; he had related a hilarious story about a skunk and the name held him captive. For ever after he was *Skunk* to us, a friend who was athletic, smart at school and a credit to any group who happened to be on the in with him.

Rubot was one of four staying in my dorm room. I'd no idea how he got his name. Once, when dad took me to school at the beginning of a term, he came into my room. "This is *Rubot*," I said, proudly introducing my father to my friend.

"Hello, Mr. *Flappit*," said *Rubot*. I don't think that *Rubot* even knew my surname was Phillips. He certainly didn't blink an eye as he greeted my father this way.

Dad, having heard the word *Rubot*, could not bring himself to try to imitate the new name. Either that or he had bad hearing. Probably both maladies were present in my dad, his lack of ability to use anything but his British accent and poor hearing. He said, "Glad to meet you, *Rhubarb*."

"*Rubot*," I corrected my father, gently. "His name is *Rubot*, not *Rhubarb*."

"Glad to meet you, *Rhubarb*." Limitations around the contours of the British tongue derived my father of the pleasure of learning American speech patterns. If he couldn't even get the name right, how would he get to know my friend better? I was mortified by *Rubot* being called *Rhubarb*, more so than my father being called Mr. *Flappit*. Just imagine a young American teen calling dad, "Mr. *Flappit*" and never even blinking an eyelash!

* * *

One of my friends picked up the nickname, *Sausage*. Allan Hahn, or *Sausage*, was *Peanut's* older brother. *Peanut* was slightly smaller for his age, whereas *Sausage* may have acquired his nickname because of a stocky build. *Porky* was their younger brother. Nicknames always went beyond the boundaries of logic.

Sausage was at least four sizes larger than I was, perhaps twice as heavy. At times he acted towards me in a kind way. At other times, he could be mean. A favorite trick was catching me while making my bed. He'd come from behind, catch my arm and twist it behind me until I was bent over the bed, helpless. Then he said, "Say, 'Sorry, Uncle'."

"Blast you, I don't have to say sorry for anything. I'm not sorry! You're not an uncle!"

He turned up the pressure. My arm was now in the shape of a "V", with my hand against my shoulder on the opposite side of my back. The outward physical pain was nothing compared to the inward resentment and rebellion that was building up.

* * *

Treks up the hill into the forest above the railway held endless fascination because of long vines hanging down from some of the trees. It was easy to see how these got their names, monkey ropes were attached to the tops of the trees.

One of our Saturday morning pass-times involved hiking up to this part of the forest. We would hang onto the vine, about the thickness of a person's wrist, and swing out into the dark space of the forest below. The hills behind Kijabe station were steep; I would be at ground level hanging onto the vine, then swing out into open space, only to find that I was 20 or 30 feet above the soft red earth at the outer orb of the swing. Huge red dirt stains on our *bags* showed that we had been sliding down hills on our bums, out of bounds.

The patient African men in the laundry could not dissuade students from spending their free time sliding down steep mountain paths. We were incorrigible. If the Point System couldn't stop us from filling up our laundry bags each week with stains on our clothes from the forest, then nothing would change us.

The constant work of that wonderful staff meant that each week our clothes came back clean and ironed, cleansed of the red dirt stains that must have been so difficult to remove. Thanking African staff workers for their work was something I hadn't yet learned.

* * *

Our African kitchen staff did their best to provide us with healthy meals. Ma Senoff bought food from African women who brought vegetables, carried on their heads in a colorfully woven *kikapu*, basket. For breakfast we had three cereals: *posho*, a corn meal served hot and steaming, oatmeal, often served with the husk that looked like a toenail, or *wimbi*, another hot grain cereal. Toast came as a soggy reminder of bread, since it had been made on wire plates hovering over charcoal, on blazers that in a previous life carried 40 gallons of petrol.

* * *

Early in my years at RVA, milk was brought each day on a cart pulled by two donkeys. Later, the donkeys retired to a softer life, feeding on the grass around the school. Earlier on, their purpose in life was to haul several gallons of milk each day, rain or shine. Now, however, they lived the slower life of grazing. Occasionally, the animals recalled their previous life, the torture of pulling the cart up steep hills. When they conversed with each other like this their braying might interrupt a prayer, a spelling class or a science project. The braying of the two dirty brown beasts brought many quiet snickers, and we attempted to copy them in their loud enthusiasm, starting with a loud cough, which gradually subsided.

Having just read a book about bucking broncos and cowboys in the USA, I decided to jump-start my new career. Perhaps I could be a cowboy; taming a donkey would be a good start. One of my friends loosened the rope which was keeping one donkey tied to a stake in the ground near Westervelt Dorm. The donkey raised his head; in a jiffy I leaped onto its back, but the stubborn beast had other thoughts about having its will dominated.

The moment I jumped on its back the animal jumped forward and reared with its hindquarters high at the same time, its hind legs kicking the air. I had nothing to hold onto. An instant later, I got off the ground, where I had fallen; to avoid those fearful legs I raced away quickly to get out of harm's way. I hadn't even been on its back for 2.5 seconds.

I learned a lot that term besides the history of Greece and Egypt. I was sad to see another career go down the drain. I would never move to Alberta to become a cowboy in the Calgary Stampede.

* * *

Most of the time we got along well, because life had its own regular rhythms and the schedule kept us busy from 6:00 in the morning until 10:00 at night. Life at RVA involved a small community, focused on education.

We Grade Nine boys were the newcomers to Westervelt Dorm. A few tentative forays into the larger world provided insights into business, various occupations and industries. Field trips took us to the wider world, in which Europeans held power and prestige, capital and stock. When Europeans used the word "stock", for example, it referred to banks, industry and the markets. The same word, when used by the Masai also spoke of their wealth, except their cattle were kept close by, protected in a *manyata*, so lions couldn't eat them. A simple word, "stock", could be used in so many different ways.

Field trips took students to several locations: to the Bata School Factory in Limuru, to a Pyrethrum factory, where the yellow flowers were processed into an effective insecticide, and to a cement factory where round rock-hard clunkers were formed, only to be crushed into the Portland Cement, which was used all over the country.

At the wattle factory the noise of the machinery was a constant roar, so loud we could hardly hear the voice of our guide as the heavy, pungent smell of the wattle was processed into tannic acid. We were careful not to touch any instruments. Sometimes we toured the Kikuyu experimental farms run by the government.

Each field trip gave another perspective on life. Some Kenyans made their lives by crushing sisal and producing rope. Others earned their livelihood by cutting out identical patterns all day, making runners at the Bata Shoe factory. Many occupations came together; some people worked in production, others in sales and still others as accountants.

Increasingly, the talk often came around to the times in which we were living, "When the Africans get their independence they will need good leaders, but what will happen when all these colonies get their independence?"

* * *

By mid-1960 we knew were living in momentous days. Colonial regimes began to fall, one after another, something like the game of dominos we played at times. New nations were being born. I heard the names of colonies and countries in West Africa for the first time. And all this was happening at the same time as we ourselves were experiencing our own changes of puberty. There were changes that were happening in us as we passed from child hood to youth: changes in our minds, our bodies, and our emotions.

Some changes came more easily than others. Whenever students would come back from the States they brought back new fashions, new clothes, new slang and new ways of looking at things. All of us were fascinated by the great improvements that these fashions had upon the unchanging monotony of our school uniforms. The girls were unable to show off their beauty, so they felt, in the grey overalls and white blouses that they had to use five days a week.

About this time changes were taking more quickly in youthful fashions in the USA. One of the changes, late in getting to Kenya, was that of short hair for the girls. Dot caught on with a sudden urge to the new winds of change. She was always quick, ready to try something new and in our family we were always captivated by her ability to get things done so fast.

Having found that thick braids were no longer in, she made a decision about her shiny, brown, long hair. One afternoon her braids came off. She wasn't Dorothy to anyone. She was now Dottie. Shirley Lasse helped my sister with her new hairstyle, so now Dot didn't have to spend fifteen minutes every morning and every night on her hair. She could simply use a brush a few times and she would be like the other girls. The day after Dorothy became Dottie, we had a family picture taken. Our parents came from Limuru for the Sunday.

Mother, whose black-grey hair had never, or hardly ever been cut, was "grieved". Mother would have made a good Pentecostal missionary if the length of hair had been a criterion of absolute obedience to the commands of God. She was grieved that Dorothy was following the ways of the modern world. Mother could never get around to using the new name, "Dottie". Short hair was not in the Bible, not for women. However, mother took the cutting of Dorothy's hair a lot better than she accepted my crew cut years earlier. In fact, when Pearl went the same way of modern trends there was hardly a word, but I was sure she suffered a grief when Pearl followed suit.

Even mother was changing. She was becoming more patient, or perhaps she was resigning herself to the fact that change was in the air.

* * *

In the dorms we had long conversations as we lay on the bunk beds. "Why are the s*imbas*, so cruel?" someone asked. African warriors fighting Belgium soldiers in Congo gave themselves the mighty name: *Simbas*. The name meant "Lions", an identity that included both conflict and victory.

"Did you hear about the things that they have been doing in Stanleyville?" another student chimed in. He gave the details of the slaughter where burning, looting and raping had taken place. Unlike the Mau Mau rebellion in Kenya six years earlier, the resistance troops in Congo were overwhelming the Belgian colonial administration.

A picture came to my mind. I imagined a lion jumping at the throat of its prey, taking the jugular vein between its sharp teeth. A deathblow was not needed, for this victim, the foreign Belgian power, simply fell down its knees, crushed by a greater power. Belgian Congo was the prey already dying; it was the simbas who were wreaking havoc, pillaging, murdering and slaughtering. What hope was there that the Belgium taskmasters, who had been so cruel in the jungles, would be able to maintain their hold on Africa?

The second disturbing element seemed to be the inability of the newly independent Africans to agree with each other. If Congo was becoming independent then the whole of colonial Africa would seek independence. New winds of hope were sweeping the land, a fierce wind, blowing into towns and cities; the newly birthed winds of freedom blew everywhere.

On the one side the minority Europeans tried to hold on, although an absolute minority. On the other side, Africans claimed their traditional lands. The whole complex, gigantic colonial structure had dominated African life since the first colonial impulse instituted slavery, almost five hundred years earlier. This elaborate system, agreed upon by European powers in 1895, was coming to an end.

The empires of Italy and Germany were over. Britain, France, Spain and Belgium would lose their colonies; new nations would be born. A great tide had come in and now it was rushing out. In Congo the fury may have been directed against the heads of state in far-away Brussels but it was the local people who got it in the neck.

The resistance reminded me of our climb up the Mount Longonot. There, before us, the empty crater was born of a sudden explosion from deep within. True, (to use one of Pa Simmonds' favorite words), true, Congo was a land racked in pain, bleeding, because of the brutal attacks of the guerilla warriors, the *Simba*. A human volcano of unbelievable ferocity had exploded in Congo. Other nations also groaned in birth pangs, such as Algeria. Would these explosions leave a permanent scar, a crater, an unbelievably deep pit of human grief? What would life be like after independence?

* * *

In other nations, including Kenya, independence matched onward like the slow, relentless progress of flowing lava, that other volcanic action. The push for independence in all the lands around us was grinding onwards, gradually pushing the British and French out. The desire for freedom from colonial rule was an unstoppable social event, like the flow of lava oozing down the side of the mountain, covering everything in its path. The call for freedom would not be resisted. The best that could be hoped for was to ease it along, just as the railway managed to move heavy loads up and down steep hills. The best that could be hoped was that the end of colonial rule would come without an accident.

Increased cruelty was even breaking out in the two colonies owned by the Portuguese, and in response the colonial powers there imposed harsher restrictions, further subjugating the Africans. Only the Portuguese were holding on; they intended to keep Angola and Mozambique as colonies. The next year, in 1961, civil war broke out in both Angola and Mozambique. Even the Portuguese colonies felt the initial convulsions of an impending volcanic-like explosion.

* * *

A lovely girl from Lorenzo Marques, started to attend the youth group in Nairobi. She was one year older than I was, and I was trying to stop myself from being shy when talking with girls but in Grade Nine I was a bit bashful.

I met Maria at the Theological School in Limuru when about 20 young people came from Nairobi for a weekend retreat. The new little Baptist Church was making an effort to include young people in the fellowship. Maria came for a four-day retreat with others her age. Her parents were evangelicals in Mozambique, that distant Portuguese colony to the South.

She was the first girl who caught my eye in a serious way. At age 15 she didn't want to talk about the cruelties going on in Mozambique, though. She was very spiritual and wanted to talk about the Gospels, and her family. My interest in her was something I kept to myself; for a long time I kept dreaming I might see her, long after her family left Kenya, which had been only a stop off point for the family as they tried to decide their future. They could return to Mozambique, to continue their work with the colonial government, or go to Lisbon. I wrote to her at her school in Nairobi. She wrote to me at RVA, and I read and reread her short letter. After that she didn't write to me again.

Her family believed a huge explosion was about to take place in Lorenzo Marques, the capital city of Mozambique, and they left for Portugal. I never saw Maria again, and I never mentioned her to my parents, siblings, or anyone else at school.

* * *

I had a more urgent concern. Too often I was on my back with Sausage on top of me. At times he seemed to be such a good friend. At other times he beat me up just to keep fit. "There isn't going to be much stomach left if you keep that up, you great big gorilla," I jeered. He rolled me over and twisted my arm another notch. I thought my arm would stay in a permanent "V" shape behind my back.

The next day he trapped me again. "How is your stomach today," he asked, jumping on my solar plexus. A crowd of boys instantly gathered at the door to see the spectacle. If the word, *Fight!* rang out, the door to that dorm room would be filled in a second, blocking out the sunlight as a dozen, or more heads, peered in.

I learned that there was more than one way to win a fight. One way was to be stronger physically than the other person. However, in my case, that was impossible. Another way was to "squeal". But you just didn't do that now that you were in the Westervelt Dorm. The only other way was to hurt more deeply, in another way. "Why don't you go and bully on someone your own size?" I asked.

"Because it's so much fun to sit on your lungs," he said, bouncing.

"No. It's because you are chicken. You just want to prove what a coward you are."

"I'm not a coward. I'm just sitting here, calm, cool and collected." It was his favorite phrase; using it he described his emotional, physical and intellectual progress all at once. He didn't know it but I had just cornered him, got him where I wanted him.

"You're not calm, cool and collected. You're crud and crap and corruption!"

The faces crowded in the door let out a great roar. They appreciated a sense of competition. And competitions came in verbal, as well as physical, onslaughts. I'd won, really, using the sharpest weapons of all: hurtful words. Sausage gave me a couple more blows and then stopped. He never used my rib cage as a trampoline again.

I had learned that words wound far more than fists and put a lie to the rhyme we had learned earlier, "Sticks and stones might break my bones, but names will never hurt me."

* * *

Now, as a freshman at *swot*, I was much more interested in the Africans around me. Africans were beginning to take on more responsibility in mission stations all over Kenya, Uganda and Tanganyika. My previous questions, about respect for authority and learning how to live within the bounds of the mission station, now included something bigger: who would eventually run all the mission stations? Someone had to have the last word; that was why authority was needed.

My new questions dealt with relationships between Africans and missionaries. The question hit me when I was returning from a hike in the forest, below the soccer field. I had been out of bounds on my own, exploring animal trails.

An African sauntered by, walking to Kijabe Township. After I greeted him, saying, "*Jambo*," the thought came to me. "Why do we have so little contact with the Africans at RVA? Why is there such a wall of separation around our school?"

* * *

An important decision had recently been made that included Africans. Jubilee Hall, used for worship services was large enough for the foreign community, with some space left over and African young people could come for the Sunday Service at 4:00 p.m.

However, when Africans were present there were just too many people to fit into Jubilee Hall. At their church their solution was to cram people closer together. In Jubilee Hall, it was absolutely clear: only one person could sit in one of those fold-up grey chairs. No, there was no question of accommodating two people on a single grey, metal chair!

So, the Africans began arriving early to get a seat. Missionaries were used to arriving just a few minutes early and they always sat in the same place, usually close to the back. Now they had to come early, hunting for four or five chairs empty seats, otherwise they would have to stand for an hour. Jubilee Hall was packed, overflowing.

It made so much sense. African young people wanted to learn English and they eagerly reached for our hymnbooks. They wanted to sing our hymns in English and would squish together, two on a chair, in order to stay. More and more Africans attended our services.

* * *

One Sunday no Africans came to the church service. What had happened? Why the separation? Whites had come from so far away to preach to Africans about the Savior but could we not worship the Lord together? The sharp wall of barbed wire had come down five years earlier, but it seemed that another wall, an invisible one, replaced it.

One day we had a special concert; a group of four violinists came from the USA on a short-term trip. They were so well dressed, wearing black suits with black bow ties. Their shinny lapels went from their necks down to their waists. I had never seen such a shiny, fancy suit before. After playing for us in Sunday School in the morning, we were invited to listen to them again at the African Church, AIC, Africa Inland Church, lower down the hill.

The AIC church building had a capacity for about 800 people, but more came; "Always room for one more on the bench!" Normally, the church overflowed. Built of cut stone, it was similar to all permanent constructions around the mission. Offering a gentle pastel shade of browns, grays and at times yellow chips, the cut stone needed no additional decoration; plaster was never used.

Today the church building was completely packed; the missionary families went to hear the special music which included familiar hymns as well as new pieces. It was a church service that left my heart pounding with enthusiasm and anticipation. Wouldn't it be wonderful to have violins, or an orchestra, like this all the time?

The service was over and a swarm of young Kikuyu boys made a beeline for the platform. There we were, Africans and whites, admiring the instruments. One little fellow, more courageous than the rest, asked the tall American violinist if he could play the wonderful violin. "No," said the American, gently but firmly.

"Please, I just want to see if I can make some music on the violin." The African boy was about my age and couldn't take his eyes off the instrument that made such wonderful music. An hour had passed with endless notes enchanting us all.

"No you can't play it. It takes years to learn to play one of these. You'd just make awful screeches."

"I think that I could play it. I watched everything you did. I can play it!"

"No, I told you that it takes years to master a violin!" The answer was final, but there was just no giving up on the part of the young fan. He had to have his hands on the violin! Anguished lines appeared on the visitor's face. He had come to entertain us; he had come to help these little African kids worship God during an afternoon service. How could he now let his precious instrument, worth thousands of dollars, be held, and possibly spoiled, by an African lad whose bright eyes were dancing with excitement?

Finally, the tall American gave in. He placed the violin under the chin of the little lad, balanced the bow in his little outstretched hand and waited to receive the instrument back - in five seconds. The rest of us stepped back with amazement. The little fellow moved the bow as though it was something he had done for a long time, at first a little wobbly, and then with a little bit more assurance. There were some awful squeaks, but he was able to play a few notes on the violin. He'd never even come near one before.

The American visitor was now in an immense quandary. The other three men in black suits were standing at the door waiting for him to join their party. The generous musician, the one with the biggest heart, faced the most impossible conundrum; he looked at 200 outstretched arms. Every African boy wanted to play that violin. After all, why could their friend play a few notes and why could they not have their turn?

* * *

I reflected on that situation for a long time. So many African boys and girls wanted to study. They didn't have much in the villages where they had come from. Perhaps their parents had a few cattle, a small herd of goats and banana trees. Didn't they deserve the same opportunities we had? How could they be treated fairly? These new questions were only the beginning.

Obviously, they had talent for music. They had to learn to speak English as part of their schooling. Yet they couldn't worship with us in English. Were we too "good" for them? Were we too high and removed from them? Couldn't we find a way to bridge the gaps that kept us apart?

What brought about divisions between people, anyway? Would there always be separation between people whose skin colors were different? What if Jubilee Hall had been built to accommodate more people?

Even the location of our school, being built on the highest part of the mission station, spoke of separation, yet everything had a reason. We occupied the highest ridge of the mission station while the African children studied on the larger, flatter ledge. Certainly, it made sense because their seven schools needed that huge area for so many dorms and class rooms. They were grouped around their large playing fields.

Still, couldn't that little fellow have chance to play a violin? Our school had trumpets, trombones, French horns, clarinets, and drums, as well as violins. We had so much and Africans had so little. Why?

I didn't tell these questions to adults.

Instead, my personal conduct was despicable because I knew that deep down, I couldn't really criticize anyone. In fact, I was a complete hypocrite.

* * *

My initial experience in greeting Mike Hall continued to distress me. Mike Hall was the first African American at school. His parents had come from the States, like the moms and dads of all my friends. Like the others, Mike's family had come to Africa as missionaries under an American mission agency. He arrived about the same time that students came from Congo. Mike was wiry and had hair just like that of the Africans. He could run like the wind. There wasn't a faster runner on the field than Mike Hall.

I arrived on the first day of school one term and Mike was playing Ping-Pong on the table tennis table occupying its space on the veranda, just outside the dining room. That was just where my watch had been broken two years before. Mike had been playing doubles, wining everyone. Who was this black guy at our school, who spoke with an American accent?

I don't know how the conflict broke, but a friendly fistfight that broke out at the far end of the table, one student trying to take the paddle from another, all in fun. Mike Hall's face showed the intense concentration of a winner, concentrating on his game. He leaned over to hit a well-placed Ping Pong ball and accidentally hit me as I stood against the railing.

"Sambo!" I cried out, "Watch what you are doing!" Instantly, I was struck dumb by my sudden outburst. I was more racist than any one there! I had been brought up with the Tugen kids, with Wilson, who was my best friend. I learned the Tugen language from Wilson and interpreted it when sick people arrived at the medical clinic in Kabartonjo. Some patients lacked front teeth and complained of pain; I would tell mother what their complaints were, translating that difficult, tonal language.

Yet, here I was, making a terrible comment against a new kid just because of his skin color. Clearly, I was prejudiced! How did that happen? How could I be concerned about the seeming injustice towards the Kikuyu, with righteous indignation, and then turn around and display the worst form of racism towards Mike Hall at our school?

Mike Hall became one of our prized players on the Rugby team. He had a unique sense of timing, enabling him to know whether to tackle the opponent or to attempt an interception, taking the ball from the opposing team as they ran against us.

When Mike intercepted a pass from our opponents' team he would run down the field for another try. He inspired us and we cheered until our lungs were tired. At times I called him *Our Gazelle*, but that nickname didn't stick. What did stick was a sensation deep in my heart. I had been mean to him the first time I saw him.

* * *

I never forgot the terrible prejudice on my first meeting with Mike. What was worse, I recognized the pride in my spirit and didn't ask him for forgiveness. If I had been in Grade Four my father would have told me to ask forgiveness, as he had done when I spoke against Ma Coder. Left alone, on the first day of High School, I recognized within myself those defects that I criticized in others. I knew I was a hypocrite and I seemed powerless to change that, or anything else.

Mike Hall never needed a nickname. He was just Mike Hall: fleeting, like the wind, swift like a cheetah, he could leap and weave, bringing us victory again as he sped towards the upright goal posts at the end of the rugby field. He made try after try in the rugby games and was one of our top players; he was often the reason for another victory against heavier, more experienced teams. Mike Hall won not just Cindy Simmons' heart; he finally won the hearts of everyone. But, he did it through his skill, determination and a bright personality. He showed me friendship and I ended up being jealous of his happy laugh and quick wit which brought him so many friends.

His presence though, was a stinging rebuke to my own prejudice for a term, and long afterwards. I could, and did, criticize missionaries for not letting Africans share in our Sunday services.

But, racism, a strong reaction when Mike had only hit me accidentally: where did that come from? How had it got into me? Something far deeper lay within me, something that could come to the surface, actions that I would regret later on. I learned that the simple resolution to behave well would not save me from regretting my actions. I needed something more than sheer will power.

***

I was becoming aware of the complexity of these questions as I avidly read *Time*, *Newsweek*, and the *U. S. News and World Report*. Magazines arrived at the library each week and I pounced on them, hungry for information on current events.

We followed the progress in the struggle for civil rights in the southern USA. The Kennedy / Nixon debate was a memorable event. American missionaries generally agreed that the USA would never be the same if a Catholic candidate won the presidency. We had a short discussion in class; I found myself becoming more interested about the world, but I also realized that I knew more about America, and little, if anything, about Canada. Because we studied England in history class, and kept referring to the Protestant Reformation I had a better understanding of the USA, Great Britain and Europe.

CHAPTER 20

SLING SHOTS AND A USEFUL LITTLE PRIMUS

*F*ew dreams impacted me as much as the one I had one night at the end of our holidays about a year later. We lived in another house in Limuru, a house located only one mile down the lane from *Karibuni Cottage*, between "D Route" and "A Route".

The owner of *Karibuni Cottage* rented it to a teacher connected with the Theological College. At the same time another house came up for rent. Dad moved us from one amazing residence to another. This second house in Limuru was a English home overlooking Limuru Lake. The property of our new home was spacious, covering the top of a hill and the entrance was at the top of a fairly steep road. Kikuyu women walked up that long road every afternoon, bent over under a load of firewood slung to their foreheads, the heavy burden resting on their backs.

Mother placed a 10-gallon steel milk drum at the entrance to our gate. If we didn't have enough space for ten widows to work, we at least could give cups of cold water. The drum was filled with fresh, cool water a couple of times each day. Women drank often and deeply from the water inside that large vessel, taking a rest after climbing the hill.

A splendid rock garden decorated the spacious property, dropping by degrees down the slope. Flowers abounded. The bedrooms of the house were at the high end, the living room and dining room in the middle and the garage and storerooms were at the lower end, nearest the gate. It was a dream house come true.

* * *

Perhaps my dream was the result of having studied the story of David killing Goliath. In my dream I made a sling shot, not the kind that we used at school, the kind Carl Barnett had taught us to make. That was called a *catty*, a catapult. This slingshot, the one in my dream, was the one David used; I saw it clearly, a long cord between the pouch and the fingers of the hand, and it was able to fling a stone further than a *catty*.

After breakfast I walked from our front door, across the wide parking area, to the garage. Two old leather soccer balls had been left by the previous renters. There, right before me was all the leather I needed! Then I went into the supply shed beside the kitchen and found a long piece of string, about six feet long. Dad had his eye on it for a "nice little parcel" as he'd say, while I had my eye on it for a nice little sling.

Behind the garage lay the vegetable patch, not a very good place to find round stones. Beside the vegetable patch a charming little guesthouse had been turned into dad's office.

Since there were a number of glass windows in the guesthouse, the nicest office my father ever occupied, I couldn't very practice using my slingshot close to that building.

If I hoped to become a good shot with a slingshot, I needed lots of practice. I looked at my feet where small bits of crushed gravel covered the perfectly manicured garden path. Not a single stone was to be seen, only tiny bits of grey gravel. What should I do? I went back into the garage and found a small round potato poking its eyes out of a bushel basket at me. "Just the thing, or 'just the job'," I thought, imitating one of my father's favorite expressions. Each potato was about two inches across, with a smooth, round shape that would scar any old Goliath. It was the perfect object for target practice.

I took aim at a cyprus tree at the end of the garden, where the garden stopped and the cow pasture began. My sling went round and round and I let go of one end of the cord, but the potato had dropped to the ground. Again I tried, this time feeling the potato leave the sling, and I waited for it to splatter against the tree. Nothing happened. I looked around. Nothing! What had happened to that rotten little potato?

A quiet sound behind me in the vegetable patch let me know that my deadly missile had landed in mom's tomato patch; it fell straight out of the sky. Never mind, I just needed a bit of practice, so I chose another potato, about half as big and it shot off at an angle of 60 degrees. I tried another and unfortunately it came down on the roof of our house, about 120 degrees off. This was harder than I thought; a lot more difficult than it was in my dream.

A half an hour later, with no more potatoes to sling away, I looked around me, at the yard and the garden. Bits of potatoes lay splattered over the parking area. During a morning with no clouds in the sky, food had literally rained down from God's heavens, except it wasn't manna. The bushel basket was completely empty. I didn't even have time to properly reflect on my actions, before mom told me how disappointed she was to have lost all those potatoes, which she was going to use for planting the vegetable garden.

* * *

Climbing Green Tree was beginning to get boring now. There were organized sports in the afternoons: baseball, basketball, volleyball and running and track and field. Depending on the time of the year there was a greater emphasis in one sport or another. I wasn't good at some sports, such as basketball. Others came more easily, like long distance running, which led me down to First Ravine on a daily basis, and sometimes to Second Ravine. Of course, that meant going out of bounds.

I watched Don go to his dorm, pride welling up in my chest. He seemed to be getting along fine with students in his dorm. The Hatchery was no longer being used for *titchies;* the little guys stayed way up the hill, in the KLD Dorm, which meant a walk of several miles a day, rain or shine, walking to meals, to class and then back at night to their dorm.

Ma and Pa Senoff still had care of them, the last building before the forest grudgingly engulfed everything but the railway tracks. Don was well appreciated by his energetic group of friends. While they must have had many of the same little arguments that we had but we didn't talk about them much. Boarding School effectively separated siblings, even at meal times.

Pearl was known as a good little musician. She was doing well in piano and a number of teachers mentioned it. She had her own set of friends. At times I was aware of cruel names that were given to her because of her brace and the limp resulting from her polio. I'd become proud of her. She was known for her writing, her poetry, extensive reading and her memory work.

* * *

Sling Shots And A Useful Little Primus

In the *big guys* dorm, known as Westervelt Dorm, we were almost thirty fellows in Grades Nine to Twelve. Naturally, fires, or anything dangerous, were prohibited in our rooms. That fire in the Stevenson's Dorm had been too much of a close thing. Of course, the prohibition included firecrackers and anything inflammable.

However, and that was a big word, as a reward for enduring the many hardships in dorm life, several of the older boys used a *primus*, the little stove the Africans used every day in their homes for cooking food. A primus ran on kerosene and once pumped up it produced a bright flame. Students, who had endured five study halls a week, deserved a treat. What could be better than a can of Sweetened Condensed Milk, which, after being boiled, produced tasty caramel syrup? This treat was a favorite and any room in Westervelt Dorm possessing a primus was most fortunate.

As far as the fire hazard was concerned, a basic questions existed in our minds, but was never asked of staff or answered by our teachers: If Africans could use a primus for all their meals without burning their houses, how could a simple, hour-long use of a primus in the middle of the floor in our room, in a building built of cut stone, present any danger?

* * *

Pa Simmons always worked hard while he supervised us during the two hour study hall; he prepared his classes for the next day and marked endless essays and spelling tests. He would look with a scowl across the green ping-pong table if someone talked or made a disturbance. At 8:45 p.m. students might leave for the bathroom. One or two would return having fired up the primus, preparing a tasty treat for students who had to suffer so. Life after study hall, from 9:00 to 10:00 p.m., was best lived enjoying fresh, hot caramel syrup.

During the previous year I felt jealous since some guys were fortunate enough to possess a primus. But, how could I ask dad for a primus? "Why do you need a primus?" he would ask. If I told him, "I want to boil Sweetened Condensed Milk each night after study hall, making a treat in our bed room", he'd see what I was up to. He might even warn me about the dangers of a fire.

So, to get a primus I would have to earn it myself. However, I didn't want to take any money out of my Life Savings in the Post Office. Someday I might need that money.

* * *

Shortly after arriving back at school I took my slingshot down to the trees near the new out doors baptism area. Solid stones lay around, left over from the construction of the outdoor baptistery. No longer would we use the cow trough for baptisms; things were improving a lot at RVA. This outdoor baptistery was a fine piece of work, plastered inside and outside and a small amphitheater fit into the contours of the hill sat 150 people.

I aimed my sling at a tree. No one would be hurt; no one would see the stone I threw, and so no one would laugh at my target practice. Gradually a callus formed on finger and the pain in my hand didn't bother me anymore, I eventually got the stones to go forward about 95 % of the time.

A week later a magnificent boulder, heavy and sharp, about the size of my fist, slammed into a Eucalyptus tree. The stone hit smack on my imaginary target. The tree boasted a huge gash under a branch that had been Goliath's head. If I had been shooting at that giant in the Bible, I'd at least have hit his Adam's apple instead of his forehead.

The time had come to make some serious money; every cent would go towards the purchase of a primus. I called Don; we talked on the path outside the dorm, not on the dorm property, because if he came into the Westervelt Dorm area he would go through the paddle machine. This was another way of keeping siblings apart; I thought it cruel that a long row of *big guys* would paddle a *titchie* just because he had come to speak with his older brother. That happened to Don once, and guys who wanted to keep their area free of the younger brothers handed out even worse forms of punishment. Many little guys had sore bottoms for days after such treatment.

After explaining my idea to Don he agreed to sell slingshots to his friends. He would deliver the slingshots; I'd get the money, a shilling, or about $0.15, at that time, for each one. The green, red and yellow plastic string I needed came from Nairobi. Ever so patiently I braided long strips of cord. A number of old soft balls were thrown out of the sports cupboard one day; Pa Simmons didn't like "junk" lying around. He was in charge of sports that term and organized a mighty clean up, for which I was very thankful. I had a good way to recycle the leather from old soft balls.

* * *

Talk about motivation, I worked like mad! I may have even caught up a bit to all the braiding that Dot and Pearl had done on their hair. Hundreds of hand movements went into the formation of each cord. It was attached to a soft leather pouch at one end. One by one I gave them to Don and he kept coming back to me with another shilling. I counted them up one day; I almost had enough money to buy a primus, kerosene and a tin of sweetened condensed milk.

One day I made a super long sling for my Canadian friend, Gordon Johnson. He was tall, a little unsure of how to use a sling. He bent down and forced a large stone out of the parking lot, the side where water accumulated during the rainy season. In order to level off that small basin, where rainwater sat for days on end, many stones had been placed to raise the level of the ground. The bolder he chose was the size of my fist and he placed it carefully in his slingshot. Being the first time that he had ever used such a weapon, and not knowing that he had something in his hand capable of killing an Ephriamite (you just had to ask a left handed Benjaminite in the Bible about that) he took aim.

The crack of the slingshot came at the same minute I fell face down on the ground. I couldn't move. He had been behind me and I had the misfortune to be at a 50-degree angle away from him as he aimed for the tree. The blow on my back threw me down and had me on my stomach; a second passed before I was able to move. Soon, I was up again and we were swinging stones around and around and firing them off.

* * *

By now 22 boys in Don's dorm had a new toy, which was actually more than just a toy; it was a throwback to the days of yore. I pocketed my money and asked one of the guys going into Nairobi on the regular Saturday trip to buy a primus. That evening I took a spanking new, bronze colored primus out of the small cardboard box and poured in the kerosene. *Sausage, Peanut, Campbell* and I laid back on our beds, happy to have caramel milk added to our regular RVA diet. For about a month the four of us in our room enjoyed delicious refreshments after study hall.

One day, Don called me urgently. "They're going to take away all the sling shots. Too many of the windows at our dorm have been broken."

I felt the shock of having had something go terribly wrong, or of having being found out, so I protested, "But I thought I told you to tell those guys not to go near any buildings when using a sling!"

"Well, some guys sort of forgot about that. They used the slings close to our dorm, instead of in First Ravine or in the forest. An investigation is going on; all the sling shots are being confiscated because they are too dangerous!"

The *titchies* lost a precious shilling from their allowance, but they had their own memories to keep from their experience, together the disappointment of loss. Meanwhile, *Peanut, Sausage, Campbell* and I shared our treats until the end of the term.

* * *

Packing up the primus presented a new conundrum at the end of term. Should I take it home? How would I explain it to dad? It had been used a lot. The blackened rim gave that away. I didn't want dad saying, "What's this, a primus? Look, it's been used ever so much! Hazel, dear, do you know anything about this?"

So, I left it at school during the holidays and returned the next term, but by then my primus had disappeared. Like the *titchies,* all I was left with was a memory.

* * *

The locust plague came again. They were such small insects, so greedy, never satisfied with what they had already eaten. They jumped into the air, then flew a little further, and then started munching again. Their strong hind legs catapulted the insects into the air. The only good thing about them was the bulging back leg. With just the right pressure the leg would kick outwards suddenly, even after it was no longer part of the pesky little creature. The lower leg possessed sharp barbs, which we would try to inject against sensitive flesh of another guy's arm or leg.

Pinching ants marched every year and their bite came from two very sharp pincers. When these ants came in the millions we would capture one and we hold the tiny body against our shirt pockets. The ant would bite the khaki and at that moment we'd sever the ant's head from the body. The strong pincers kept the ant's head firmly attached to the shirt. Some guys had an artistic collection of on ants perfectly spaced on their shirt pockets, or all the way down their shirt, between the buttons. This came to an end when the laundry staff complained to the administration.

* * *

The *big guys* no longer seemed so big, or so clever. However, I was jealous of them for one reason. They would soon be going on their own Senior Safari.

I began to pay more attention to what students did after they left RVA. They talked about school in the USA: Wheaton College, Moody and Biola. I heard the *big guys* talking about their future and started paying attention. For the time being I had no idea what would happen to me after RVA. How did you go about planning your future in a place half a world away?

CHAPTER 21

WARTS, DUMAS AND HUGO

A certain daily "chore" in Limuru wasn't a chore at all. Bringing the mail from the Post Office in Limuru meant riding three and a half miles to the township and coming back again. Riding my bike was good exercise and I brought back letters each day; often a parcel arrived. Dad had more time in his office while I watched the endless procession of African life along "D Route". Life was never the same from one day to the next.

I never got tired of the scenery going to Limuru and back. Just at the head of our Karibuni Cottage there was a pyrethrum field belonging to our neighbors. A high price was paid for a crop of white flowers. Who lived in that farm? It seemed that no one had seen the two English women who were said to live there.

Once onto "D Route", I rode past the campus of the Theological Seminary where some 100 students studied behind the closely clipped cyprus hedge. Mother and dad were friends with many students, always inviting some to our home for Christmas. These were men who were too poor to go home to their tribal areas at the end of the year.

The Theological Seminary was very large. One section of the campus hosted special groups for conferences. Limuru was becoming a center for church conventions. An elementary school served African children up to Standard Four, since the British had imported their system of education. Kikuyu children arrived home from school each day with newly learned words of English. It didn't matter that they were proud Kikuyu, who were told at home that their tribal customs were the best in the world. To live in Limuru meant they also needed Swahili and English. They went to school, passing Standard 1, 2 or 3, while their mothers came from the forest, carrying firewood on their backs to prepare the evening meal fire. Their children walked to school to learn the rules of English grammar, English History and Robert's Rules of Order.

After passing the Theological College I cycled past the tree-lined entrance to the land of the Edens. I longed to be free from piano lessons that took us up there each week. Mrs. Eden, Senior, would insist that you sat up straight at the piano. The first thing in playing the piano was a straight back and curved fingers. I found it more interesting to hear her stories, trying to piece together the two-generations of a Kenyan settler family, than to sit up as straight as she did herself. But piano lessons were for later on in the week.

Another half mile took me to the base of a steep hill. Trains going "up country" lumbered through a long "V" cut through the hill. The train reappeared behind a small wattle forest and headed towards the long tunnel that would swallow it up. The train would emerge from the tunnel, arriving at Limuru. I kept going up the steep hill, past luscious green pastures, finally coming to the small Post Office. As I sped along, I looked at the two small, ugly warts on my left thumb. Nothing had been able to rid me of those ugly bumps.

* * *

It was impossible to get bored along this road. There was a constant stream of life. African women carried everything; they bowed under loads of firewood, cut in pieces, about two feet long. The pack of wood was thrown up onto their backs, usually with the help of another woman. Suspended on their shoulders by a brown leather strap that wrapped around the forehead, a woman bore the burden of the day; it was the fuel for the fire at night. The weight of these homeward bound cargos was more than I could manage; I tried to lift a load of wood once and found it embarrassing to have to quickly lower it to the ground. Kikuyu women carried that kind of a load every day.

Women walked in a slow waddling motion, supporting the load on their backs as they leaned into the future, hopeful and optimistic. A two-inch wide line indentation formed in their foreheads, speaking of the amazing stamina and dedication to home life. By the time that old age had arrived, the deep indentation across the forehead showed how much energy was needed to keep the home fires going.

Sometimes I saw a Kikuyu family moving house. The head of the family walked ahead proudly, carrying only the address of his new home. Walking ten paces ahead he showed his wife the way. His wife and kids followed behind. The wife carried the bed frame and other belongings on her back. A Kikuyu woman carrying a bed frame forced trucks and cars to pass carefully. With that bed frame taking up space in the road, she might be whisked away to beyond the grave in the case of an accident; and the car might lose far more than just a headlight.

The Kikuyu man sometimes carried a tail whisk, a symbol of authority. He probably had reason for walking well ahead of the bed frame. Their ancestors had hunted lions, meaning the man walked proudly into the future, not looking back. Women never hunted lion; women were meant to be followers; men were leaders. Women carried beds.

* * *

Riding along on my bike I still worried about the warts on my left thumb. I had tried picking them off, but infection dissuaded me from doing that again. I tried hot water to no avail. Nothing would get those two wretched little growths off my hand.

One day, as I was starting a new Christmas holiday (Christmas was always the best holiday time) I rode to town. Rugby was the new sport at school. Memories of pushing in the scrum reminded me that I needed to be fit for the upcoming term so I decided to make my daily run to Limuru and home again in record-breaking time. Each day I would go a little faster; by January I'd be faster and stronger, perhaps even strong enough to make it onto the "A" XV team, moving up from the "B" XV team, which was my current standing.

I tore up the lane, turned right past the Divinity College, and strained as I headed up the long hill. Now the long hill up was behind me. The Post Office came in view; letters were posted and I mounted the bike in a flash, starting home.

The best part of being on a bike was going down hill, fast! When I got to the bridge over the railway tracks on my way home, I never even looked at the railway train entering the tunnel below. The road was passing by at break-neck speed. I rode along the very edge of the road, the smoothest bit because the bare feet of Africans along that section kept the dirt absolutely smooth. This ride was fabulous.

My head was facing straight down along the smooth dirt strip along the edge where the Africans walked. I pumped as hard as I could, hoping to have a new record for the daily trip. Coming around the curve into the long straight section down hill I couldn't go any faster. I leaned forward, constantly gaining speed beside the train tracks as I neared the bottom of the steep hill.

The rock on the path might have been avoided if I had been seen it, but that day I had tossed caution aside. Everything seemed to happen at once. My front wheel hit the small boulder and stopped. The back wheel kept going, though, at the same speed as it had been going at the second of impact.

I hung on for a crazed moment, looking at the ground with my head straight down, a quick second that didn't last long. My hands hit the ground after a complete flip. My left hand took the worst beating. My leg was somehow wrapped into, or around the frame. Correspondence from P.O., Box Number 1051. Limuru, Kenya, lay scattered across the ground. The front wheel wouldn't go around. Worse, my left leg wouldn't move. I waited, ever so angry at myself for once again getting into a pickle.

An African passed by who was a friend of our family. He called dad, who came quickly and I was soon at home, getting my wounds attended to. By some sort of a miracle there were only bruises; no bones were broken. A bandage covered my thumb and left wrist, and another bandage was wrapped around my left knee.

* * *

Christmas was coming. Don liked Mecano building sets and Pearl was fond of books, I wanted a balsa wood model airplane and Dot liked little things for her hair. Mother and dad went to Nairobi to buy Christmas gifts and that morning I decided it was time for a general clean up. I was not meant to be a carpenter; cooking was out of the question. Perhaps I could be a supervisor! I made a promise to Don, Dorothy and Pearl. "One shilling goes each person in the cleanest, neatest room!"

Seeing the possibility of doubling their weekly allowance, Dorothy and Pearl set to cleaning their room with a vengeance; this was a quick way to earn money at Christmas. Books from their huge bookshelf lay in piles all over the floor. Each one went back in the bookcase; Enid Blyton's books covered half a shelf but we had outgrown her books and dad now had us into great authors, Charles Dickens and others.

Don and I set to; we'd have our room cleaner and brighter than our sisters. We swept the floor, made the beds without a wrinkle, and put all Mecano screws and bolts away. Both rooms were now spotless. However, in a quandary over how to judge one room to be neater than the other, I took the easiest out. "Its a tie", I declared. "Your room is just as neat as ours. No body gets any money!"

"Why, how about that!" exploded Pearl, as she looked around her spotless room. Flowers graced their room. I hadn't thought of decorations, or flowers. Girls looked for beauty in life. "You are the great, big judge!" she continued. "How do you judge, eh? And anyway, who made you the judge in the first place?"

She was really incensed, certain her room was cleaner and neater than ours. Her wrath just had to be appeased. The answer was obvious. We loved big parcels at Christmas time. American kids got big parcels at Christmas time and they were forever going back and forth to the States. Christmas was almost here.

* * *

Dad and mom never took a furlough; they just stayed on and on in their work. Dad would write home to all our relatives, "We are so happy here in our literature work that we just don't feel it would be *right* to come home now. The monthly *Kesho* magazine is selling well, and Hazel is doing so well at the Sunday School typing up the Bible lessons."

Kesho, the periodical dad produced, was one of the reasons that we were the longest running kids at the mission. Everyone else traveled to the States and back, so their styles and clothes were always up to date. We had Christmas parcels that came from "home", yet "home" in Canada was so far away.

* * *

Every time that I went to Nairobi, Alexander Dumas was one whose books I'd linger over. However, I was positive that neither Alexander Dumas, nor Victor Hugo, would be at home with me at Christmas, unless I specifically asked for one of their novels. I was too proud to ask for my own present so I had to plan something different. I had a small savings in the Post Office. Sometimes dad deposited a bit of money in our accounts; my life savings account had reached 140 shillings, about $20.00.

I went to the Post Office in Nairobi to draw out part of my savings. My first signature was made at age seven years. I was 14 now, and thanks to penmanship classes my writing had improved. The Post Office clerk was doubtful that the signature before him and the one in the savings booklet belonged to the same person. He examined my name in the passbook carefully, written seven years earlier, when I was just learning to write. The two signatures didn't match! My heart beat fast.

Could I put into effect the plan I had for secretly getting Alexander Dumas or Victor Hugo for Christmas? I needed to make up for having disregarded flowers in Pearl's room, meaning that she didn't get a shilling for having cleaned her room so well.

The Post Master, a hearty Asian man with a turban and a smiling face, believed my story. He gave a slight nod to the clerk and I walked out of the Post Office with money held in my sweating paw.

Then, I started on the really fun part. I found Alexander Dumas' massive work, *The Count of Monte Cristo*. The cover was a bright dark green. I could hardly wait. Dumas had battled Hugo to see who could write a longer novel. French novels needed 900 pages to spin out the long yarn.

* * *

I bought a double set of presents, for myself, for Dot and Don and Pearl. Getting the packages into the car was the next problem. Mom said, "My David, you bought a lot today, didn't you?"

"Mom, these are just the wrappings. You know how certain things have to come with thick wrappings, don't you?" Perhaps I left her wondering what gifts might be coming for her kitchen. Fibs just couldn't be avoided in this adventure.

How could I explain the extra gifts? I found an old cardboard box, just the right size, in the attic above the garage. I packed all the presents in it and sealed it with a big sheet of brown paper, addressed to "The Rev. Kenneth N. Phillips, Box Number 1051, Limuru, Kenya." I glued Canadian stamps from my stamp collection, the same ones I had removed from previous parcels that came from Grandma Hill two weeks before. The stamps bore the postmark, but the brown paper on which the stamps were pasted didn't match the complete the black circle of the postmark. I hoped my family would think the package had cleared the post office in Winnipeg.

"Look at the package on my bike!" I called out as I took the package from the carrier of my bike. The parcel had come all the way down from the garage, a distance of fifty yards. Dad and mom assumed it had come through the Post Office in Limuru.

"Who sent it?" mother asked. "It says, from Santa Claus!"

"It's from Canada," said Don. They didn't send kids to RVA for nothing; he could read the name on the stamps that he had been examining in my collection two days earlier.

Over lunch the conversation was a cheerful glow of expectation. A parcel like this was so mysterious! Who was our Santa Claus? Did it come from the Devitt family? Perhaps it had come from the Drysback family, in Seattle, Washington. The elderly couple could hardly stand us, four small children, closing in on her fancy tea cups seven years earlier. That was impossible; the stamps were from Winnipeg, Canada, not Seattle, Washington.

Dot said definitively, "It came from Canada!"

I added my own a suggestions. If I didn't say something, they might catch on that something was amiss. Christmas came and we left Santa Claus' gifts to the end. "Goody!" I jumped up and down, surprised. "Just what I wanted! Alexander Dumas! I wonder how Santa Claus knew what I wanted? Look, it's *The Count of Monte Cristo!*"

Dad wanted to see the book. He didn't know I was interested in French literature from the 19th century. "Glad to see you are progressing," he whistled and the little "S"s were a sign of approval. It was amazing how Pa Simmons could motivate kids who had never been interested in literature before. I grabbed the book from him just as he began to examine the inside page. Most people would look at the first page, then the index and then thumb through the book. Dad, however, was full of the publishing details and he wanted to know technical things: when it was printed, how many copies, what type of print and the city where it was printed. I could understand Mr. Cook's struggle with my father's insistence everything be printed perfectly, and I felt a bit of pity for my father's colleague who had to put up with dad's perfectionism.

I didn't want dad to take up detective work on Christmas day. The last think I wanted was to hear him ask, "How could a book printed in Oxford have been sold in Canada and sent to Kenya?" I grabbed the book; he was a little surprised and gave in. He examined the little penknife sent him from the North Pole. Pearl had a gift picked it out just for her, my way of paying her back for disappointing her about the prize money that she really should have won. Girls really do clean up their rooms better than boys. They instinctively knew how beauty brightens up a room.

* * *

As I settled back to read the great novel *The Count of Monte Cristo*, I felt an itchy feeling under the bandage on my thumb. The scrape on my leg was almost all better. That was all that remained from my bike accident; I remembered the verse, "Pride comes before a fall." Before reading the thick, new novel, I removed the bandage from my thumb. There was no sign of warts! Both had been left in the dust on "D Route"; a new scar had formed, covering the place where they had taken root.

I had gained a blockbuster of a nineteenth century novel and I lost two warts, but I didn't solve the mystery of Santa Claus. There were a couple of delayed attempts to solve the whole question. Dot, who kept working on the puzzle, trying to figure out the existence of items available in Kenya, finally guessed. "I know! *David* is Santa Claus," she said before we went back to school.

I put her off, though. "Then what about those Canadian stamps on the parcel?" I responded. No one ever had the answer to my question: "How did those presents come in a parcel with stamps from Canada, eh?"

CHAPTER 22

A SECRET SWIMMING POOL AND THE BEGINNING OF THE SPACE AGE

Strictly speaking, once past First Ravine, a student was out of bounds. After the sharp, hairpin curve around First Ravine, there were two other deep gorges, Second and Third Ravines. All three were full of mystery, animal life, strange sights and sounds. A pleasant hike included exploring one of these three ravines. The road to the commercial area of Kijabe Township wound around those sharp bends; cars had to use care to round the corners at each ravine.

At First Ravine we still might find a shell left from the target practice of the King's African Rifles during the Mau Mau, years earlier. Hundreds of swallows chased their meals in the air, never tired by dramatic acrobatic performances. They would swoop down from the high cliffs above and finish their dive-bombing action with a flourish of a wave past. King fisher birds occupied the lower section of the ecological niches.

Just down from the road at First Ravine one of the *olden day guys* had discovered a cave. Thousands of bats inhabited the dark, grimy cave. We marveled as they sped in and out of the cave. We squatted down close to the floor as they flew over our heads. We had started to learn about nature from Moody Science Films; one explained how bats navigate. We tried to imagine their amazing radar at work, but try as we might we couldn't hear their high-pitched squeals. Appreciation for the creation all around us included bats and birds, cheetahs and leopards, crocodiles and giraffe. There was only one thing awkward about a desire to appreciate God's creation up close: most exciting events were out of bounds.

* * *

At some time or other an African trail had been formed. It started on the long shelf on which Kijabe was situated crawled through the forest past Third Ravine and burst into the sunlight at Kijabe Township. One Saturday, when we were out on a hike, we followed the trail where it forked to the left, instead of going to the town. It ended at a cliff. *Peanut* spotted something. "Hey, Everyone! Here's a path down the cliff. Let's go down!"

Holding onto roots of trees, balancing on the points of protruding rocks, we sped down to the rocky mass of boulders below. A stream, endlessly practicing its music, called to itself in little jumps, singing a wonderful melody. We leapt like monkeys, from one side of the stream to the other when suddenly we came upon a large enclosed area.

"Wow!" exclaimed *Fish* who was at the front of the line. "Just look at that, will you!"

"Our very own swimming hole!" breathed Gord.

"Are any health problems here?" questioned *Crimson*.

We debated the possibility of damming up the stream, making the swimming hole larger. It was too much of a risk to swim in stagnant waters, but we knew we had a first class secret.

For several Saturday mornings we hiked to our secret water hole, the owners of a great treasure. Many times, after school in the afternoon, I ran by myself down the trail, below First, Second and Third Ravines, and then ran down the cliff, jumping from one stone to another to reach the swimming pool; then I ran up the cliff and reached Westervelt Dorm just in time to get cleaned up before supper. I trusted my ability to jump and run, to get back safely, even though no one knew where I was.

* * *

I knew many trails. The loneliness of the forest, birds crying in the trees and monkeys jumping overhead: all these were part of appreciating the outside world that made up such a limited universe on the steep sides of the Rift Valley.

However, I misjudged my running abilities. A joint sports day was planned, bringing together students from RVA and the African schools. I signed up for the one-mile race, confident that I would win one of the top spots. Looking at the runners before the beginning of the race I saw that they were tall Kikuyu guys, my age. They were slender, deep-chested young guys with determination in their faces. They lined up at the starting line. Within 20 seconds they were in front, gaining with every long stride. They ran twice as fast as I did! No matter how much I ran I still could not catch up to them, I came in last. When it came to running long distances, none of us possessed the deep reserves of energy and strength that these young men had in abundance.

They were the true sons and daughters of Kijabe, the owners of the land. Their struggles in life would involve learning how to divide their lands, how to live as Christians in their own society and finding a job. My struggles were not that much different, except I didn't even know where I was going to live or what my calling in life might be.

* * *

Our chapel services were continuing daily, as were other activities in our agenda. We ran through the scriptures, frontwards and backwards, in the morning, at noon and at night. We learned the stories of Daniel, the disciples and the early church.

The mysteries of the tabernacle in the wilderness were uncovered, layer upon layer, as we learned the means by which God had spoken to "the fathers" about heavenly things. At times, I had doubts about some of the teachers' interpretations of the tabernacle, but I kept them to myself. Why make others doubt about things that weren't too significant?

January meant the arrival of AIM missionaries for the Annual Convention. Only RVA was big enough to accommodate missionaries from all over Kenya.

* * *

We were back at the school for the Annual AIM Conference and for the second time, our family slept in my room, this time in the Westervelt Dorm. I felt awkward at having all six of us in the tight quarters of one room in the Big Guy's dorm.

On Sunday, the last day of the meetings, mother and dad called me aside. "We don't think that you should take communion this afternoon. As long as you show a rebellious attitude, you need to think what the body and blood of Jesus Christ really mean."

I let the elements go by. Never had I desired to participate in the communion service so much. The correction was good for me; there was contrition in my heart and a tear in my eye as we drove away. Another AIM Conference had come to an end.

* * *

However, I was deeply disturbed, for another reason because I had listened outside the window for just a minute when some mission business had been discussed. The words said by some missionaries seemed similar to what I might say in an argument at school. They had a more polished manner of saying things. I could tell that different agendas lay behind various arguments.

After a little while I moved away from the window at Jubilee Hall, so as not to be caught. The topics were like hot potatoes. What should be done with mission properties when independence came? Some wanted a more open attitude; others, believing that Africans had not yet mastered their own affairs, disagreed. Consequently, there was a real tussle because questions about properties and programs, cars and money, authority and job assignments were not easy matters to solve. I wasn't the only one with an attitude problem.

* * *

Returning by car to school for a new term a few days later, I knew more about the human heart. Our hearts hide many things. Unless one spoke about hidden things, others had no clue as to what was really going on inside another person. It was easy to tell a fib, to disguise the truth, to stretch the limits of truthfulness. Words, after all, were a window to the human heart, showing what was inside a person.

Why, even though we had all this great amount of Bible information, was there such a gap between my knowing and my obedience? It was, as James would have it, that we looked in the mirror and then forgot the shape of our faces.

* * *

One fellow who did not follow the rather nasty ups and downs was Ray Davis. He arrived back at school with a "breath-taking" story. His family had taken holidays down at the coast, just south of Mombasa. Having waded out to the reef late in the low tide, he was some 800 meters from land when he discovered a low tide pool and started to explore it. He examined the hundreds of sea-life forms, but suddenly a wave lifted him off his feet.

He had been out too long from shore before his return. He struggled as waves of the in-coming tide cleared the reef, rising rapidly, making a smooth walk back to the shore impossible. He swam, wading, looking for the best path back to the beach, as the waves rose and the tide came in. He went down under the rising waves and at one time almost didn't make it back up for air. As he struggled against the waves, trying to reach the sandy shore south of Mombasa he thought to himself that it was his final day. He considered it a miracle that he made it to shore.

The effect of Ray's testimony was electric. I sat on the edge of my bed. There was a quiet moment and then he said, "From now on, I'm going to live like a real Christian." He had drawn his line in the sand. Ray was a piano player in the chapels at youth meetings on Sunday nights, and in many other meetings. I respected him for his firm stand, his quiet manner, and his persistence at the piano. If he made the occasional error in the notes on the piano, at least he was pursuing a definite goal.

Somehow, Ray had managed to get past his First, Second and Third Ravines in a metaphorical sense. I was still coming along somewhere in the woods, if one wanted to push the analogy. We were on the same trail, but he was much further ahead. Ray had passed through his low point and come out safely.

* * *

Some actions were not that serious, only pranks. In the dorm we became experts in rolling up the towel after a shower in order to flick someone's butt with the small, wet end. If the towel emitted a loud crack, at the same time that it left a small red bruise, then the look of dismay on the face of the guy who had just been nicked was worth the wrath that immediately filled the room. Some guys made their towels sound like a whip for horses.

Other actions were strictly forbidden, such as peashooters. An endless supply of bamboo from up on the hill served as peashooters. One could either fire a spitball, made by chewing a bit of paper and aiming it across the room. At certain seasons of the year, the pepper tree provided plentiful dark-brown seeds, more ammunition than one could use. The benefit of peashooters was their accuracy. From the back of the classroom, over to an opposite row, one had a pretty good chance to hit a guy square in the neck. The downside was that getting caught using a peashooter. That could result in detention for one week, thus loosing all the free time between the last class and supper.

* * *

More serious was the neglect of homework and low marks. Sometimes low marks were the result of other actions. I enjoyed a growing appreciation of paperback novels. Tim Udd and several other guys had many exciting novels about the American Wild West. The variety seemed endless. Some were fans of Edgar Wallace or Agatha Christie; detective novels made the rounds. I often read a novel a day, having learned to speed read in order to get through the novels, while not losing time for studies, but my home work was often late.

The result was obvious. Put simply, I wasn't trying hard enough at school and at the end of the second term in my sophomore year I was not allowed to go to *Rendezvous*. I looked on sadly at the other 150 students as they enjoyed roasted corn and then another Moody Science movie in Jubilee Hall.

There were only three others in the back of the truck and it was our responsibility to carry out dirty chores, to help other students enjoy the greatest feast of the term. I loaded more charcoal onto the back of the truck. I looked out of the window of the blue Chevrolet truck and wound the window down as a drizzle fell lightly on the smoke rising from the smoking fire. To the west the sun was going down and to the east, over the top of the escarpment, an angry billow of black cloud swirled in the early evening. A small rainbow momentarily broke through the drizzle, which I took it as a promise from God. If God had made a promise to Noah, then He could be making one to me, too.

"Look, a little patch of blue sky," I said. Pa Entwistle was at the wheel and he looked at me, and I trusted him, as much as anyone. I even wanted to tell him a lot of things, while a strong emotion filled my throat. It was the only *Rendezvous* I ever missed in the eleven straight years at the school. I had not been honest with my teachers. Sitting in the cab of the old Chevy truck brought me close to an adult. I wanted to change the message going home to my parents: "David has an attitude problem. He must stop sassing his teachers." I decided to keep my feelings to myself and wound the window up, without starting a significant conversation about why I had missed out on *Rendezvous*.

CHAPTER 23

MODEL AIRPLANES, PIONEER CAMP AND A STOLEN SALARY

*D*uring the previous year I had become increasingly interested in aviation. Roger Crimson made airplanes at home school, dreamed of them by night and breathed about them by day. He had slim arms and legs and didn't mind getting teased. He laughingly turned distasteful comments about his lack of athletic abilities into jokes about Cesnas and Beachcraft and other aviation topics. No one could dent his good humor; he seemed incapable of hiding a sour, vengeful spirit.

Roger bought his models at toy stores. With infinite care he cut the tiny parts out of balsa wood and glued the fragile structures together, bit-by-bit. The fuselage was made first, then the wings, the ailerons and the tail plane. He covered the wings and the fuselage with a fine paper that shrunk tightly when it dried. His little plane was as light as a feather; he knew how to make it fly and twist, dance and conquer the sky. Roger was more than a craftsman; he was an artist.

* * *

I watched fascinated and wanted to make my own model planes. Back at home, when I had a chance to make my first model plane, I was careless while using the razor to slice through the light balsa wood as I cut against the grain. It was sheer carelessness. I broke several tiny parts that were vital to give the necessary strength to the fuselage. I wasn't as careful, or patient (thorough, as dad would say) as Roger. But, finally, my first plane was been ready to fly.

We stood in our back yard in Limuru, facing a wide, green lawn with Don watching. I wound up the propeller: 88, 89, 90 times. Then, I threw it forward like *Crimson* did and my model plane went up and glided down, the elastic band having done its work of providing the energy to fly. I wanted my tiny craft to land on the flat area used for badminton in our back yard, landing on its two small black plastic wheels, rolling to a stop. A real Beachcraft would have taken a dip and come out of the clouds gracefully.

Instead, my plane landed with a thump on its nose. Then, to see what it could really do, I climbed on the roof and wound it up, 88, 89, 90 times. "I'll just wind up the prop 105 times," I said to Don, who stood close by, thrilled with the first performance of my little craft. I wound it up: 100, 101, 102, 103 times, and then a terrible thing happened. The rubber band was wound too tightly; the model plane collapsed as the propeller snapped against the tail with a shuddering sound. My little Cesna model had imploded in a single, terrible flash. Light-as-air balsa wood parts were crushed in a tangled mess; I could do nothing about it.

* * *

That had been at the beginning of the holidays. Now, here at the end, after working hard, and carefully, I was finishing another balsa model, a Cesna 150. The weather was cloudy and overcast as I set the paper over the wings and glued the last parts together. This time I was very careful with my sharp razor as I cut the tiny balsa wood parts. I didn't break a single part, having learned my lesson the first time. Carefully holding the fuselage in my left hand I finished the project, pushing the dowel through the aft part of the fuselage. The prop was ready to wind up, the rubber band in place. There, my model was ready; tomorrow she was going to fly!

The next day dawned wet and cold and rainy. The monsoon rains had arrived. Not to be put off, I moved all the furniture out of the way in the living room, making a landing space; I stood at the edge of the dining room. I'd have the plane do only a short flight. That way, if it hit some furniture, it wouldn't do any damage. I wound up the propeller: 35, 36, 37 times; there, that was enough. Taking careful aim I let go. The Cessna went better than I could hope, sailing forward, straight as an arrow, then slowing in a flawless landing. The balance was perfect and it rested at the door, where the hall started.

"Yippee!" I called out. "My plane flew perfectly." I ran to pick it up.

At that very second Dot was coming from the kitchen holding a tray of knives, forks and other items to put back in the dining room cupboard. She came into the living room, and as always, she was quick about everything. She hadn't seen the little airplane landing under her feet, so she stepped on it. One wing snapped off, destroyed. Crunch! My little Cesna met with an unexpected fatality on its first flight! I didn't have time to think of what the owners of the Titanic must have felt at their disaster. Facing my misfortune, I exploded, "Why don't you watch where you are going?"

"Why play with your model airplanes in the living room where people come walking through all the time?" was her quick reply. "Anyway, I'm sorry!"

Her question contained sounder logic than mine, but I was bigger and older.

* * *

I was determined not to let things go, but naturally I became even more miserable for not being willing to forgive her. I told myself that I wouldn't let her have the satisfaction of her contrition. A cold rage burned down deep in my heart.

In fact, it got worse as hundreds of new words in spelling class seeped into my study hall assignments. Pa Simmonds demanded good spelling and our best performance. He knew all about SAT tests so he insisted on strict discipline. I tried hard but still had difficulties so he kept me copying those words out, over and over. Once, after I had spent a whole study hall working on impossible English combinations of vowels, he took my masterpiece and tossed it in the waste paper basket without looking at it, which left me with sweaty palms.

* * *

Dad found a way to help me, not with spelling but with "difficult" attitudes. Arrangements were made to go to Pioneer Camp near Eldoret. Dr. Lee Ashton, a good, long-time friend of our family, had worked with dad in Eldoret; many times dad had attended the little Brethren Chapel, not too far from the Eldoret Hospital. Lee Ashton grew up under the influence of young Christian men and women at Cambridge and Oxford; they took responsibility for their Christian lives in university, and now he was the expert in Kenya in directing camps for teens. Dad told me that a scholarship had been arranged for me. When I was 15 I went to Pioneer Camp for the first time.

Pioneer Camp helped me come to understand spiritual truths. Days were loaded with fun, and I appreciated the wonderful skits and the "limy" songs. We sang *It's a long, long way to Tiparary,* and dozens of other British songs, most of which I had never heard. I already knew scores of American folk songs and now I was learning British songs. Here was a new world of music, friendships and variety. An excellent speaker at camp spoke to us with messages based on the book of Joshua. His talk on Achan and the theft of forbidden objects at Ai spoke to me; I had taken books from a bookstore. As the camp went on, I was drawn in in a strange, new and authentic way, to the Christian faith.

We almost fell off our chairs with laughter at some of the skits. In one of them, a strange, huge wonderful rare creature "Rary" grew and grew until it had to be destroyed at the edge of the Grand Canyon. "It's a long, long way to tip a Rary", exclaimed Dr. Ashton as he concluded the skit. We loved this gentle doctor who was so at home with adolescents. I was asked to participate in some of the skits. Camp counselors listened well and I found out that many other students my age also had similar attitude problems.

My only real problem came as I peeled spuds for lunch; I cut off more of the skin of the potatoes than I needed to. Listening to the stories of the British boys studying at other boarding schools in Kenya let me know something of what was going on in their lives. In the afternoons I played on a rugby team. The British boys were much better in the scrum than I was. A few guys spoke lots about sex and drinking, about prostitutes and they seemed to think that swearing had to be included in every sentence.

* * *

The *Rag* after supper was a masterful combination of stories produced with finest British wit. In the on-going story, read each evening, we were treated to the best of *Punch,* Eldoret style. One of the lady counselors was called Miss Paste. She was single. So, in fact was one of the male counselors. The *Rag* recounted their "courting" adventures, as well as those of all the campers. The story finally maneuvered them into a ridiculous situation. "'Squeeze me', he said as he got into the train, 'and I'll meet you out side of the Tube.'"

One needed to know British allusions and American subway terms, sports and literature, French and Latin in order to get all the jokes. Laughs came in so many ways, combining British, American and African words. We campers roared with delight, and approval as each new adventure unfolded on the heels of the events that had happened right up to the tick when we sat down to our evening meal! Keswick and Pioneer Camp, Inter Varsity style, had made a lasting mark upon my life.

On the next-to-last day of camp, one of the white settlers invited us to his farm. He made dozens and dozens of Swedish pancakes for 200 hungry teens. We gobbled them up faster than he and his stout wife could lift them from the hot, blackened stove. We played British Bulldog, which I understood well, and by the end of that afternoon we were sunburnt, tired and thrilled to be part of a community of people who loved the Lord.

* * *

However, a very different event took me past Eldoret less than two weeks later. Dad had continued working with Fanuel from the time he worked in MacKinnon Road and now, he was an experienced colporteur. Fanuel could sit in any market place and, using his knowledge of so many languages, sell Christian literature. He was my hero, able to communicate with Africans, Asians and Arabs all over East Africa.

Fanuel told how some Africans, Luo tribesmen, had been so angry when he set up his Christian bookstand in the market place that they attacked him on a hilly road. They tied him to the frame of his bike. On the back were three large steel trunks, full of Bibles and books in many languages. Fanuel and his bicycle had been thrown over an embankment, but he was saved in a providential fashion. Someone had watched the attack as it occurred and called the police right away.

That was not the only tight corner he had been in. He had dozens of stories that showed God's faithfulness. Fanuel's life had been miraculously saved on more than one occasion and he was one of dad's best colporteurs. They were real colleagues, friends, praying, planning and sharing together.

Mother would pray for Fanuel and his family, "Loving Father, keep Fanuel safe in Thine loving and everlasting arms. We know Thou art able to undertake for him in the many dangers in which Thou hast placed him." I admired Fanuel, this courageous African man with a dozen little mouths to look after at his home across the Ugandan border.

* * *

One day, while we were busy at school, dad became disturbed. His money orders to Fanuel had not been arriving through the Post Office. Fanuel wrote to say that he had gone for many months without a paycheck from the Literature Department.

Dad immediately decided to take a trip to Uganda and I wanted to go with him. We went up country, past Nakuru, Eldoret and across the Ugandan border at Tororo. From there we set out for his little farm. Fanuel was so glad to see dad. They talked in Swahili; dad carried the receipts for the payments made through the Post Office and they learned why the money orders had not arrived. The Post Office manager had been systematically cutting open the registered letters and emptying them. After he had been caught, the manger was in the hands of the police.

Fanuel, though, had gone for ten months without pay. During this time of great trial one of his children, a teenage girl had run away from home with a man from a nearby farm. They had not been found so Fanuel had problems that were more acute than just stolen payments.

Dad preached in Fanuel's little church. There were about forty people in attendance. Even though many folk could not understand everything in dad's Swahili, since they belonged to the Toro tribe, there were six folk who accepted Jesus as their Author and Finisher of their faith at the end of that evangelistic service. Dad was not only good at explaining the gospel, he took every opportunity to teach and preach. His exposition of Hebrews 12:1-2 was understood even by his son in Swahili that day.

* * *

We drove back and I wanted to tell dad about the conflicts I faced at school. He seemed to be in a pensive mood, wondering what was going to happen to his best colporteur, and how to make good on ten months of back salary.

On my part, there was a little imprisoned sentence in my throat. I was bursting to tell him about events at school. Every time that I started to mention anything about girls, I felt a small red fever creeping up my neck. A bit of shyness held me back, though. Another opportunity for sharing and learning from one another was lost.

* * *

My fever was not only caused by a reticence to talk about girls. Dad called a doctor who diagnosed a serious case of malaria. While I dealt with sweat and chills, Paul White, the author of the famous *Jungle Doctor* books, came to visit. He was so bright and cheerful and came into my room and did tricks to cheer me up. He told wonderful stories, too.

After my bout of malaria I noticed I could not easily run those long distances. As I ran towards First Ravine sharp pains stabbed my right side, stopping me in mid-stride. At first I thought it would pass, but the pains started about 10 minutes after I began, so I knew something was wrong. My liver had been affected and for a year I didn't compete in any races.

* * *

The term was already one week old when I sank into my seat at the back of the physics classroom. A flood of emotions hit me. After having visited the African homes in Uganda I wanted to learn Swahili, longing to chat with Africans. I lived in their land but now I began to realize that I knew so little about them. Every tribe was different. People came from larger tribes, such as Kikuyu, Luo, Luhya, Kamba, Kalenjin, Kipsigis, Nandi, Tugen, Marakwet, Gussi and Meru. Altogether forty tribal groups co-existed in the country. I had heard about the Pokot and the Turkana people many times lot since dad's friend, Tom Collins, had worked in that difficult desert region for so many years.

How could God know all those languages? How was it possible for Him to know each African tribe? Did he really care about their customs and fights, their dreams and aspirations? How could God see into the hearts of all those folk, those *wogs* as we called them, and love them all?

Thinking about different tribes made me wonder how God viewed people. For example, if one person obeyed God, then God was happy. If another person disobeyed, then God was sad. Since some people were always disobeying, God was unhappy with them. How could God always be happy and unhappy at the same time? And what happened to "God's heart" when the bad person became good and the good person became bad? I couldn't begin to understand the possible flip-flops that must take place in God's mind. I began to appreciate how God lived beyond the limits of our time and space. The words "eternal" and "infinite" began to come into my vocabulary.

* * *

Leaving theology aside, which only left me with more unanswered questions, I asked mother for a grammar book in Swahili. I wanted teachers at school to help me a little; now I rushed through my homework and opened my Swahili grammar book, trying to learn vocabulary and grammar on my own. Mother also loaned me her manual in Short Hand. Suddenly, playing battleships during study hall was unthinkable. I wanted time to learn Swahili and Short Hand and so much more.

One day, in the library while I was studying lesson three of the Swahili book, I had a new thought. "I am becoming more interested in the words Africans speak. If I think about my self less, and think about others more, then maybe I'll begin to see a change."

CHAPTER 24

THE RADIO TRANSMITTER, CLUBS AND RUGBY

One term I brought my new bike to school. My old bike, which flipped me head-over-heels, needed far more than just a new wheel, so dad bought me a shiny new bicycle with handlebars that bent down and back, a speed bike with ten gears. Dad was all right. He might not be able to get his tongue around "Rubot", said with an American accent, but on the day he bought a new bike that didn't matter at all.

By now a whole row of couples stood on the porch in front of the windows over looking the Valley in the dying hours of the day. Couples could stand there and talk after supper, but not hold hands and certainly not kiss. Boys and girls were supposed to stand 18 inches apart, but I suspected some couples were "out of bounds" on this matter, just as I was in riding my bike outside the school boundaries.

No girl would spend time with me, so a new form of manhood was needed to let girls know a guy was interested. Anyway, I wouldn't know what to talk about with them; I made up for the lack of attention from the girls with experiences on my bike.

Peanut also brought his bike to school that term. There was hardly time now in our schedules. Classes, chapel, dish washing after meals, study hall: each day was full of activities. *Peanut* and I obtained permission from Pa Simmons to ride out to Kijabe Township and around the valley road and back. It was the same route we had taken on our daylong trek four years previous. We tore down the road one day, past the Asian's stores after threading our way around First, Second and Third Ravines.

Careful not to skid on the slippery, grey gravel, which might mean heading over a precipice, we zoomed down to Kedong Plains. The wind blew through our T-shirts; the secrets of the morning were ours alone. We peddled south along the Eldoret-Nairobi highway, past the Catholic chapel, and made it to the entrance to the station. That was as far as we would go up the escarpment road. Those were magical hours, arriving before the noon bell calling us all for lunch.

* * *

With the arrival of the Simmons family the social life improved greatly. Special activities took place on Saturday nights. Most families living on the mission station opened their home for nine clubs: photography, cooking, leather and crafts, radio, sewing, quiet games, Bible Study, dramatics and rifle. Pa and Ma Simmons knew how to get the maximum out of their colleagues, not just from their students.

The Radio Transmitter, Clubs And Rugby

In the Bible Study Club, which I attended one term, we studied the book of Hebrews. We wrestled for weeks over the problems of Chapter 6. Could a person be saved, then lost and saved once more? I had a particular interest in this thorny question since I most definitely did not want to go through the Great Tribulation. My close call with the Rapture in Nairobi gave this question urgency.

It was to the credit of our hosts that they didn't just say, "Look, theologians have been arguing over this for centuries. Here's what they say." Instead, they let us work through that passage in relation to the rest of the book, and in relation to the rest of the Bible. They helpfully directed us to the texts we were trying to find, when we searched for a passage. When asked directly, they gave brief answers. Chapel services, which had seemed so boring, were suddenly a reservoir into which we dipped freely and often.

Where we had hardly been able to sit through a 15-minute message, some of us now debated hotly. Then hot cups of steaming chocolate milk came from the kitchen of our hostess, accompanied by hot coffee cake from the oven. We had to be careful not to burn our tongues, but our hearts were warmed. The Scriptures were becoming so interesting.

* * *

Other lads were in the process of picking up radio skills in receiving and transmitting. They had extra classes on Saturday mornings. I was so proud of *Peanut* and *Rubot* and the other six guys who were attending the Radio Club. Imagine! One day they might even learn to put a transmitter together!

The various clubs were getting better all the time. The Radio Club, for example, was increasing in its scope. The Radio Club demanded more mathematical skill than any of the others and these students even had extra classes, on Saturday mornings.

The radio transmitter was set up in *Rubot's* room, overlooking the little field between our dorm and the Girls' Dorm. Several boys offered to be radio announcers. Everyone who had a collection of records sent them into room "1", on loan of course. The night came that the little home built transmitter was ready to go on the air. The girls were told to turn on their radios after study hall. We all turned on our radios in our rooms and knew that the girls were listening. We lay back on our beds at 9:00 p.m. with freshly boiled sweetened milk. This was the life!

"The Voice of RVA is now broadcasting" came a bright, expressive voice. "Welcome to the opening show of the year." The accent was a perfect imitation of the professional African broadcaster who opened his nightly show, the popular "Top Ten and Your Requests." Everyone knew it was a takeoff on the Voice of Kenya, VoK, the Government Radio station with broadcasting studios in Nairobi.

A second voice came through, a perfect imitation of an Indian Singh, complete with the accent produced by the tip of the tongue flipping backwards. "Try Oatmeal for breakfast", came the announcer. "In case you haven't had oatmeal for breakfast in the last two years, we have just the thing for you to start your day. There aren't more than two toenails in each spoon! It's been perfectly cleaned of husks. Call us and we'll give you a supply for three years for free."

We sat back on our bunk beds and roared with laughter. Oatmeal was our regular breakfast fare. It wasn't always cleaned properly, so frequently it had the feisty husks remaining that were just the texture and size of toenails.

"Now for Number Ten on the hit parade", continued the first announcer, "It is Elvis Presley singing *Jail House Rock*. It comes from 'Grieving Heart' and is sent to Joanne with this message, "Why are you so quiet?" The voice was a matchless imitation of the African Voice of Kenya broadcaster who used every ounce of energy as he went through the Top

Ten every night. His voice was set back in his throat, his mouth open like a cave to produce just the right Kikuyu accent of an African speaking the Queen's English. Elvis was warming up a wind-swept ledge of rock on the edge of a great African Valley.

"Why are you so quiet?" was the Kenyan way that a boy had of saying to a girl, usually through the long distance of a letter to the radio station, "I want to hear from you!" It had to be said with the right polish. A thin veneer of politeness covered just a twinge of accusation. Why would that girl not talk to that boy? Such a message always intrigued, adding mystery: someone's unknown broken feelings were becoming known.

Every night one of the boys, or more than one, would send a message to the Girls' Dorm with the inevitable final refrain, "Why are you so quiet?" *Rubot* read another coded message in a Luo accent. He said, "To Sheila, Mya Dea, Eet ees soo longe dat yuu note tooke too mee. Whyy ees iit? Don'te yuu wante too havee mee wiithe yuu? Don'te bee soo colde. Whyy aa yuu soo quieete? Frome youre brookeen harte." (My dear, it is so long that you not talk to me. Why is it? Don't you want to have me with you? Don't be so cold. From your broken heart.)

Someone said, "Is Jon sending another message to Sheila?" Back came the answer, "Naw, maybe it's *Flappit* sending a message to Martha." Who could be sure? Would she guess who was the admirer? The girl had to figure out who her respective admirer was. She had to decode the references that were made in such an indirect fashion.

At night the brave little radio kept up it alternative accents and wide variety of music. The variety was stupendous: American jazz, Negro Spirituals, Rock and roll, Kenyan Hill Billy, Classical Bach, Country and Western, Roaring '20's. There was even a bit of "jundi", Hindi. No one could accuse our radio station of racial prejudice, of leaving out any form of music, formal or informal.

A British voice would give a summary of the latest news from London. Then an American twang would make an advertisement for Jeans from New Mexico. Finally, we'd move from *Got to Take a Sentimental Journey*, a record from Ted Simmons Jr. collection, to *Swing Low*, a fine rendition from Philadelphia loaned by Mike Hall.

At 9:50 p.m. our little radio transmitter from the Boy's Dorm to the Girl's dorm said "down and out". Lights were out and we all lay in the dark laughing with sides that ached for the next ten minutes. There was so much laughter, and since laughter is the best medicine, hardly anyone got sick that term.

* * *

One day the police arrived. They went to the Principal's office. Herb Downing rubbed his slightly balding head and invited the white soldiers to sit down. The point of the visit was known immediately. "We will come to the point without any formalities, Mr. Downing. It is our duty to report that an illegal radio station is operating in this area. One of our men picked it up by accident when he was down on the plains. At first we couldn't believe it. There are no registered stations in this area. However, we have taken several directional finds, and they all point to just this place."

Herb Downing, a law abiding man, the one who enforced the Point System, making it function like a well regulated clock, promised an investigation.

* * *

The word was out in a flash. At the boy's dorm all the records were returned to their respective rooms. Jazz records went back to Ted Simmons, Jr. Elvis Presley's music was returned to Kenton Fish and finally, most painful of all, the jack was unplugged from the back of the little, home-made broadcasting machine.

Kijabe lost its best accents. Southern, British, Australian, Scottish, South African, German, *Jundi* Asian and *Wog* African: all those accents were lost from the air, blown away with the winds of change. Those fine accents were partially inspired through Pa Simmons' fantastic renditions of *Giuseppe the Barber,* in perfect New York Italian and *Casey at the Bat,* in Boston New England drawl, but how could they be lost from our hearts, our minds, or our tongues?

No one was caught for the inexpensive jaunt into radio-land. No one was punished for the little pirate station. Had anyone maliciously invaded the British public domain, those air waves that were owned by the Kenyan Government? Who could have guessed that the Government "owned" radio waves? Or, that within the small confines of RVA mission station something illegal, of that magnitude, was going on?

The mixture of voices of British police, New York Negroes, Western cowboys: all of those were just innocent pranks, weren't they? But what a lesson! You could be out of bounds even when you were in bounds!

So we lost our little radio station and that night we laughed in the dark. *Sausage* said it best, pronouncing his obituary for the little radio station, on which his brother *Peanut* was one of the stars. The lights were off the voice came in a marvelous African accent, a final tribute in five heart-felt words, "Why are you so quiet?" Then we roared in laughter and hit the sack. Who could know what tomorrow, or next term, might bring?

* * *

We were always proud of our running. We thought that we could run well; after all, we had soccer and basketball and track and field. We even imagined ourselves as athletes, that is, until Dave Reynolds arrived as a new teacher. Dave's parents had been pioneer missionaries in the olden days. Dave's older brother had died as a young man. The Reynolds family had made a name for missions, having come from South Africa and working in the highlands, around Eldoret. Then the family went back to South Africa.

Now Dave arrived, an adult, seen as taking the place of his father. That he arrived with a limp was not a surprise; his leg had been affected by polio. He had overcome the handicap and he was an enthusiast in physical training to build up muscles. He ate rugby and slept rugby. He even dreamed rugby, and, when there was nothing else to dream of, he dreamed of restoring antique and vintage cars. He had part of his father's blood in him at any rate; he had that connection with the olden days.

When there was nothing left to dream about in rugby, and when there was nothing left to be done in renewing the upholstery or putting a new steering wheel into a Model T Ford, Dave descended to the earthly level. At such times he became our chemistry teacher.

* * *

Coach Reynolds didn't lack in the competition department of his mind. He wanted to form *two* rugby teams to compete against other schools in Kenya. Each team, the "A" team, and the "B" team, needed fifteen players and this was a challenge, but he was up to it since there were only thirty boys in the high school dorm. There were about another seven boys in the homes of the kids that lived on station. His pool of available material was extremely limited. Unlike the Prince of Wales, which had almost 500 boys and the Duke of York, with its 450 residents, our Coach started from a disadvantage.

No matter. Even with his short leg, Coach Reynolds had made it into the South African Springboks, the top professional team of South Africa. He showed us how to do a scrum "properly" one day. It was a rainy day and we had to practice indoors. We pushed the tables aside where we usually spent our evenings bent over our textbooks during study hall. He formed two scrums, determined to show how to do things "properly". We crouched down, eight on a side.

"Push!" he yelled. The sides were equal, but he was not satisfied that we had found our potential so he stood in the place of one guy in the second row. He straightened his weak leg and set his strong leg at the "proper" angle.

"Push!" he yelled as we huddled in the scrum, pushing against him. He almost had us out through the glass windows behind us before he stopped. "What's the matter with you guys? You don't know how to scrum properly!" He accentuated his limp back to his chair. If he could do that against us, and do it with a partially withered leg, and if we were whole, what were we capable of doing? Coach Reynolds had strange teaching methods but after that demonstration we had a higher standard against which to judge our achievements.

Still not satisfied, he said we needed extra training. Our "warm up" run consisted of running down the hill to the roundabout between the Pa Cook's printing press and Pa Teasdale's Bible Institute, then up the long hill around the missionary's residences, up the still steeper hill past the single ladies' house, past Jubilee Hall and the Downing's home, and then back to the goal posts where he waited with stopwatch in hand. Coach Reynolds still wasn't satisfied with our progress! "If you ran 'properly' you could get it done in the same time as running around this field!" The playing field was level. The three-mile track he made us use was torture. How could we run up and down steep hills?

For him this was just a warm up but he was up to the challenge of forming an "A" XV team and a "B" XV team. In order to do this he had to persuade 80% of the healthy teens to risk their necks, arms and legs. Anyone who could persuade almost all the *big guys* to take their lives in their hands had charisma.

* * *

A few fellows couldn't, or wouldn't, take on the majestic calling in life that rugby demands: crushing your shoulder bone against the on-coming femur of an opponent twice your weight, tackling a heavy full back as he slams his outstretched palm into your nose, risking damage to any part of your unprotected body. Those were just the incidental risks of attempting to make a try. Coach Reynolds got his two teams, but I was still so thin that he put me on the "B" XV. The "A" XV was the better team.

We had five weapons on our side. One was George Belknap's mighty hoof. He could boot a ball from any where inside the half, the centerline. Any infraction by the other team could cost them their lead. Since we only had a few guys to act as back up, George was like the secret-weapon that an army uses to inspire fear in the enemy.

Our second weapon was the altitude. Kijabe stands at 7,200 feet, while Nairobi is lower, at 5,000 feet. Since Kijabe was so much higher than Nairobi, we were generally in fitter condition and could run circles around our opponents after the second half.

Mike Hall and Hal Boone were also secret weapons. A British team came, having spent too much time in the pubs, not enough time in the gym. Perhaps that was why I gazed with eyes open at their over-hanging bellies. With their extra weight they could push our scrum back to our goal line at will. However, Mike Hall would weave and jump, thread a fraction of an empty space, lope across a field, intercept a pass and then flog them for another loss. With Mike, Hal, Danny Schellenberg in the backfield, and Ray Davis as left wing, we had a team as swift as a herd of gazelles. Our backfield more than compensated for our lightweight scrum.

Overall, then our weaknesses and advantages averaged out. We were lighter in the scrum so the opposing side got the ball more often. However, with guys more agile, much quicker in the backfield, we always stood a good chance of winning. When it came to lineouts we had taller guys, and our lack of experience was compensated by having to bend into the constant wind of Kijabe. Rugby demands that constant bending forward into instant danger and we transferred our energies into a Renyolds-sized desire to win. When all else failed, *Sausage*, our fifth secret weapon, was our full back. That was one time in the game when it was good to have *Sausage* on your side.

* * *

Our first game was played on the African playing field because our rugby field was not yet finished. The visiting team from Nairobi won, much to our chagrin. We couldn't get over the pace of how fast the scrums were formed and how fast the ball was thrown in on a line out. We still had so much to learn and so we were thrilled that Coach Reynolds had come to RVA to teach rugby. We didn't mind it when he taught us the mysteries of Chemistry, a subject that he mastered as well as restoring his old cars.

We lost again, in Nairobi, in the second game, but then we began to win. The other teams, although drawing from a larger pool of players, began to fall to worse defeats. We played Saint Mary's Academy, Prince of Wales, Duke of York, and other teams. Within a very short time rugby became a passion. With rugby and basketball competitions now taking up Saturdays and clubs filling our free evenings we found RVA had too many options, too many things to occupy our time.

* * *

I was on the Young People's committee, which meant trying to think up interesting Christian programs for the Sunday night activities. Later on in the year, before I finished the Tenth Grade, or sophomore year, elections were held in Westervelt Dorm.

One of my friends nominated me as a sub-prefect, which meant that I would have to impose the Point System, be a model of Christian behavior and set a high standard. When the nomination was made I felt an urge to speak up; I should have said, "You don't know what you are doing. I'm not the person to enforce the Point System! Please withdraw the nomination!" That's what I should have said, but the second passed quickly; my name was written the board and the election proceeded.

By the end of that Friday evening I had something else to ponder. Lying flat on my back I looked up at the dark ceiling. Starting in my junior year I was to be one of two sub-prefects. Next September would come and I would have to be a different person. I was amazed that people had placed trust in me for the responsibility of upholding the Point System.

* * *

It was almost holiday time again and the next term I would be in Grade Eleven, starting my junior year. Mom and dad had booked the AIM bungalow at the beach in Mombasa. We took the train, called the Boat Train, from Nairobi. This train was timed to arrive in Mombasa with time to spare, unloading passengers who were leaving on the next sailings to Europe and other destinations.

Unfortunately, our train stopped in the middle of the night. We were in Voi, half way to the ocean. A train had become derailed after hitting an elephant. That cargo, three miles towards the coast, was a load of cattle. We waited all day in the hot sun of Voi until a repair crane lifted broken cattle wagons back onto the tracks. Water on our train reached the price of gold. When we did get going, the next night, the engine pulled the train slowly past the place where a hapless cargo had met its death. Below us, beside the tracks near the bridge, the presence of dead cattle made itself known, in spite of complete darkness. The smell of rotting carcasses filled our nostrils and I coughed for many minutes.

Mombasa was awash in the endless splashing of waves, the eternal joy of the rise and fall of tides. When the tide went out we waded in the tidal pools, examining the colorful sea creatures, and when the tide came in we swam along the edge of the shore. Dot was learning to swim; we tried to swim further each day. It was hard to hold a grievance against her at such a moment. After all, her stepping on the fragile wing of my model plane had been an accident. I didn't express forgiveness but I showed her many species of sea cucumbers and starfish. Don found endless varieties of shells and sea life. The tidal pools were an exploding mixture of green seaweed, little colored fish, rippling waves in the breeze and tiny crabs with their eyes constantly moving, forever on the lookout for trouble.

* * *

One day, the sun beat down with such intensity that it was almost impossible to bear the heat. On the ferry to the city of Mombasa we watched a Muslim lady dressed in black, calmly holding her child, looking out through just her tiny window of space. Even her nose was safely tucked away out of sight of the glances of men folk.

African men heaved sacks full of grain onto their backs and walked down steep gangplanks in the old harbor of Mombasa. Their black backs, covered with fine yellow dust, ran wet as long rivulets of sweat grew during the increasing heat of the day. African men heaved bags off their shoulders into the holds of old wooden Arab dhows.

Arab merchants supervised the African workers. The dhow's single mast supported an old, dirty sail that flapped lazily. The dhows sailed with the monsoons, from Asia to Africa, returning as seasonal winds changed direction. Some of these Arab merchants watched from the quay, wearing ankle-length, sparkling white robes and twisted, black rope holding a headpiece in place as protection from the sun.

Indian agents wore turbans, red and white and yellow, an amazing variety of silken beauty. On their fingers they wore shiny gold rings with green and red stones. Some sparkled in the sunlight for a tiny second, bright as the sun playing with its own lights bouncing off the waves. The scene took me back to Sinbad, the Sailor, whose stories of magic and far off lands seemed to be alive just beyond the enchantment of Old Mombasa Harbor. The entire scene was a tide of humanity where Islam, African tribal religion and European civilization came together in little pools, much as the tidal pools boasted many species of life. The Muslim religion was strong here, with calls to prayer sounding five times a day. These calls stopped and a few minutes later loud, raucous voices bartered for better prices. Arabs and the Indians dominated the commercial areas of life, while Africans bore the brunt of the burden in moving goods from one place to another.

* * *

How was it that some people settled down into printing, others into banking, still others into trading at sea? How did some people, like the Brits, gain colonial power? Why did others, like the coastal Africans, accept colonial rule, whether that of the British now, the Portuguese before them, or the Arabs, hundreds of years before?

So many questions went through my mind. I asked dad how Africans came to be subservient to Arabs, Indians and Europeans. Back at home, during vacation, the talk around the table-talk turned to who the first president of Kenya would be. The general consensus was that Jomo Kenyatta would become Kenya's first president in spite of his association with the Mau Mau, and connections with Moscow.

The British were there to enforce democracy; they had to respect the wishes of the people who were setting up their government. Dad seemed reticent to talk more about his political views, saying he had come as a missionary. That meant he had to stay away from "political chitchat"; obviously, Kenya's future was "political chitchat".

However, at night, after we were supposed to be in bed I occasionally heard dad and mom chatting about their fears of the future, then praying for the country. I drifted off to sleep, sometimes worried by what could happen if things went wrong, sometimes comforted by the fact that God would take care of the new country.

CHAPTER 25

ENFORCING THE POINT SYSTEM, AND THE LASSE FAMILY

*V*acation was over too soon and I returned to school as a sub-prefect. Certain things automatically brought points off. One was arriving with scruffy shoes at inspection at 6:25, just before breakfast. One day, I decided that I was going to put into practice the teaching of my father and the increasing good influence of Dave Reynolds, to do things "properly". Just before breakfast everyone stood in two lines to make sure that uniforms were properly done up. I walked down the *back* of the line my fellow students, not the front, examining the back of students' shoes instead of the toes.

All the guys were in a straight line up, their hands at their sides. I spotted dirt on the back of Tim Udd's shoes. He hadn't been doing things "properly"!

"Aha," I pounced. "Points off for not polishing your shoes," I was jealous of his good marks and here was a way to get one up on him.

"I polished them," he growled.

"Points off," I pronounced pointedly. As he went to breakfast I went to his room, found his closet and Point Card and wrote in the appropriate column, "-.1"

When I arrived after breakfast he had erased the mark. I wrote it back and a day later it had disappeared again. He did not respect my authority. So I wrote it down again. Once more it was wiped from history. The space on the card was getting a bit thin, ragged and worse for wear. When I went in to write it down once more, he stood in the way.

I looked at his shoes. They were polished. It was just the time to call a "truce". Since he had learned to polish his shoes properly, there was hardly any more reason for taking those points off.

The days were bright. Points off were being taken off as Ray Davis and Malcolm Collins and I inspected shoes, uniforms and beds, making sure everything was in order.

* * *

I'd had a crush on each of the girls in my class at least once, probably in alphabetical order, too: Andrea, Diane, Linnea, Patricia, and Ruth. Since there was still no girl with whom I could stand on the porch to watch the dying minutes of each day I decided to compensate in another way.

* * *

Since I was sub-prefect, I gave myself permission to "go out of bounds" (there were side benefits to this position) and headed down to the plains on my bike. I went on the same route as my escapade years before when we found so much bubble gum. Up the hill I raced at the turn to the Kijabe Township. It was a long trip up hill, climbing almost 1,000 feet. My weight flipped from one side of the bike to the other. I had visions of myself climbing the Alps, chasing the leader on the Tour de France race. The others would trail behind me. Dreams filled my head, for I'd be catching the rider with the yellow shirt, who would be just a half a wheel ahead of me. All the other 200 bikers would struggle to catch up. Then, just ten meters from the end of the day's run, I'd catch up and pass by, winning by the slimmest of margins. Tomorrow I'd wear the yellow shirt.

My daydreaming ended just then. My handlebars broke and I fell of the bike. The metal of the handlebars couldn't take the stress of racing up the eastern flank of the Rift Valley. Getting back just in time for supper was the least of my problems. I had to run all the way pushing a broken bike. How could I explain that I had to take points off my own point card? Sir Walter Raleigh had, unknowingly, lent his name to the bicycle industry in Great Britain, but materials used in manufacture of export items were inferior to his character and his famous name.

* * *

There was a fine mechanic at our school, who used wrenches and screw drivers and every kind of tool. Whenever the lights faded slightly, a sure sign that the diesel generators were just breaking down during study hall, he shot off his seat, a rocket who hit the door of the generating station just as the begrudging motor was initiating its final sputter. We owed our two hours of uninterrupted study every night to his constant running back and forth to the diesel engines.

I decided to ask him to fix my bike. "Can you fix my bike?" I asked. He wasn't one for rugby or long hikes. He preferred to look face at the bottom of a car engine parked about three inches above his nose. "Yes, I'll do that in return for your washing my socks during a whole term." He knew how to bargain.

Having no choice, I had to make a considerable concession to my pride. I washed more dirty socks that term than ever before. His socks had an added weight; they kept getting full of grease. His heavy woolen socks would have made good protection for Russian and American explorers, who were arriving at the Arctic Pole in the International Geophysics Year of Global Exploration.

I learned something important through that event. Bargaining demanded a quick mind and ability to trade, either physical assets or skills. Because I was slow in arriving at conclusions, my bargaining abilities could only go one way, towards improvement. He got his socks cleaned for 13 weeks; I got my bike fixed once. I thought it humorous that he wanted clean socks so he could slide under another dirty car chassis.

* * *

By now, I had become accustomed to the cycles of terms and holidays. Life with Dot, Pearl and Don at home meant family outings, trips to Nairobi, showing an evangelistic film to the neighbors in Limuru and enjoying Mombasa.

In contrast, life at *swot* meant endless chapel services, classes, study hall and meals predictable for their monotony. Laundry still came back a little bit damp, especially during the rainy season. One accepted designated chores, such as taking our place on the dishwashing teams and cleaning up after meals.

We lived in two worlds. Our relationship as siblings almost vanished at school, unless we took intentional steps to include each other. I was David at home and *Flappit* at school. Mom and dad knew almost nothing of what really went on at school. It was the same the other way around. None of my teachers or classmates knew what a paradise we lived in. Not only that, though; who knew that mom employed twelve widows each day, working half a day and receiving a full day's wages, thus enabling about 70 people to live because those women tilled the fields and then kept the harvest for their children?

* * *

By now our class had a huge store house of memories tucked away: field trips to the Museum in Nairobi, the Wattle Factory, annual trips to the Hodson's farm, the Agricultural Fair Ground, the Billy Graham Evangelistic Meetings, and Saturday trips to Nairobi, only 40 miles away. Hundreds of visitors had come to the school for brief visits of a day or two, including some well-known names in the Christian world.

Tim Udd said something about his home area one day and I was amazed to see how much he knew about Nyasaland. I knew of his skills as a speed-reader. Quiet and serious, he had the best grasp of general knowledge in our class. I realized one day how little I knew about him, or any of the personal lives of our students in their own home locations.

Tim Udd, Dan Shellenberg, Ray Davis and Jon Arensen kept us entertained with the quartet they had organized; Carol Schuit, Sheila Propst and Winnie Brown sang as a girls' trio, and occasional trumpet trios were played at chapel by Bob Hollenbeck, David Ness and Dan Shellenberg. The choir had more than 32 lovers of music, learning new vocal skills under the direction of Pa Hollenbeck. The band, which was learning to march in formation on the sports field, was complete with about 35 musicians. With special contributions needed for chapel, Sunday School, church and young people's meetings every week witnessed the constant expansion of musical talent.

Junior-Senior banquet opened me to American culture even more. The theme chosen for the banquet was "Song of the South". David Campbell entertained us with spontaneous humor as a Mardi Gras fortune teller. Pa Simmons, for the evening changed into the person of Senator Fogbound W. Claghorn III, introduced us to subtle shades of truth-telling, those only a Southerner would know. RVA's social life was growing.

Junior-Senior Banquet was a smashing, and delicious, success at the end of the last term. The only thing wrong, of course, was that I had to take another twenty shillings out of my life savings, using the money to buy a new pair of grey pants. How could I tell mother and dad that I didn't like the clothing they bought for me; that, if I wanted ask a girl to go to the Banquet with me, I needed a certain kind of grey pants? My Life Savings was evaporating quickly.

* * *

For a while all interest in pranks disappeared. Competition for influence in the world seemed fairly balanced, until Russia launched Sputnik. The *big guys* became more interested in rocketry, but teachers stubbornly refused to add another club to the Friday night activities around the mission station. Rocketry was going too far.

The disappointment of not being able to delve deeper into rocket science was made up for in two ways, one passive and one active. The passive means was through reading. *Popular Science, Popular Mechanics* and other journals kept us abreast of extraordinary new developments. *National Geographic* took us to far-away places.

The time came to begin talking about sending a man into space and Westervelt Dorm had its own method of winning the Cold War. Americans and the Russians may have possessed superior financial resources, but nothing could beat RVA ingenuity.

A small hole was bored through a tin can and the fuse of a firecracker stuck out, awaiting its match. The tin can, when placed on a bowl of water, went straight up in the air after a small explosion. The purpose of the water under the tin can was to direct the thrust inside the can in only one direction: high into the air. When a small bug, such as a ladybug or grasshopper was placed on top of the tin can, the sudden explosion of the firecracker launched that unsuspecting species into near-space. President Kennedy didn't know to what extent he had inspired teenaged boys, joyful in their briefly successful launches. Perhaps we didn't see a human go into far-away-space, but the thrills of tin cans exploding above Westervelt Dorm matched the excitement felt at Cape Canaveral.

The Cuban Crisis came and went with prayers being said daily in chapel and especially on Sunday afternoons. Meanwhile, news from the Southern States brought new ideas about civil rights and marches for justice. Massive change was in the air, not only across Africa, where colonies were becoming countries, but in the USA as well.

Suddenly, the assassination of President Kennedy in 1963 hurled the entire mission station into a state of shock. By this time I was well aware of the significance of current events; we were constantly glued to the radio, listening for every angle on the story. Everyone commented on the calamity. I felt sorry for American friends whose president had suffered such a needless fatality. A cloud hung over the school for weeks. The ongoing story gripped us all, and in a flash I felt as if my president had been killed.

* * *

At the end of Grade Eleven I went on a hike to think things over. I began to realize how selfish I really was. How could I be sub-prefect again, in Grade Twelve? I needed to get a lot of things straightened out in my life. Before nominations began I stood up to declare that I would not accept any position in Westervelt Dorm.

It was time to take stock. I was now one of the *big guys* but it didn't feel important. I would soon be studying in Canada, although I didn't have any ideas confirmed.

Don had reached Grade six. The day that he learned to tie his own shoes seemed so long ago now. Why, he and his classmates, Martin Downing, Peter Eklund, Kenneth Lewton, Curtis Teasdale and Robert would soon catch up to Doug Adkins, Meryl Bainbridge, David Beatty, James Ness, John Propst, Thomas Shumaker, Allan Davis and Paul Frew. I wasn't familiar enough with the girls in his class to know their names, but in a few years they would all be known as the *big guys*!

Taller than most of his classmates, Don was now one of the leaders of a little group. He commanded respect by his easy, informal manner. I enjoyed those few quick moments when I slipped him soggy toast, covered with jam, as I left breakfast. It was against the rules to pass food to those lined up, waiting to get in, but I couldn't remember anyone getting points off for passing food on to younger brothers.

Pearl was in Grade eight, a budding musician. I had been so proud of her when she was received her certificate for the Presidential Physical Fitness program. President Kennedy believed in setting a common standard for students: running, throwing, jumping and other activities. There she was, struggling with a handicap of a brace, and keeping up to almost all the kids her age. I almost burst with pride when I learned how well Pearl had done. She had a happy disposition that I wished was mine. She wrote stories and understood words so well. Many of Pearl's classmates had the same surnames as those who had already graduated, or were in school at the time: Vic Downing, Liz Allan, Amelia Smuck, Dale Dorrell,

Cam Arensen, Steven Barnett, Harry Johnson, Carol Schumaker, Carol Waggoner and Jim Propst. Almost all of her class signed their names on my copy of the year book; they were an outgoing group, now moving into Grade Eight.

Dot was "standing on the porch" after supper, which meant she had a boyfriend. Being sociable was definitely one of her strong points, even as a Grade Nine student. I could see her becoming more popular all the time. I didn't know if mother and dad knew about her boyfriend, so I stayed away from that subject at home. Her classmates, like mine, had moved up to the senior dorms and their abilities were already being noticed: Steve Schellenberg, Rebecca Mills, Beth Ann Glock, Lee Downing, Carol Barnett, Phyllis Dilworth, Susan Boone, John Carlson, Carl Ebeling, Mary Johnson, Steve Machamer, Ruth Belknap, Betty Ann Campbell and Harold Dorrell. RVA's enrollment included family units with many families having three, four or more students across the grades. Dot's classmates were almost all siblings of students in the other grades.

* * *

Perhaps the awareness of African tribes and customs, the changing political times in Kenya and the rest of Africa, as well as missionaries in family units with siblings at school combined to make me feel more sociable and outgoing. Maybe the change came, too, because of ongoing hospitality of the teachers and mission staff who often served us hot cookies or coffee cake after Sunday School.

"We were going to start off the year in a big way," stated Dave Reynolds with a confidence that had grown with each win, both at home as well as away. He obviously had been dreaming of rugby during the long weeks in August. He had acquired several vintage cars and these *jitneys* were parked under trees beside his house. One of them was parked in the direct sun; this Model T beamed after hundreds of hours of shining dedication. The seats sparkled, upholstered with new brown leather. The black, thin, almost-new tires, gleamed in the sun, were ready for service, but not a church service.

"Isn't Dave Reynolds' home a great place to come to after Sunday School?" I was whispering to *Peanut* one Sunday morning, visiting his home. I added, "Dave is generous with his home and Bobby is a good sport to go along with all his crazy ideas." Bobby had served us tea. She was quieter than Dave. At least a dozen of us sat in a circle, making ourselves at home in their living room. Some read *Life* magazine, others chatted with Dave about his dogs.

"Why don't you go out and warm up the tea for us, *Flappit*?" instructed Dave as he talked about rugby with some of the guys. I felt privileged and went to their kitchen, turning on Bobby's electric stove. I placed her gorgeous china teapot on the center of the red-hot element and went back into the living room to wait for hot tea.

He sure was a cool guy. How was it that we referred to most people by the name Pa or Ma, while you could never make Pa stick to Coach Dave Reynolds? Conversations in the living room varied from one corner of the room to the other. Someone was talking about new *gogs*, or glasses, and how much *jink*, or money, it would cost to restore Dave's *jitneys*. New clothes, boyfriends and homework were the topic for some. I was plowing through *Life* magazine when a horrible clatter came from the kitchen. Bobby Reynolds came running back into the living room in and her voice was quivering, "Our best china tea pot is in a hundred pieces all over the top of the stove!" Everyone went rushing in to the kitchen to see the mess. I couldn't even warm up a pot full of tea properly! Dave could fix a thousand parts on an old, broken Model T; his wife could make a dozen teens feel at home, but all I could do in the warmth of their home was to ruin her best teapot. Lanny Arensen, Joe Friberg, Mary Barnett, Jon Salseth, Irene Lincoln and Janet Johnson, and a dozen others, had witnessed my inability to do anything right in the kitchen.

"Well, if I wasn't good at things in the kitchen," I deliberated as I climbed the hill very crushed, "what was I good at? How do you find out what God wants you to do in your life?" I'd heard Proverbs 3:5,6 and a hundred other verses in the Bible about finding God's will for you. But when it came right down to it, I didn't have a clue as to what God wanted me to do after RVA.

* * *

Carpentry? No that was out, because I bent nails before they were fully embedded in the two-by-fours. Being a cowboy, breaking in horses was impossible; I couldn't even ride a donkey. Aviation? I had no success in that area; I couldn't keep a model in the air. Mechanics? No, I couldn't stand looking at engines just three inches from my nose. Some guys enjoyed keeping the diesel engines going, providing the station with electricity, but I didn't like getting my hands blackened in grease. Science? My marks in physics hadn't been bad, but I had to work for them so hard that I knew that this would not be a career for me.

Perhaps sports? I had been on the "A" XV now but no one even had to compete against me for my position in the scrum. Dave practically begged us to get on the team.

Besides that, recently I had twisted my ankle on a line out, practicing an illegal move in rugby, having someone boost me in the air, lifting me by the rugby shorts. An extra three or four inches extra height in the lineout made the difference in retaining possession of the ball; getting it back to our running backs. I had practiced the illegal move many times. Once, as I went up high, I lost my balance slightly. My ankle snapped and I lay on the ground. My ankle, which stayed swollen for weeks, kept me out of the game for the rest of the season. "Both Dave and Bobby Reynolds are disappointed in me," I thought as I climbed the hill back to Westervelt Dorm. I didn't have a broken ankle, but the pain kept me out of the game.

* * *

New teachers had arrived, among them Geraldine Stocum, or Gerry, as people called her. She was an extremely gifted musician. Her hands simply danced on the keyboard of a piano and her knowledge of music was vast. The first time I heard her my eyes opened wide and my mouth hung open. Jerry had been saved as an adult. Having been in nightclubs for many years before coming to Christ, she brought unusual skills with her when she found God taking her to Africa; one of her skills was theater. Like the oither teachers, her glass frames were dark, with a slight shape of sea gull wings. Her caring personality and broad smile were needed for teaching boys and girls who were 12 and 13 years old; I knew her best as the sponsor of the dramatics club. How could one aspire to anything less than excellence when she could play almost any musical piece ever written in America, and play it with adrenaline-added bounce, at that?

Shortly after arriving she announced that she was going to hold tryouts for a three-act play, *The Barretts of Wimple Street.*

Gerry Stocum held the tryouts in her house, located between the Propst home and the KLD dorm. All the roles in the play were available; I wanted a role requiring a good bit of versatility. I was to be Mr. Barrett, the father of Elizabeth. In the true story, Elizabeth was being won over by Robert Browning, the famous English poet, and, as the father of Elizabeth, Mr. Barrett discouraged, opposed and forbid the relationship. Of course, he was unsuccessful and eventually Robert and Elizabeth eloped. I, as the severe, authoritarian father, was left thwarted, stricken by the power of love between the two well-known English writers. The story was a true one, inspiring very deep feelings in the audience.

The three-act play, *The Barretts of Wimple Street,* was presented in Jubilee Hall and, it was well received by the missionary community on the mission station as well as many guests from other places.

My problem, which I did not tell others, involved intense nervousness. I had trouble remembering my lines. They were important, since my character, Mr. Barrett, was supposed to stop the infirm, but beautiful daughter, Elizabeth, from marrying such a rascal as that nasty Robert Browning. I left out one line, halfway through the play; other actors picked up after me as if nothing had happened. My memory failed me at a critical point in the baptism, and now, again, I didn't have the memory required for acting. I would never find my livelihood as an actor. I didn't have enough confidence in being on stage and I had a weak memory; many events showed up my poor abilities in that regard.

Kenton Fish was singing solos all the time now, so I knew he would go into music, but he was not part of our graduating class, for both he and Crimson, who was headed for aviation, were doing their senior year in the States. Carl Barnett, Mary Barnett, Sheila Hutchinson, Danny Schellenberg and Faith Stauffacher had also spent time in our class over the years, and they too were graduating from other high schools in the USA, so seven of my friends had already gone away.

Andrea Propst had developed a sickness and graduated later from RVA; I felt so sorry for her being part of a family whose father was a doctor, but not being able to graduate with us.

Hal Boone was interested in medicine and we knew he would become a doctor. He was miles ahead of me; Latin and medical terms were beyond me. Ray Davis did well in math so, *natch*, a career in engineering was up his alley. Danny Schellenberg excelled in soccer and he might be a star in a USA college. Dianne Dilworth, Ruth Schuit and Linnea Johnson each had a future in nursing. Bob Hollenbech wanted to go into the military; he'd do well waking soldiers up each morning with his brilliant trumpet call.

It seemed that half the graduates from RVA went to study in Wheaton or Biola: Wheaton, Illinois, if your parents could afford that college, or Biola, if your parents came from Southern California. Students from the USA had their future decision taken care of, even if the final decision of a career was postponed another four years.

So, how could you understand what God wanted you to do? Did the Lord start speaking in dreams? Did he really "hit you over the head with a Bible verse", as one ex-graduate said one day in chapel as he returned to see his old stomping grounds?

* * *

I decided to talk to Phil Lasse about it. Phil and Shirley Lasse were two of the kindest souls at RVA. Phil's fingers painted unbelievably meaningful paintings. Phil and Shirley were living in a rented house and decided to build their own house about a hundred yards below the out-door baptistery. I admired Phil almost like a father, and in order to help him I accepted his offer to help dig the foundations for their new house. I watched him set the square lines in place to set the location of the trenches that would form the foundations of his Kijabe home.

One day he showed me how he did his artwork. He worked in the office close to the printing press. "When it's time, God will show you what to do," said Phil. "God always takes care of you, and he tells you what you need to know for just this little bit of a time.

Make a list of the things that you do best and show it to God. Do the best with what you have right now. In the future God will show you more."

I listened even more closely to devotions at their house. Their kids were still young, but Phil read through a lengthy chapter in II Chronicles. I deeply admired this Christian family that made me feel so comfortable in their home.

* * *

Special speakers often came to speak at RVA. Corrie ten Boom spoke at church one afternoon, riveting me with her story of having been imprisoned for helping Jews escape from the hands of Nazi cruelty. She held up a tapestry, showing how the threads on one side hid the real picture and then turned the picture to us, hiding the loose ends.

About the same time I began to listen more carefully to the messages brought by Howard O. Jones, Pastor Harrison, Jimmy MacDonald and a full week of meetings by Mr. Herringshaw.

* * *

When the time came for us to choose all the positions for the senior class, there was excitement in the air. We were in the classroom where I had passed so many hours; Clara Barrett had taught me here, then Verity Coder and finally Trumbal Simmons. That room was inextricably bound up in my mind with spelling lists, grammar workbooks and, best of all, the hot fireplace. Sometimes the fire was so hot that it burned one's legs. Jonathan Machamer was chosen to plan senior safari. He needed three people to help him.

Finally, the position of editor of the year book came up for election. Everyone had already been assigned to some job or other. There seemed to be no one left for the year book. I accepted the nomination and five minutes later was in charge of preparing the *1964 Kiambogo*. It meant working closely with Phil Lasse. Several students were skilled in photography so they could shoot photos to record events during the year. Sports days and rendezvous were recorded in pictures, as well as many other scenes around RVA.

CHAPTER 26

SENIOR SAFARI

Sports Day and Rendezvous were the best part of every term because they signaled the end of a 13-week stay in the dorms. However, there was an event that we looked forward to more than anything else. Senior safari topped everything. It signaled the end of our time at RVA, time for the senior class to sneak away undetected from the other students. At the end of each year, sometime in the final term, the entire senior class would sneak away at night. Senior safari meant being given permission to go "way out of bounds", not just with permission, but also with the blessing of the administration.

Preparing for senior safari was like getting one's first passport. It signified a turning point, a new identity, an affirmation that young adulthood was real. Our teachers would not have to teach Grade 12 classes for a week. Pa and Ma Simmons, our class sponsors, would be with us the whole time. We would be leaving school in the back of an open truck, heading for a distant place, living in tents and having our own adventure. This would be a trip surpassing all other RVA events.

The rules were unwritten, but everyone knew them. Seniors had to wait patiently, never speculating about the date. On the day before the trip we would be told where to go. A truck would be waiting for us, hidden somewhere on the station. We knew it would happen, but the day and the hour were unknown to us, except for the three seniors who had planned it all in conjunction with our class sponsors. This seemed even more exciting than the Rapture.

* * *

Graduation was only another three months away. A shiver of both exhilaration and fear went down my back. How did anyone plan the future? Why didn't dad talk to me about what would happen to me after I left RVA? Why didn't mom ever give her opinions about studying in college in Canada?

I would not go to England to study. That was out of the question and I had no connection in the States to Moody, Biola, or any other school so university there was impossible. That left only one possibility: Canada. That left me satisfied; I didn't need a clearer definition about my future.

* * *

Each of the students in the graduating class of '64 received an assignment before the yearbook was typeset. Each one stated their extra-curricular activities, where they were going to study in the States and wrote a few words as a final statement.

There was one advantage to being the editor of the school year book. I had a crush on a girl named Martha. She didn't like me so I couldn't very easily ask her for her picture to keep in my wallet. One day, in the dark room where the pictures were being developed for *Kiambogo*, I asked the photographer for six pictures. He picked five at random. I pointed to another one. The sixth picture was a portrait of girl I was interested in.

Martha didn't even know that I had her portrait.

I showed the picture to mother over the Christmas holidays, taking care to not tell her how I had come by it. Perhaps I was progressing; I hadn't really stolen the picture. It was a "right" of mine as yearbook editor to see the pictures before they were printed up. Every disadvantage in life must have an advantage, I told myself. Her picture was tucked into the cover of my Bible. In the photo she had a fleeting smile playing at the corner of her lips and I felt a slight ache in my heart.

* * *

Only three people in our class knew the destination of senior safari, when it was to start, and how it was to be arranged. They would carry out all the arrangements. No other student was to find out. If a student from the junior class learned, then the Grade 11 guys would do everything possible to prevent us from leaving. If word got out, we might find that the Grade Eleven students had removed the battery from the truck. The tires could be flat. Perhaps something worse might happen. Not even the seniors dating juniors could tell their girlfriends when they would see them again.

At the beginning of term we brought a special kit, which included clothes and blankets. I gave my bundle to Jon Machamer who took care of it from then on. These were our clothes for senior safari. He and two others had done all the planning.

* * *

One Friday we seniors were told one-by-one, "Tonight is the night!" Jon had it all worked out so that no news could get out. I knew what Jon should choose as a career. He would go into spying for the USA. He'd be successful in spying on Russians any old time. Cold war or no, he'd out smart, out think, any spy vs. spy vs. spy.

Study hall had never passed by so slowly; I was so excited I could hardly sit still. "After devotions," we had been told, as if the future success of the Cold War depended on our discretion, "go down to the African Church. Go two by two. Make it look like you are going for a walk. Start off in every different direction, but end up at the African Church. The truck is in the parking lot."

We snuck into the darkness. When the lights went off everyone would miss us, but by then Jonathan would be rolling down the hill, ready to start the engine. No one would detect our departure in the darkness of the station. Besides, where would they look for us? The plan was perfect! Ma and Pa Simmons were waiting for us to arrive.

We found the truck and I was amazed. Tents, poles and boxes of food: everything needed for camping for a week was stuffed into the truck. How had Jonathan and his friends managed this? I felt nothing but admiration. I changed his career from spy to a general in an army, no longer just an ordinary spy.

Duffel bags, spades, tents, food, water: everything had been thought of and packed with care. We were piled on the back of the five ton, blue Chevy truck, speeding down the highway, across the Kedong Plains and up the other side of the Great Rift Valley, the far away rim that I had seen every day but never climbed.

We didn't even know where we were going. Jon had done a stupendous job of organizing the entire expedition; he had access to all the tenting and camping through his father. Under the cover of darkness we left Kijabe at 10:00 p.m.; in the truck supplies for 24 people for a week were carefully packed. All the details had been taken care of. My father couldn't help in that way, and I felt a high respect for Jon and his family.

* * *

We were heading towards a new game reserve, the Masai Mara Game Reserve. Opened only two years before, it brought the public into very close contact with nature. After driving all night, we arrived at 6:00 a.m., just as the sun was dawning. We tumbled out, dusty and dirty, from eight hours on the back of a truck. The African game warden showed us where to set up the tents, away from the permanent camp facilities where he lived, but close enough to the game wardens if there was a run-in with animals.

Three tents were lowered from the truck. One was for the *dames*, the girls, and one was for the guys. The place occupied a clearing with about 75 meters of clear space, a semi-circle that hopefully provided safety from wild animals. During the night a fire would keep hyenas and other animals away. Space was dug for a *choo*, a restroom, beside each tent.

As someone went down to the stream to *fagg*, or fetch, water, an elephant pounded through the bush. He had been drinking there when we arrived. We had set our tents up in the area that was home to a large bull elephant.

Our little campground was quickly set up; in less than an hour plates, knives and forks had been laid out on a long table. Each person had at one responsibility. We accepted Jon's leadership. He seemed able to do anything in this environment.

Bob Hollenbeck was to blow the trumpet to get us up in the mornings. Hal Boon and Linea Johnson offered to do the morning dishes together, which came as no surprise to anyone. Pa and Ma Simmons were both in a sporting good mood. The others, Malcolm Collins, *Peanut, Fish,* Tim Udd, Wilfred May, John Arensen, Pat Marsh, George Belknap, Mike Hall, Ray Davis, Bob Robinson, Diane Dilworth, Ruth Schuit, David Campbell, Jon Salseth and I, were divided into teams with responsibilities, preparing food, cleaning tables and keeping the camp clean.

* * *

As the day got under way I forgot about being tired. We had all been up for 24 hours without sleep, but our first big day was just beginning. After breakfast the truck headed out into the game park. We wanted to see the largest species of African game: elephants, lions, buffalo, leopards, cheetah, giraffe, hippo and rhino. Other animals in the park abounded, especially antelope.

Hundreds of birds flew in bushes and trees. Giraffe gracefully loped from one tree to another; elephants lumbered along slowly. At night hyenas slunk off, their sloping shoulders making them look as if they were permanently scarred by a guilty conscience, condemned to dig through left overs. Hippos yawned tiredly in the morning sun, as if it was far too early to get up; then they dipped back into their watery bed again. Crocodiles kept their mouths wide open, as if at a dentist's appointment, their sharp teeth attended to by their faithful nurses, little uniformed birds dressed in white and black, flying in and out of their great gaping mouths.

Open savannah spread out in every direction, further than the eye could take in. Topis and impalas, gazelles and hartebeest fed in herds. Near the river birds of all kinds flew or waded in the water: bee-eaters, cranes, herons and hornbills. Ostriches kept a watchful eye; and two secretary birds guarded their nest, one of them flying back with what looked like a snake.

Two Masai wardens were assigned to be with us at all times. They knew this territory better than anyone. The girls in our class hung on to the cab and we, seventeen guys, were clinging to the sides and back. Actually, sixteen of us guys rode in the back. Jonathan was driving and Ma and Pa Simmons rode with him in the cab.

* * *

On the second day the wardens spotted the pride of lion. There were 23 in the pride. The great, bushy brown-yellow male lay on his side in the shade of a tree. Beside him were bones from a wild pig, or perhaps some another animal.

Several lionesses watched as the cubs rolled over on the ground in wrestling matches. They bit each other's tails and played tug-of-war with stalks of grass. Some played catch-as-catch can with the tails of grown up mothers. The hairy tip was fair game and the mother flicked it this way and that. A young cub nuzzled the legs of one mother, climbing over her body and she accepted the playfulness of the cub; she licked the cub and lay down, so other cubs could climb all over her. The sight was one of untroubled family life, lion-pride-style. The animals had been successful in their hunt the previous night and now, at rest, they occupied a fairly large area, perhaps 40 yards across.

Our truck came closer. The pride awoke to this intruder, smelling of diesel and tires. They stood up, opening up a path. One of the larger lionesses moved away, watchful and slightly anxious. Our game warden, wearing a smartly pressed khaki uniform, and a two-inch wide black leather shoulder harness over his right shoulder, held his shining rifle at the ready. Jonathan inched the vehicle forward; we heard a low growl and the bushy male leaped up. We were too close to the lions for their own comfort. The huge male looked slightly belligerent, possibly ready for an angry encounter. Slowly the hair around his shoulders stood up.

I wondered aloud, "In trying to get out of the area has Jonathan driven over the tail of the male lion?" I couldn't be sure because of my position at the back of the truck. We paid attention to the snarling male; for a moment I forgot the lioness that had been the first to move away from her pride. I was standing at the very back between Malcolm and *Peanut*. Malcolm looked around and there was the lioness; crouched down, angry, whipping her tail slowly this way and that, ready to pounce. She turned her head and looked at two cubs, then lowering her head, stared up at us in the back of the open truck.

Jon was our driver and he was looking over the fender on the passenger's side at the male lion in front. Just then he wasn't concerned about what was happening at the back of the truck. Our lioness' tail had stopped waving. The tip of her tail stood up in a straight little point, rigid, at attention! Now, everyone on the open back was aware of danger.

Bob Hollenbeck stood near the cab. "Boot it!" he growled loudly, and that caught Jon's attention, but the noise of Bob's boot against metal startled the crouching lioness. The three of us who were standing right against the rear of the open truck looked down on the lioness, which once again held her tail stiff.

"Boot it! Boot it fast." Bob repeated, demanding immediate action. The truck moved forward and lions moved away from us. The lioness that sensed the greatest danger followed the truck, her front paws flipping up as she walked, then down and around as each huge paw met the ground. I watched, mesmerized by the sight of those powerful paws gently touching the ground, enabling the creature to trail us. What mighty, powerful paws! When she walked her paws made little circles in the air before raising dust on the ground. We eased our way past the shade of the acacia trees.

We arrived at our camp at the end of the afternoon. After a delicious supper under the open sky we piled into the truck for a brief ride to the swimming pool. Under the floodlights we jumped into the water, some showing off their skills in diving, others creating a splash with mighty cannon balls.

* * *

At night the red eyes of hyenas starred from a distance. We sang choruses and songs as the flames leaped into the air. We took turns stoking the fire so that there would always be a good flame to scare away the animals. Suddenly, there was a distant roar. The ground shook as we heard lions hunting in their wild freedom. They had no limits, no bars, and no concrete walls. This was not a zoo. The open sky above, the seasonal rains and the herds of animals migrating: this was their world. A keen sense of smell and skills in hunting as a pride enabled them to survive in this wild land.

Vulnerable animals such as zebra, bushbuck, eland, duiker, antelope, hyrax, kongoni, Tommie and wildebeest were kept safe by being part of a herd. The skills used by the hunters, the lions, leopards and cheetahs, to ferret out the weakest, the youngest or oldest, from a herd, were essential for lions to survive. The open savannah of Masai Mara Game Park provided both freedom and constant danger. Each animal had its own means to stay alive, being either the hunted or the hunter.

* * *

The third morning in Masai Mara yielded two new discoveries. First, we learned how close the lions had been to us the previous night when they made their kill. The roaring lion seemed to shake the ground. Second, we could see how strong a lioness' paw is when used together with her teeth against the jugular vein.

The game wardens had taken us to a spot not even three hundred yards from their guards' compound. A giraffe lay sprawled out on the ground, awkward in its final position as it fell. I marveled at giraffe running across the plains, looping with their massive bodies and long necks. However, this giraffe lay in a grotesque position, its neck twisted backwards where it had fallen to the ground, breathing its last. Vultures were already gathering around, ready for their part after the kill.

Beside the half eaten giraffe, the male and a lioness lay fast asleep on the ground, their bellies breathing up and down. Flies filled the air. We were so close to the sleeping lions that several students got close up pictures in which the head of the beast filled the entire slide. The window of our truck was less than five feet from the massive beasts as we reluctantly drove away.

* * *

The following day, our fourth day there, we witnessed a kill. It was in yet another part of the park and the sun was falling towards the horizon. We had seen thousands of creatures during the day. "Just one more little jaunt over this way," said a warden.

We drove slowly across the savannah, and arrived at an area enclosed by trees and brush on three sides of a very big open field. A lioness was running toward a herd of antelope. The animals scattered, wild with fear. Suddenly the lion veered to one side; she had captured a baby gazelle. Next, the distraught mother gazelle ran back and forth between the lion that was carrying off her young, and the herd that wanted to leave immediately for the distant protection of the open field. We watched enthralled. The mother, indecisive, scampered back and forth, pulled one direction by fear, unable to leave its off-spring because of affection. Again, she edged towards to the lioness, her mouth filled with the limp neck of the small animal; recognizing her danger, she exploded in a great leap back to her friends.

It was a pathetic dance, stepping between frenzy, grief and inequality. Even the animals feel the loss of their kind. I took her dance between courage and fear as her wordless obituary to the young she had borne.

* * *

We hadn't seen any buffalos. Of course, by this time we had heard an animal story from each student. From some guys, especially, scores of animal adventures poured out. I was surprised because I thought that our family had a lot of stories to tell, but my tales were nothing compared to my classmates' adventures. Here, under the endless, open skies I didn't feel jealous or inferior. I felt proud for the breadth of their experiences: on robbery-prone streets of Nairobi, on hunting trips or wide-open savannah grasslands.

They would manage their transition to the USA in just a few weeks. I still didn't want to think of my move to Canada at the end of July, with the trip planned through Southern England to meet dad's brothers, so I put that out of my mind.

Buffalo seemed to have migrated far away. Our game wardens took us to several spots. I even prayed to see buffaloes, "if the Lord willed", of course. On the fifth and final day, the head warden took us to another place, to the top of a small knoll. On the plains below were *thousands* of huge black bodies. The sharp outward turning horns of the buffalo were visible, unmistakable. Five thousand beasts were calmly going about their breakfast. Five thousand *kiambogo*! Their pointed horns, like the set nailed above the door at our school, made them among the most dangerous of Africa's wild animals.

Would this paradise wilderness continue as an endless treasure trove of African animals? Elephants were becoming the victims of poachers who shot them and left them rotting. Having lost their long, prized front teeth, the rounded bellies of dead elephants were considered useless by poachers.

Ivory was the source of fortunes to unknown, shadowy figures in Hong Kong, Bombay and Singapore. Hunters wanted that sharp up-turned horn of the rhino; bent-over, old men bought rhino powder after marrying 17 year-old girls. I felt angry that anyone might want to spoil these natural settings. Death had to occur, of course. The more powerful animals hunted the smaller ones, as we had seen. Mostly, it was the older, weaker animals of the pack, or the younger, helpless ones, that were killed by the larger hunters. But, hunting for ivory was altogether different. That was deliberate destruction.

* * *

On our last night in the park we had a great bonfire. David Campbell sang the song with his own significant changes, "Home, Home on the range, where the deer and the buffalo roam; where seldom is heard, a discouraging word, and the skies are not cloudy all day. How often at night, with the stars big and bright, have I wandered alone on these plains?"

Then we sang what had recently become my favorite hymn, "O Lord My God, When I in awesome wonder, Consider all the worlds Thy hand has made." I was lost in wonder. Up high, wherever we looked a thousand galaxies flickered beyond the Milky Way.

We burst out laughing as Campbell favored us with his crazy compositions. "Who put the toenails in the oatmeal, who put the toenails in the oatmeal, who put the toe nails in the oatmeal. . .to make it a brighter day?" I laughed so hard tears streamed down my face. Sitting on the tarp covering the bristly brown grass in the distant Masai Mara Game Park we were still students of RVA. We were a long way from school, gaining another perspective, examining our experiences, enjoying humor, accepting pain, understanding some of the rawest events one might ever see in Africa.

Under that vast empty sky dotted with a million pinpoints of light, there wasn't such a thing as an "American" or a "British" song. Nationality was only one way of defining a person's existence; each nation's tradition brought some other source of satisfaction. I lay back on the ground with my face up to the sky, my head held between my hands.

The roar of lions hunting at night shook the ground. Wild animals roamed all around us, but we were safe. Jonathan and game wardens had planned this. This was a safe kind of trip. In fact, we were still "in bounds", even though we were so far "out of bounds" because we had our Senior Class sponsors with us. No one had to be worried for our being so far from the school. Safari meant spending a week in freedom, another kind of learning.

Morning came all too soon. Exuberant in their joy, the birds sang to us. Spontaneous choirs flew to other perches constantly, always keeping up their rehearsal. Birds tried out first one choir loft and then another, this time higher up. Suddenly, they were lost from view as they flew to another tree.

Grade 12 was almost at an end; that was the deepest meaning of senior safari. Like the birds, which practiced their songs first on one branch and then another, we too would soon be flying, leaving our perch for other lands. The five days away from RVA provided a brief window into the panorama of open liberty we would soon enjoy.

The guys' tent came down. The other two tents were also folded up. Our final meal of pancakes and syrup was both sweet and a little bit sad. Then followed the long ride back to the Great Rift Valley, the slow descent down the western side and there, in front of us was the turn off the main road, the dirt track to our school.

Now Masai Mara Game Park, like the previous 11 years of school, was a memory.

* * *

The Junior-Senior Banquet brought out other emotions, ones of expectation and excitement. Jubilee Hall was transformed for the event. The juniors chose the theme of "The Wishing Well" for the night, focusing on American culture in the 1890's. Marvelous food was followed by hilarious skits, which culminated in the play, "Egad, what a Cad!" The evening was a total success. The Grade Eleven students crossed our paths each day, in the dorm, the dining room, in band, sports, clubs and many adventures and now they had put on an unforgettable banquet for us: Harold Felton, Valerie Clark, Norman Smuck, Judy Machamer, Richard Sauffacher, Jim Morrow, Susanne Walter, Lewis Trout, Roland Giddings, Martin Van der Heyden, Catherine Boone, Richard Mills, Prilla Wegmueller, Jim Camp, Joe Friberg, Jim Gaunt, Tim VanNattan, Beth Alber, Janet Johnson, Ann Pearson, Mary Simmons and Stanley Arms.

* * *

Now, final exams were in the past. The last Sunday had dawned. We seniors sat in the front rows for the last church service at RVA. The Junior Class, which had done such a splendid job in providing the Banquet to honor us, sat behind. Our graduating class was made up of 19 students and the Junior Class had 18 students. Because this was a formal occasion the sophomore class sat behind the juniors, and I realized how the enrollment at RVA had grown in the last 12 months. There were 31 in their Sophomore Class and 33 in the Freshmen Class. Enrollment had been 154 students in 1962; now, as we began the final events leading to graduation, we were 206 students in Jubilee Hall.

There were Ted and Mary Simmons, our English teacher from whom I had learned so much. In truth, he learned more about me, my weaknesses in adverbial phrases, spelling, composition, literature and grammar. Mary was my French and typing teacher. They made a great impact on my life.

Sam and Kay Senoff greeted us all warmly. I remembered his last joke in chapel, just two weeks before. He said, "A little girl had overheard high school graduates talking. One said, 'I'm free, I'm free!', and the little girl replied, 'So what? I'm four.'" His little jokes somehow made biology, math, geometry and physics a little bit more bearable in the corrugated classroom he built years before. Pa Senoff had moved from speaking without notes to using well-planned notes. Even though he lost himself with his own laughter, he didn't let chapel out early that day. Apparently, RVA was good for teaching teachers survival skills.

Phil and Shirley Lasse blessed me with warm words of encouragement. I was glad to have learned many things from them. Without Phil's help in getting the *Kiambogo* put together we would not have had a yearbook. I had no words to thank them both for their patience and dedication.

Jim and Vivian Hollenbeck were smiling, as were all the other teachers. Even Ken Downing seemed to be in a good mood.

What would the future hold for each of us, those were the *big guys*, and those who would leave RVA in the next few years? Where would we go? The previous year John Homes had spoken to us during Spiritual Life week and recently an African pastor, Mr. Guchuha, explained how God guided Abraham and Isaac and Jacob. How would God guide each of us?

This Sunday afternoon service, a few days before the Graduation Exercises of the Class of '64, began with my favorite hymn. I had looked to John Newton many times in the last several years.

Amazing Grace, How sweet the sound
That saved a wretch like me,
I once was lost, but now am found,
Was blind, but now I see.

God's mercy had become more real and I could say that he "saved a wretch like me". He'd touched my life once when I was depressed and wondered if I wanted to live. He took me as I was, a thief, proud and concerned too much with myself.

'Twas Grace that taught me heart to fear,
And Grace my fears relieved,
How precious did that Grace appear,
The hour I first believed.

God had taught me through parents, school and friends. Many Africans were part of it, too: Fanuel, with his dozen children and ten languages; Hanna, who advised mother about the neediest of the widows; the cooks and men in the laundry, cooking food and keeping our clothes clean. They were an important part of my life and I hadn't even stopped to thank them. I felt a sense of shame for that.

I knew that God didn't operate on a point card system, but he did have a Great Rendezvous, one day in the future, planned for his children. God had shown me his Grace System.

Through many dangers, toils and snares,
I have already come,
'Tis Grace hath brought me safe thus far,
And Grace will lead me home.

The barbed wire, the King's African Rifles and the first days at school, when the Mau Mau was active, came back to me as we sang the words "safe thus far". A quick succession of experiences passed through my mind: steep ravines; an almost broken ankle when practicing line outs for rugby; a lioness poised on the ground behind our truck and two warts scraped off when my bicycle flipped over completely. Yes, God had saved me from many dangers. He would lead me give me a home. The last verse was a confession of my faith.

The Lord has promised good to me,
His word my hope secures,
He will my shield and portion be,
As long as life endures.

If John Newton could compose that hymn after a life contaminated by slavery then I was going to sing and live the same faith.

* * *

Graduation day arrived and I wore my new suit. For once I didn't mind a suit. It seemed natural. I hardly noticed what was happening in the graduation service, except that finally my name was called. And the name on the High School diploma was David Phillips, not *Flappit*. I had passed all the final exams.

Our teachers and staff sat together, 21 people who influenced me over the years: Clara Barrett, Sam and Kathleen Senoff, Ina Reed, Jim and Vivian Hollenbeck, Shirley and Phil Lasse, Herb and Mildred Downing, Trumbell and Mary Simmons, David Reynolds, Gerry Stocum, Ted and Mary Honer, John and Jessie Barney, Edythe DeYoung and Roy and Judy Entwistle. Verity Coder and Gladys Bellinger were on furlough. The graduation was a whirl of events, with speeches, music and the handing out of diplomas.

The time came for congratulations and we stood in a long line. Many people came to wish us the best in the future. The Grade 12 girls grabbed everyone's attention with their dazzling white dresses. They stood in a row in the front line for the final photo. Standing on the slight embankment beside Jubilee Hall for our graduation picture, we guys stood behind the girls. This was our last minute together.

We had traveled together a long way and now our class of '64 had come as far as we could go as a group. From now on we would find our own limits and set our own boundaries.

Mike Hall, our class president; Ruth Schuit, our secretary and Dianne Dilworth, our treasurer; stood for the photo with Bob Hollenbeck, Bob Robinson, Danny Hahn, David Campbell, George Belknap, Hal Boone, Jon Arensen, Jon Machamer, Jon Salseth, Linnea Johnson, Malcolm Collins, Pat Marsh, Ray Davis, Tim Udd, Wilfred May and I: there we all were and, now, the final photo was taken. We left our places, where we had stood together for the last time.

We would never be together again.

CHAPTER 27

OVER NIAGARA FALLS

The sun shone on us from directly above as graduation photos were being taken. I looked down finding that I was standing on my shadow. Cameras snapped in front of us and I grinned. Parents were as proud as we were, the graduates of the RVA Class of ' 64.

Stepping aside I joined the rest of my family for a family portrait. Dad was smiling, proud as could be, one shoulder just a little higher than the other, the result of his polio, the same defect that I had because of the polio fever I had survived 12 years before.

Mother kept putting a little stubborn hair into place under the bun at the back where her long braids were done up perfectly for the day. She licked her lips getting ready for the picture. Her head was tilted slightly to one side and a half smile was playing on her lips; it was her sign of feeling pleased.

This was our last family picture before I went to Canada. Dot, Pearl and Don were to stay at Machakos with Ruth Peckover, a single lady missionary, a friend from Toronto, and a life long friend since our days at Kabartonjo. Dad, mom and I were to leave Nairobi later in the month, on the way to Canada, stopping off in England to see dad's relatives first.

Dot was radiant. Her smile, quick and spontaneous and true, was so encouraging. Pearl had just completed Grade 8. She was proud of her big brother and her bright smile meant more to me than the prize that she earned. She had passed with honors. Don, casually placing hands in his pockets, laughed, "Congratulations, man." It was the best thing I could have heard.

One by one the students loaded up their trunks into their parent's cars and left, waving, shouting brave words to each other. The overcrowded parking lot began to show its true colors; green grass once again became visible around Jubilee Hall as cars left for a hundred destinations. Each vehicle left in a cloud of swirling red-brown dust; dust was our parting wave from Kijabe, the symbol our final RVA experience and the fragility of life itself.

* * *

A student spent a whole life at RVA and all that was left after the graduation ceremony was a storehouse of memories, friendships that might last, or might not, and the dust billowing across the road and the playing fields. Across Kijabe the ever-present winds still blew hard.

One by one my classmates left with their parents. Ray Davis called from the window of his car as his father drove off. Ray waved, calling out, "Bye, *Flappit*. God bless! See, ya', *Flappit*." I waved back. I had said good-bye to everyone else and now I was saying good-bye to one of my best friends. I waved as he disappeared from view, the Davis' car heading went around the far bend, past the soccer field. I said nothing for a minute and for a second I held my breath.

There was Jubilee Hall, our church, our auditorium, our assembly hall, the bell and the diesel generators. A small clump of trees beyond the bell, at the edge of the hill, had once been my favorite place for playing Cowboys and Indians.

Beside me the *big guys'* dorm, Westervelt Dorm, would take in the new Grade Nine students when they arrived in five weeks' time. By that time I would be in Canada, ready for college. Above the forest, where the thick undergrowth and tall trees climbed to the top of the Rift, huge white clouds prepared to roll over themselves in their excitement, to disappear as they floated over the Valley as the hot air beneath made them disappear. The place was well named, Kijabe, the Place of the Wind. That's what graduation did; it took real people and dispersed us forever, like a cloud disappearing into thin air.

Slowly, I let my breath go and breathed normally. Then, I walked towards our car. Ray had said his good-bye, calling out to me. Ray had given me my nickname, giving me my school identity. In a mysterious way he took it away, too. He was the first one to use it and now, as we left for 19 different destinations, he was the last one to use my RVA name, *Flappit*. I was thankful it turned out that way.

* * *

A great turning point had come for all of us. We would remember each other by the nicknames we invented, the situations we encountered and the adventures that had formed us into a school community. I closed the back door of our car, and dad said, "Congratulations, my boy. We are so proud of you!" He was so British. Mother turned around from the front seat and she smiled, with genuine gratitude.

I found that I could not swallow. I rolled down the window and looked out at Jubilee Hall for the last time. I didn't want Dot, who was sitting in the middle of the back seat, to see the tears in my eyes. Now the dust rose from dad's car, just as it had for students who had already gone.

My first decision was to find a job in Canada and my first income would go to pay the storeowner in Nairobi whose seven books had disappeared from his store through the generous space provided by the huge pockets in my bulky khaki *bags*. I felt genuine remorse and repentance for having *hocked* those books, walking out without paying for them. My conscience told me restitution was in order. I could never *cob* things again; the pain in my conscience was too great. I decided right away to pay restitution double for those books, "which had gone missing". Dot didn't know it yet, but I would ask her to help me to pay off a debt. I counted on her ability to get around Nairobi, to find that store, and make things right.

* * *

Room number "6" in Westervelt Dorm had been my home away from home for the last two years. Our car was right alongside it, close for a second, and my head was out the window, watching it fade away, as our car sped along the road close to the rugby - soccer - baseball field. Kiambogo, the building central to our existence, and Green Tree occupied the same space that they had when I arrived 11 years before.

One last glance before rounding the bend, near First Ravine, gave me a final view of the school grounds, still being swept by the wind. What was left to show that we had spent our days there and now had been scattered to the four winds? Only memories remained. I rolled up the car window, feeling more alive than ever.

In no time our car had gone past the hospital, the African schools, around the sharp corner at Dames Stream, and along the dirt road out to the Nairobi-Naivasha highway. At the highway dad turned up the escarpment towards Nairobi, to the airport, and to college in the future.

* * *

A week later Dot, Pearl and Don had moved into their new temporary home in Machakos. A few days afterwards more than one hundred AIM missionaries and children boarded the plane from Nairobi to Paris. The airplane was a Constellation, noted for its unique tail with three fins. During that day, as we flew towards Europe, many new ideas crowded in. I leaned back and closed my eyes. Each of us would have to set our own boundaries, learning what our own boundaries would be. The Point System was over; there was no longer the promise of *Rendezvous*.

For three terms I had been sub-prefect, giving me the authority to "take points off". I thought about it as we flew through bumpy skies, over the desert, towards Cairo. Points were always taken off, but they could never be awarded. The Point System was an external system with regulations, meant to enable everyone to live in harmony. The Point System didn't go deep enough, though. It only hinted at an internal set of values. Somewhere along the line, self-control would have to become one's internal compass.

In the end, it was impossible to control everything through the Point System. Perhaps, in a way, that was what graduation meant, although no one actually put it that way. A future awaited us, beyond the boundaries of our school.

Our dorm parents, teachers and the administration had set boundaries for us. Something far more deep within us was needed. My conscience, trained through all those experiences, would have to guide me now. In a way my nickname represented one important part of me. My nickname, *Flappit*, was no more but it would remain in my memory, holding me close to eleven years of Boarding School.

* * *

The Constellation airplane, the gracefully designed *aeornave* with three tail fins, landed in Paris, and from France all the families headed to further destinations. Because so many missionary families had left Kenya at the same time, almost the whole plane was occupied with AIM families taking their sons and daughters back to the USA for higher education. A photo was organized with all the AIM families together before the flight. About half of our graduating class was traveling on the same plane.

The plane rose into the sky and I looked down at Nairobi National Park. I would not see lizards and crocodiles, serval cats, foxes and jackals, baboons and vultures again. Those birds! Egrets, guinea fowl and hammerkops, pelicans and spoonbills, crown cranes, bustards and starlings were now in my past. Some guys had cameras and were taking photos of the wild life back to the States; I carried memories of my butterfly collection with immaculate specimens, their long tails a marvel of delicate creation.

The updrafts shook the plane several times as we sat in rows, each of my classmates close to their mothers or fathers. Already the separation was happening, for I couldn't talk to them on the plane. Anyway, what would I say, now that we were going to so many different destinations?

We landed in Paris and families quickly found their luggage. A quick "good-bye" was my final word to a few; France was a quick stop-off and now the parting was forever.

Mother, dad and I spent several days in Paris, partly to visit mom and dad's friends who were in mission work in France. We saw a few sights, mostly parks. Three days later, a short train trip took us to the English Channel and a ferry brought us to the white cliffs of Dover. For three weeks we traveled the land that dad called his home. He took us in a rented car to the green hills of Surrey, to the landing place of Norman, the Conqueror, the sights of London and sparkling gardens in around London and Eastbourne. Several wonderful encounters with my aunts and uncles in England, together with cousins, left me wanting more of life in England. However, that was not to be, since I was to fly to New York in a few days.

A day after landing in England mother wrote a letter to the AIM office in New York to let them know that I was coming on a BOAC 707 jet plane to America. I was to stay a night at the AIM guesthouse, and the following day I was to fly to Toronto, and then connect to a flight to Winnipeg. She wrote all those details in the letter, and gave me a list of those who would be meeting me in the airport in New York.

* * *

Dad had given me $20 to go to North America; he was certain that this was sufficient for any eventuality for international travel to the USA and on to Canada.

It was hard to imagine that in March 1947, when I was three months old, I had sailed on the great Queen Elizabeth, on a sea voyage from New York to South Hampton, or that I had sailed across the Atlantic, both ways, when we came on furlough in 1953.

We landed in New York. My luggage came and I waited in the arrivals area for someone to come from the AIM office. However, no one arrived. After waiting four hours I stepped into a taxi for the trip to the International Office of the AIM, but after going less than halfway around the airport the taxi meter already read $2.50. I told the taxi cab driver that I didn't have enough money to get me to my destination; I had decided to go back to the terminal. This brief encounter provided me with my first experience of colorful vocabulary in New York.

A bus trip from the airport through Queens left me close to the AIM office. I was met at the desk with the words, "No letter has arrived to tell us of your arrival!" The next day the letter arrived in the office, just as I was leaving by bus for the airport.

* * *

Something terrible was awry in New York! I was to fly on Trans Canada Airways, but after searching the airport half a dozen times I was ready to give up. Mom and dad had bought a ticket for me on a carrier that didn't exist!

The only counter that had the word Canada on it was Air Canada so I stopped to ask for directions. "Oh, Trans-Canada Airlines changed its name to Air Canada today! It's a good thing you arrived just now. Five minutes later and we would have closed the counter for this flight. Hurry, you'll barely make it onto the plane."

The airline was renamed and expanded on that day, August 31, 1964. With my heart pounding, I sat down in a seat by the window, bound for Toronto. The farming areas of New York below shone as green pastures and forests sped by. It was heavy with dark foliage at the end of the summer weather.

At the border the plane flew over Niagara Falls and a white cloud of mist hovered above the never-ending waterfall. Mist rose high into the air, dancing slightly according to the convection of air currents, always holding its place steady over the Horse Shoe Falls. Here was my first lesson: a chance to turn over a new page! This occasion would certainly be different than returning to RVA for a new term. Attitudes and achievement were such important markers, with Point Cards reflected our behavior, and Report Cards indicating how well we had done in class.

A new life lay spread out before me; I didn't want to spoil it. I looked down on the mighty cataract below, marking in rushing water and age old rock the border between Canada and the United States.

"God, I love you," I whispered, "I want to live for you every day," I breathed slowly. "You are Lord, and I will live for your Kingdom, not for myself."

Looking out the little window I felt a cleansing and a promise; a cleansing because I knew a new life lay ahead, and a promise, because the same promises given to Abraham, Isaac and Jacob were available for me.

RVA had set my limits for almost the whole of my school days. Rift Valley Academy gave me an understanding of my own limitations. So often I had disappointed others, but much more often I hurt myself. I knew that God's power would be with me in a way that had never happened before.

* * *

The summer weather was stifling hot in Toronto and I hadn't kept out a clean shirt to change into before the last flight. I would have to arrive in Winnipeg with a sweaty shirt several hours later, after customs and my last flight. Grandma Hill, Uncle Fred and Aunt Marion, Uncle Elmer and Aunt Ruth and Aunt Helen would be waiting to meet me at the airport in Winnipeg. In a few days I would be registered at college; I was returning to the city of my birth.

The Customs Officials sat in their small offices and I stood in line for my passport to be stamped. His hand was reaching out for my passport, but I sensed another hand, as well. In only a few hours, before evening, I would be arriving at my destination. I was going to trust God to guide me, to provide me with His strength and to show me what the boundaries of my life would be.

I had taken one suitcase to Canada, and packed on the top was a sweater, which I thought would be sufficient for freezing winters in Winnipeg.

I headed down the hallway of the round airport building and found the departure lounge of the Air Canada flight to my new home. I felt a clean heart inside and a sweaty shirt around my shoulders, wilting in the suffocating heat of a late summer day.

I knew that I would always be safe within the limits He would set for me. He was going before me and for now, that was all that I needed.

"After Words"

*I*t was only after our two daughters were finishing Elementary School that I made an effort to write some of my memories from Rift Valley Academy. Cathie, my wife, and I had been working for ten years in the western Brazilian state of Mato Grosso do Sul, where we brought up our two daughters, Elizabeth and Jennifer. Our assignment had been to work in partnership with the Brazilian Baptist Convention, training men and women for ministry, forming a new seminary and planting new congregations. Ten years of adventures had proven the validity of the decision made as I flew over Niagara Falls.

Now we had moved to Brasilia, the capital city, in 1987 and we faced a difficult decision. What kind of education would we provide for our daughters while they grew up in South America? This question returned constantly as our summer holidays spread out before us, a month-long trip around the nine North-Eastern Brazilian states. As we traveled thousands of kilometers on that long drive I began to reminisce, telling stories from Rift Valley Academy.

The next year, at the Baptist Theological Seminary of Brasilia, while teaching pastoral theology, Old Testament survey and church history, I began to write some African memories. My gift to Elizabeth for her 12th birthday was a book of memories.

Having been an MK, or Missionary Kid, myself, then having brought up two daughters in South America, and later serving many missionary families in many countries, I wanted to be honest about struggles involved in growing up internationally. The grace of God has been more than sufficient in my life, so I write with hope for those who grow up many miles from their parents and loved ones.

Others may have viewed these situations through a different lens. All explanations and reflections about RVA are my responsibility, perhaps part of my on-going need to correct things. I welcome the opportunity to make things right!

* * *

Dorothy completed her entire education at RVA over a period of 12 years, graduating in 1967. She went to Winnipeg and studied at Winnipeg General Hospital and completed her R.N. course. She married Jack Reimer in 1971 and they have two married sons and two grandchildren. Dot and Jack live in Victoria, British Columbia.

Pearl also completed her entire schooling, 12 continuous years, at RVA, graduating in 1968. She studied at the University of Winnipeg, became an elementary school teacher and married Dennis Thomas. Two sons were born to them and she lives in Winnipeg.

Don also did most of his studies are RVA, returning to Canada to finish his High School. He studied at the University of Winnipeg and University of British Columbia. He married Sylvia Kool. He is a teacher in Vancouver, British Columbia.

* * *

A word of deep appreciation goes to each of my teachers at RVA, whose lives were lived sacrificially. However, I rarely understood that, since I was overstepping bounds so often. Looking back on those events, I recognize the hand of God in giving me each person as a coach, mentor and teacher in a special way. So many lessons in life keep going back to teachable moments during which these teachers and dorm parents interacted with me.

I express my deep appreciation to those who were my classmates and to those who graduated before 1964 as well as those who came afterward. My admiration of their qualities has not dimmed with the passing of almost five decades. Having been raised in Kenya, spending time with other missionary kids at Kijabe, enjoying African friends who taught me their languages and being part of the African-Indian-European foreigner society was a privilege shared by a privileged few.

Photos and other resources:

An extensive file of photos can be found at Jim Hoover's (RVA '67) Facebook site. This collection has received contributions by many alumni of RVA.

RVA Memories is a fine collection of memories of former students, complied by Richard Mills '65, Dorothy Phillips Reimer '67 and Jim Hoover '67. This work contains a bibliography complied by Wilfred Danielson (RVA ' 55) of no less than 32 pages, listing books about RVA, books by RVA alumni and other materials: articles, archival and online.

Original sources include the annual year books, called *Kiambogo*.

After RVA

*D*avid graduated from University of Winnipeg, B.A., 1968; University of Manitoba, B.Ed., 1971; and Regent College, Vancouver, 1976, M.C.S. He taught English, history and geography and was a counselor for boys at Beausejour High School, 1968-1971. David married Catherine Steinmann in Winnipeg in November 1968. Cathie trained as a nurse at the Winnipeg General Hospital and has used her training in many settings on four continents.

They carried out extensive youth ministries at Trinity Baptist Church, Vancouver, 1971-1976. David and Cathie served with Canadian Baptist Ministries from 1975 – 2011: in Brazil, 1977-1990; Bolivia, 1990-1994; and Turkey, 2000-2011. From 1995-2000 David was General Secretary for Canadian Baptist Ministries, CBM.

David's ministries included: participation in the formation of the Baptist Theological Seminary of Western Brazil, Campo Grande; participating in a extensive church planting movement in Campo Grande; the Pantanal Project in Corumba, Mato Grosso du Sul; teaching at the Baptist Theological Seminary of Brasilia, Brasilia. As Latin America Representatives for CBM they traveled to various countries in Central and South America. Denominational activities took them across Canada and to many other countries. In Turkey, David was Director of Harvest Church Ministries in Istanbul; he helped develop discipleship materials in Turkish through the Timothy Project, or Deep Change, as it is called in the Turkish language.

Cathie's involvement outside their home have included: Latin American Representative for CBM, ministry to street children in Brasilia, Brazil; Prison Kid's ministry in Cochabamba, Bolivia; involvement with MK's, in connection with David Pollok's ground breaking work with Third Culture Kids; and extensive involvement with refugees and asylum seekers in Istanbul. Her ministry involved participating in the lives of refugees and asylum seekers from over 60 nations.

They have two daughters: Elizabeth Phillips Lumkes, married to Robert Lumkes, and grandchildren: Samuel and Aimee; and Jennifer. They also raised two Middle Eastern boys as foster sons: Robert and Sylvester.

Forthcoming books from David K. Phillips:

Modern day chronicles of God's Kingdom:

Beyond Survival: The Evangelical Church in Angola
The Con Man's Last Debt, and Other Stories from Brazil

<u>The Agonizing Hallelujah</u> (A.D. 89–113) is a saga of historical fiction about Antipas, the leader of the church in Pergamum (Revelation 2:13), at the end of the Apostolic Age. The series follows Antipas' granddaughter, Miriam, her extended Jewish family and Anthony, a Roman soldier. The seven novels trace the experiences of early Christian believers through the seven cities of Asia Minor during a period of increasing persecution. These volumes come out of an extensive experience of leading tours through the Seven Churches region.

Each volume follows on from the previous novel.

Through the Fire: A Chronicle of Pergamum
Never Enough Gold: A Chronicle of Sardis
Purple Honors: A Chronicle of Thyatira
The Inn of the Open Door: A Chronicle of Philadelphia
Rich Me! A Chronicle of Laodicea
The Shadow of the Fortress: A Chronicle of Smyrna
An Act of Grace: A Chronicle of Ephesus
The Songs of Miriam: a Compilation of her Songs from the Saga

<u>Anxiety's Extravagant Reversal</u> (A.D.154-183), a saga of historical fiction, follows on from the previous seven novels. Miriam's great-grandson, Nicholas, must make important decisions, one of which threatens his life. These three novels trace the earliest developments of the Christian church during the second great period of organized persecution in the Roman Empire. These novels introduce the reader to seven cities in the Turkish area of Asia Minor in the affluent Meander River valley. The descendants of families encountered in the previous saga, *The Agonizing Hallelujah*, are featured in these three books:

A Strengthened Weakness: A Chronicle of Priene and Myra
A Joyful Sadness: A Chronicle of Aphrodisias and Alinda
A Living Sacrifice: A Chronicle of Miletus and Magnesia

CPSIA information can be obtained at www.ICGtesting.com
Printed in the USA
LVOW121247190712

290641LV00003B/3/P